Making Evidence-Based Psychological Treatments Work With Older Adults

Making Evidence-Based Psychological Treatments Work With Older Adults

Edited by

Forrest Scogin and Avani Shah

American Psychological Association • Washington, DC

Published by
American Psychological Association
750 First Street, NE
Washington, DC 20002
www.apa.org

To order
APA Order Department
P.O. Box 92984
Washington, DC 20090-2984
Tel: (800) 374-2721; Direct: (202) 336-5510
Fax: (202) 336-5502; TDD/TTY: (202) 336-6123
Online: www.apa.org/pubs/books
E-mail: order@apa.org

In the U.K., Europe, Africa, and the Middle East, copies may be ordered from
American Psychological Association
3 Henrietta Street
Covent Garden, London
WC2E 8LU England

Typeset in Goudy by Circle Graphics, Inc., Columbia, MD

Printer: Edwards Brothers, Inc., Ann Arbor, MI
Cover Designer: Mercury Publishing Services, Rockville, MD

The opinions and statements published are the responsibility of the authors, and such opinions and statements do not necessarily represent the policies of the American Psychological Association.

Library of Congress Cataloging-in-Publication Data

Making evidence-based psychological treatments work with older adults / edited by Forrest Scogin and Avani Shah.
    p. cm.
 Includes index.
 ISBN 978-1-4338-1157-9 — ISBN 1-4338-1157-X 1. Psychotherapy for older people.
2. Older people—Counseling of. 3. Older people—Psychology. I. Scogin, Forrest Ray.
II. Shah, Avani.

  RC480.54.M35 2012
  616.89'140846—dc23

                    2012002596

British Library Cataloguing-in-Publication Data

A CIP record is available from the British Library.

Printed in the United States of America
First Edition

DOI: 10.1037/13753-000

CONTENTS

CONTRIBUTORS

Catherine R. Ayers, PhD, Research Department, VA San Diego Healthcare System, San Diego, CA

David W. Coon, PhD, Health Solutions and the College of Nursing & Health Innovation, Arizona State University, Phoenix

Kim J. Curyto, PhD, VA Western New York Healthcare System, Batavia, NY

Shukofeh Dadvar, PhD, Grace Adult Health Center, Santa Clara, CA

Haley R. Dillon, MA, Department of Psychology, University of Alabama, Tuscaloosa

Mark Floyd, PhD, Sam Rayburn Memorial Veterans Affairs Medical Center, Bonham, TX

Dolores Gallagher-Thompson, PhD, Department of Psychiatry and Behavioral Sciences, Stanford University School of Medicine, Stanford, CA

Shiva G. Ghaed, PhD, MPH, Department of the Navy/Branch Medical Clinic, Marine Corps Recruit Depot, San Diego, CA

Alden L. Gross, PhD, Bloomberg School of Public Health, The Johns Hopkins University, Baltimore, MD

Ronald E. Holtzman, PhD, Bloomberg School of Public Health, The Johns Hopkins University, Baltimore, MD

Maureen Keaveny, MA, Graduate Program in Counseling Psychology, School of Letters and Sciences, Arizona State University, Tempe

Jean Ko, PhD, Bloomberg School of Public Health, The Johns Hopkins University, Baltimore, MD

Steve Koh, MD, MPH, MBA, University of California at San Diego, La Jolla, CA

Kenneth L. Lichstein, PhD, Department of Psychology, University of Alabama, Tuscaloosa

Peter Lichtenberg, PhD, Institute of Gerontology, Wayne State University, Detroit, MI

Suzann Ogland-Hand, PhD, Pine Rest Christian Mental Health Services, Grand Rapids, MI

Jeanine M. Parisi, PhD, Bloomberg School of Public Health, The Johns Hopkins University, Baltimore, MD

George W. Rebok, PhD, Bloomberg School of Public Health, The Johns Hopkins University, Baltimore, MD

Jane S. Saczynski, PhD, University of Massachusetts Medical School, Worcester, MA

Quincy M. Samus, PhD, Johns Hopkins School of Medicine, Baltimore, MD

Forrest Scogin, PhD, Department of Psychology, University of Alabama, Tuscaloosa

Avani Shah, PhD, School of Social Work, University of Alabama, Tuscaloosa

Adam P. Spira, PhD, Bloomberg School of Public Health, The Johns Hopkins University, Baltimore, MD

Kelly M. Trevino, PhD, Dana Farber Cancer Institute, Boston, MA

Irene Rivera Valverde, BS, Project PERLAZ, Stanford University School of Medicine, Stanford, CA

Julie Loebach Wetherell, PhD, Psychology Service, VA San Diego Healthcare System, San Diego, CA

Ryan G. Wetzler, PsyD, ABPP, CBSM, Sleep Medicine Specialists, Louisville, KY

LIST OF FIGURES AND TABLES

FIGURES

TABLES

LIST OF APPENDICES

These appendices may also be found on the supplemental website for this book: http://pubs.apa.org/books/supp/scogin-shah

Making Evidence-Based Psychological Treatments Work With Older Adults

1

INTRODUCTION TO EVIDENCE-BASED PSYCHOLOGICAL TREATMENTS FOR OLDER ADULTS

FORREST SCOGIN AND AVANI SHAH

Evidence-based practice (EBP) is here to stay. We make this proclamation despite the controversy that has attended this concept. Psychology is, after all, an evidence-based discipline, and we should expect nothing less from the applied arms of our field. In this book, we undertake the daunting task of summarizing the evidence base for psychological treatments as used with a particular segment of the population: older adults. Older adults comprise a substantial and rising portion of the populace, and thus it is important that we bring the best available knowledge to bear on the often complex health and behavioral problems presented by older people.

This book is a continuation of efforts undertaken by the Society of Clinical Geropsychology of the American Psychological Association (APA) to provide scholars, practitioners, consumers, and policymakers information on practices that have been systematically evaluated. This information was first published as a Special Section in the APA journal *Psychology and Aging*, in which reviews were undertaken of psychological treatments for anxiety, depression, insomnia, caregiver distress, and behavioral disturbances associated with dementia. In this book, we want to go beyond the information provided in these reviews by sharing perspectives on the implementation of these evidence-based treatments (EBTs). The authors of those aforementioned reviews are passionate about promoting the best for older adults, and it is with this intent that we agreed to create this book.

To make the content of these chapters even more valuable to practitioners, we have enlisted as coauthors persons who are actually in the business of implementing EBTs with older adults. These individuals will tell us about the challenges and rewards of using EBTs in applied settings. Thus, we hope to combine that which is at the heart of psychology: the marriage of hardnosed scholarly evaluation of the evidence base with the realities of using these interventions with the exigencies that exist in the health care world. You may recognize that this is essentially the APA definition of EBP: the synergy of the best available scientific information with the skills of expert clinicians in the context of the patient's values and preferences. Our book is an effort to dilate this aspirational synergy.

This book is an effort to provide information on EBTs to practitioners who work with older adults. We would like to provide an overview of the methods the original task force used to identify EBTs so that this information will not need to be repeated in each of the chapters that follow. Five teams were assembled to review the literature on psychological treatments for anxiety, depression, insomnia, memory, disruptive behaviors in dementia, and caregiver distress. These areas were considered the most likely to have received sufficient scientific attention to warrant review; moreover, these are problems that are of significance to older adults and those who serve them. Review teams used a coding manual developed by Weisz and Hawley (2001) for a wider effort to identify EBTs by APA's Society of Clinical Psychology. This manual provided guidance on determining what articles to include in the reviews and decisional rules on whether a treatment should be considered beneficial. In a nutshell, for a treatment to be considered evidence based there needed to be two controlled studies in which the treatment was shown to be significantly better than a control condition.

Though this task may seem relatively elementary, it was, simply put, a huge undertaking. Review teams looked over hundreds of articles and provided detailed coding on about 30 articles on average per team. Many decisions had to be made along the way, and this is where the collective wisdom of the committee was invaluable. For example, deciding what was indeed a psychological treatment was not always easy—for example, whether to include interventions that focus on exercise and respite care (we decided these were not psychological treatments). In the end, it was gratifying to find that a number of psychological treatments were indeed found to be evidence based across these disorders and problems, despite our use of a rigorous set of criteria for inclusion. In these chapters, the authors have updated these reviews with studies that have been published since the 2007 review. Not surprisingly, this did not change to any substantial extent the status of the earlier established EBTs.

In this book, we hope to provide you with information on treatments that have a substantial evidence base, but more importantly, we hope to stimulate your thinking about implementing EBTs in your work. To this end, each chapter has sections prepared by providers on the challenges and benefits of using EBTs. It is rarely so easy as to pull a treatment manual off of the shelf and apply an EBT from start to finish with unfettered fidelity (and contrary to popular belief, even in clinical trials). Moreover, we have yet to see "cookbook" protocols; at best, most provide an outline that must be filled in by the provider. Patients present with disparate conditions including wide variation in cognitive status, complicated medical comorbidities, and tremendous cultural diversity. As such, clinician expertise and flexibility are vital. At the risk of repetitiveness, this expertise coupled with the best available treatment protocols is at the heart of EBP. However, the evidence base for psychological treatments for older adults is neither deep nor broad. Clinical geropsychology is still an emerging specialty only recently recognized as such by APA, and the number of investigations that support the efficacy of our work is fragile. On at least two occasions over the past several years I (FS) have tried to help colleagues find controlled efficacy data on particular well-known treatments for common disorders, only to find that we had assumed such data existed but did not. Thus, we are not naïve in our advocacy for EBP, knowing that in many circumstances one must work with minimal direction from the scientific literature. Such shortcomings do not, however, justify a renunciation of attention to the best available information.

In any discussion of the use of EBTs the following question arises: How does an individual clinician implement specific interventions with a particular client, remaining true to evidence-based principles of care while at the same time tailoring the intervention to the needs of the client? There is no simple or entirely satisfying answer to this question. Certainly, a first step in an evidence-based approach is to be knowledgeable of the scientific literature in a particular area. Accessing this information can be a daunting task even in a relatively small subarea such as geropsychology. Systematic reviews and extended presentations such as those contained in this book are helpful. Another key component we believe is important to addressing this overarching question is a commitment to an EBP perspective. This means there must be a willingness to obtain and follow protocols that may not be familiar or in some cases entirely compatible with one's predilections. Implementing an EBT then becomes the challenge.

What principles guide a clinician when faced with implementing an intervention for an individual older adult within an EBP orientation? One guiding principle is sagely stated by our clinician coauthor, Mark Floyd, in Chapter 4; to paraphrase, give the EBT a chance to work and modify when needed. For example, in using cognitive behavioral therapy (CBT) with depressed older adults we sometimes find that clients struggle with the cognitive assignments, such as monitoring thoughts. For others, this is easy and often very productive. For those that struggle, modification of the protocol to emphasize behavioral activation and supportive psychotherapy is often a course of action. We know that both behavioral activation and supportive psychotherapy are beneficial interventions, and in this way the clinician has stayed loyal to an EBP perspective.

Other vexing questions arise when engaging in EBP. For most of the more common presenting problems, there are two or more EBTs. Which one should be selected? The quick-and-dirty answer is that it probably doesn't matter as long as whatever is chosen is implemented skillfully. The prevailing belief among leading psychotherapy scholars (Chambless et al., 2006) is that there are small differences in efficacy among various EBTs for similar problems but that skillful implementation of any particular EBT has large consequences.

Not to be ignored in this discussion of the use of EBTs is the preference of the client. Having several EBTs available for a particular presenting problem allows a presentation of options from which the client can state a preference. Of course, presenting options assumes the clinician has the background to skillfully deliver each treatment. A frequent concern for those implementing EBTs is how to adapt such standardized treatments to the unique clients that often seek treatment. Tailoring interventions to client characteristics can lead to better outcomes, but until recently there has been little guidance on ways of accomplishing this while maintaining the integrity of the treatment. For further information on this topic, we suggest reviewing the work conducted by an interdivisional APA taskforce (Norcross & Wampold, 2011) that identified empirically supported methods of adapting psychotherapies based on various client factors (e.g., patient reactance–resistance, spirituality, culture).

The chapter authors in this volume share a passion for advancing the field of mental health and aging. We also have a deep conviction that psychological treatments can provide real benefit to the quality of life of older adults. In each of the chapters that we briefly overview below, we also provide information on treatment resources, including training materials and measures used in conjunction with the EBTs.

In Chapter 2 of this book, Shiva G. Ghaed, Catherine R. Ayers, and Julie Loebach Wetherell present an overview of EBTs for geriatric anxiety: relaxation training, CBT, supportive therapy, and cognitive therapy. Clinician coauthors Ghaed and Wetherell discuss their experiences with implementing CBT with older adults in the Veterans Affairs health care system. Their presentation of "Helen" demonstrates the use of relaxation training and cognitive therapy techniques in the treatment of generalized anxiety disorder symptoms, such as worry and tension. Anxiety is one the most common problems seen in community-dwelling older adults, and it is important that we have solid choices for EBT implementation.

Chapter 3 is a presentation by Haley R. Dillon, Ryan G. Wetzler, and Kenneth L. Lichstein of EBTs for geriatric insomnia. The previous review identified two treatments: sleep restriction–sleep compression and multi-component CBT. Clinician contributor Ryan Wetzler discusses his experiences in using EBTs to treat sleep problems in older patients. Challenges identified include limited community understanding of EBTs, difficulty establishing consistent referral sources, reimbursement challenges, and difficulty applying a research model of treatment to complex clinical populations. These challenges should resonate with all psychological treatment providers, and the authors of this chapter provide us with some creative ideas to mitigate these difficulties.

Chapter 4 summarizes EBTs for depression among the older population. Avani Shah, Forrest Scogin, and Mark Floyd provide information on the six treatments identified in our review: behavior therapy, CBT, cognitive bibliotherapy, problem-solving therapy, brief psychodynamic therapy, and reminiscence therapy. Our clinician collaborator, Mark Floyd, shares his experiences in implementing EBTs in the home-based primary care system of the VA. This unique setting provides many challenges and rewards for EBP, as medical comorbidity becomes extreme and the home environment forces clinician creativity. Floyd's commonsense suggestions will be appreciated by clinicians who are interested in working with older adults experiencing depressive symptoms.

Chapter 5 summarizes the evidence base for memory and cognitive training programs for older adults. George W. Rebok and colleagues present information on eight memory training approaches to meet evidence-based criteria. These include association, visual imagery, method of loci, self-guided training, and relaxation training. Concerns about memory functioning are frequent among older adults, and clinicians should be equipped to provide the best available interventions for the oftentimes very motivated older adults who are seeking assistance. At the same time, one would likely encounter questions about recent commercially available technology to improve memory, which is briefly overviewed in the resource section of this chapter. As this is an emerging field with few sole clinical providers of cognitive interventions, Rebok shares his clinical experiences in providing cognitive interventions to older adults.

Chapter 6 reviews the evidence for psychological treatments aimed to reduce behavior disturbances of dementia. This chapter is authored by Kim J. Curyto, Kelly M. Trevino, Suzann Ogland-Hand, and Peter Lichtenberg. The clinician perspective is supplied by Curyto, Trevino, and Ogland-Hand.

Three interventions were determined to meet EBT criteria: progressively lowered stress threshold, pleasant event scheduling, and simulated presence therapy. These authors note that the implementation of EBTs for behavioral disturbances are often challenged by level of staff–family support, the resources available for the significant effort involved in the use of these EBTs, and the wide variance in the environments in which they are used.

Chapter 7, the final chapter, summarizes EBTs for caregiver distress. David W. Coon and Dolores Gallagher-Thompson infuse the chapter with considerable research experience in the area of caregiving while highlighting unique clinical experiences within a cultural framework of three clinician coauthors: Maureen Keaveny, Irene Rivera Valverde, and Shukofeh Dadvar. They note that caregivers come from diverse cultures, and awareness of their needs is critical to EBP. The case examples provided in this chapter highlight the need for cultural consciousness.

These chapters cover a broad range of the problems experienced by older adult consumers of psychological services. However, there are other areas that need attention, among them, substance abuse, posttraumatic stress disorder, and serious mental disorders. Even in those areas with established EBTs, the need for evidence on a broader range of older adults is a recurrent theme in this book and many related scholarly pieces. Many talented clinicians and researchers continue to advance our field, and it is undoubtedly the case that future efforts of the sort presented in this book will provide a broader and deeper evidence base on which clinical practice can draw. In the meantime, we can draw some comfort from the fact that our field has advanced to the point that an array of evidence-based interventions are available for consideration as we serve our older adult clients.

REFERENCES

Chambless, D. L., Crits-Christoph, P., Wampold, B. E., Norcross, J. C., Lambert, M. J., Bohart, A. C., & Johannsen, B. E. (2006). What should be validated? In J. C. Norcross, L. E. Beutler, & R. F. Levant (Eds.), *Evidence-based practices in mental health: Debate and dialogue on the fundamental questions* (pp. 191–256). Washington, DC: American Psychological Association. doi:10.1037/11265-005

Norcross, J. C., & Wampold, B. E. (2011). What works for whom: Tailoring psychotherapy to the person. *Journal of Clinical Psychology, 67,* 127–132. doi:10.1002/jclp.20764

Weisz, J. R., & Hawley, K. M. (2001). *Procedural and coding manual for identification of evidence-based treatments.* Unpublished manual, University of California, Los Angeles.

2

EVIDENCE-BASED PSYCHOLOGICAL TREATMENTS FOR GERIATRIC ANXIETY

SHIVA G. GHAED, CATHERINE R. AYERS,
AND JULIE LOEBACH WETHERELL

Despite common misconceptions, anxiety appears to be one of the most prevalent and debilitating psychiatric disorders presenting in the geriatric population. The prevalence of anxiety disorders among older adults in the community is estimated to be approximately 9% (Kessler et al., 2005). However, morbidity estimation for late-life anxiety is challenging because of variables that include comorbid medical conditions, increased medication use, inconsistent assessment, and diversity in the older population itself (Ayers, Sorrell, Thorp, & Wetherell, 2007). It is likely that there are even higher numbers of older individuals experiencing symptoms of anxiety that while not diagnostic, are still clinically significant and cause notable distress and dysfunction (Himmelfarb & Murrell, 1984). These prevalence rates may also be underestimates of true population values given the likelihood that older adults may deny, minimize (Gurian & Minor, 1991), or simply not recognize anxiety or depressive symptoms (Wetherell, Petkus, et al., 2009). Generalized anxiety disorder (GAD) and phobias appear to be the most commonly diagnosed anxiety disorders in the older population (i.e., 10% prevalence rate), and they most often present in primary care settings (Beekman et al., 1998; Flint, 1994; Kessler et al., 2005; Thorp et al., 2009).

Late-life anxiety has been linked to a variety of negative outcomes, including impairments in both physical and psychological functioning. Older men with anxiety appear to be at higher risk for coronary artery disease and experience greater mortality (Kawachi, Sparrow, Vokonas, & Weiss, 1994; Van Hout et al., 2004). Anxiety has been linked to substance abuse (Poikolainen, 2000), polypharmacy (Golden et al., 1999), and overutilization of medical services (de Beurs et al., 1999; Stanley, Roberts, Bourland, & Novy, 2001) in older adults. GAD in particular is associated with increased somatic complaints, for example, related to gastrointestinal problems and nausea (Haug, Mykletun, & Dahl, 2002), headaches (Zwart et al., 2003), and dizziness (Eckhardt-Henn, Breuer, Thomalske, Hoffmann, & Hopf, 2003). Furthermore, anxiety adversely affects subjective experiences of well-being and quality of life (QOL) and impacts daily functioning (Brenes, Guralnik, Williamson, Fried, & Penninx, 2005; Brenes, Guralnik, Williamson, Fried, et al., 2005; de Beurs et al., 1999; Lenze et al., 2001; Lenze & Wetherell, 2009; Wetherell, Thorp, et al., 2004). Suicide, in general, increases with age and may be an even more serious problem in late-life anxiety populations (Pearson & Brown, 2000; Szanto et al., 1997). Nearly half of older adults with depression have co-occurring anxiety disorders (Beekman et al., 2000; Lenze et al., 2000), and suicide risk may be up to 10 times higher in these patients than in the general population (Khan et al., 2002). For this reason, the assessment of depression and anxiety should be a priority when evaluating geriatric patients who present to primary care settings, regardless of their specific complaints.

Medications such as selective serotonin reuptake inhibitors (SSRIs; Lenze et al., 2005, 2009) are efficacious for geriatric anxiety, and some data suggest that SSRIs are more effective than psychotherapy (Pinquart & Duberstein, 2007; Schuurmans et al., 2006, 2009). Yet the impetus for using evidence-based psychological treatments for anxiety with the older population derives from a number of factors. One of the most compelling reasons for offering psychotherapeutic treatment in lieu of pharmacotherapy is that older individuals tend to already be taking many medications and often prefer not to add to a long list due to concerns about side effects and other issues (Wetherell, Kaplan, et al., 2004). In addition, there are risks from taking commonly prescribed older medications such as benzodiazepines (Klap, Unroe, & Unutzer, 2003; Mamdani, Rapoport, Shulman, Herrmann, & Rochon, 2005; Paterniti, Dufouil, & Alperovitch, 2002). Despite more recent evidence of efficacy and safety of newer medications such as the SSRIs (Lenze et al., 2005, 2009), some evidence suggests that long-term use of these medications may contribute to bone loss (Diem et al., 2007). Lenze et al. (2005) recommended integrated treatment for late-life anxiety patients for this reason, and they suggested taking a more graduated care approach, particularly in the management of somaticizing patients.

THE EVIDENCE

This section provides an overview of research that supports the use of specific treatments for anxiety in the geriatric population. A comprehensive review of the literature was conducted on psychological treatments for older adults with anxiety, resulting in the identification of several standard EBTs that have been deemed appropriate and effective for this patient population. These treatments include cognitive behavioral therapy (CBT), cognitive therapy, relaxation training, supportive therapy, and bibliotherapy. Recommendations are also made in regard to whether to enroll a patient in individual or group therapy and treatment approaches that may be more effective in patients with cognitive impairment.

Cognitive Behavioral Therapy

CBT is a general term used to classify a set of psychotherapy modalities that share in common a focus on how maladaptive thoughts adversely affect our feelings and behaviors. In a recent review, Ayers et al. (2007) evaluated 10 studies that used CBT for late-life anxiety, eight of which provided support for this approach (see Table 2.1). Most of these studies included standard components of psychoeducation, self-monitoring, relaxation training, thought stopping and thought challenging, and exposure to sources of anxiety. In addition, some studies also taught problem solving and addressed issues such as sleep, communication, memory, and life review. Overall, there was strongest support for the use of CBT with patients who were older and had a diagnosis of GAD (Ayers et al., 2007). Furthermore, in some studies, results indicated long-term and sustained improvements in not only anxiety but also depressive symptoms and QOL (Stanley, Beck, & Glassco, 1996; Stanley, Beck, et al., 2003; Wetherell, Gatz, & Craske, 2003). A meta-analysis provided quantitative confirmation that psychotherapy is more effective than attention placebo and other active control conditions for geriatric anxiety (Hendriks, Oude Voshaar, Keijsers, Hoogduin, & van Balkom, 2008).

The following section describes nine studies that provide support for CBT and one study that provides support for cognitive therapy for use with older anxiety patients. Although the majority of these studies included patients with only GAD, two studies included patients with several other anxiety disorders (e.g., panic disorder, social phobia, anxiety disorder not otherwise specified) in addition to GAD (i.e., Barrowclough et al., 2001; Gorenstein et al., 2005). In the first study, self-reported depression and anxiety were significantly lower for patients who received CBT versus those who received supportive therapy after treatment and at follow-up (Barrowclough et al., 2001). Gorenstein et al. (2005) compared patients who received medication with those who received

TABLE 2.1
Cognitive Behavioral and Cognitive Therapy for Late-Life Anxiety

Authors	Sample	Conditions	Manual	Length of treatment	Outcome measures	Findings
Barrowclough et al., 2001	$N = 55$; M age = 72; met criteria for panic disorder (51%), social phobia (2%), GAD (19%), or anxiety disorder not otherwise specified (28%)	1. CBT 2. ST	CBT based on disorder specific models: Clark, 1988; Wells, 1997; and Beck, Emery, & Greenberg, 1985	8–12 sessions of individual, home-delivered therapy	BAI, HAMA, STAI-T	CBT group-reduced self-reports of anxiety and depression significantly more than ST immediately following treatment and during follow-up.
Gorenstein et al., 2005	$N = 42$; M age = 68; met criteria for GAD (55%), GAD with panic (9%), panic disorder (17%), anxiety disorder not otherwise specified (19%)	1. CBT-MM 2. MM	CBT based on Gorenstein, Papp, & Kleber, 1999	13 individual sessions	STAI-S, STAI-T, PSWQ, SCL-90 Anxiety and Obsessive-Compulsiveness (OC)	CBT-MM experienced significantly more improvement than MM alone in phobic anxiety and OC. No difference in worry, state, or trait anxiety.
Keller et al., 1975[a]	$N = 30$; M age = 68; subjective reports of anxiety	1. CT 2. WL	CT based on Ellis & Harper, 1961	4 weeks, 2-hr group session per week	STAI-T, STAI-S	CT group showed significant declines in irrational thinking and anxiety, whereas WL did not.

Study	Sample	Conditions	Treatment basis	Sessions	Measures	Results
Mohlman et al., 2003	Study 1: N = 27; M age = 66; met criteria for GAD Study 2: N = 15; M age = 67; met criteria for GAD	Study 1: 1. CBT with problem-solving skills training, daily structure, and sleep hygiene; 2. WL Study 2: 1. Enhanced CBT with memory aids; 2. WL	CBT based on Gorenstein, Papp, & Kleber, 1999	13 individual sessions	BAI, SCL-90, Trait worry, STAI-T, GADSS	Study 1: No immediate differences between CBT and WL. CBT group significantly reduced GAD severity at 6-month follow-up, whereas WL did not. Study 2: Enhanced CBT group showed significant reduction in anxiety—worry and global severity relative to WL.
Mohlman & Gorman, 2005	N = 32; M age = 69; met criteria for GAD, had intact EF, improved EF, impaired EF	1. CBT 2. WL	CBT based on Gorenstein, Papp, & Kleber, 1999	13 individual sessions	BAI, PSWQ, STAI-T	Intact and improved EF showed significantly greater decrease than the WL on worry. Improved EF showed significantly greater decrease than the impaired EF and WL on STAI-T.
Stanley et al., 1996	N = 48; M age = 68; met criteria for GAD	1. CBT 2. ST	CBT based on Borkovec & Costello, 1993; and Craske, Barlow, & O'Leary, 1992	14 group sessions	GADSS, percentage of day worrying, PSWQ, WS, STAI-T, HAMA, FQ	CBT and ST groups both significantly reduced worry, anxiety, and depression. Gains maintained at 6-month follow-up.
Stanley et al., 2009	N = 134; M age = 67; met criteria for GAD	1. CBT 2. EUC	Stanley, Diefenbach, & Hopko, 2004	10 individual sessions	PSWQ, GADSS, SIGH-A, BDI-II, SF-12 (MCS, PCS)	CBT (vs. EUC) significantly improved worry severity, depressive symptoms, and general mental health. Similar improvement not seen for GAD severity measure.

(continues)

TABLE 2.1
Cognitive Behavioral and Cognitive Therapy for Late-Life Anxiety *(Continued)*

Authors	Sample	Conditions	Manual	Length of treatment	Outcome measures	Findings
Stanley, Beck, et al., 2003	*N* = 85; *M* age = 66; met criteria for GAD	1. CBT 2. Minimal contact control	CBT based on Borkovec & Costello, 1993; Bernstein & Borkovec, 1973; Craske, Barlow, & O'Leary, 1992	15 group sessions	PSWQ, WS, GADSS, STAI-T, HAMA	CBT group showed significant improvement on measures of worry, anxiety, and QOL relative to control. Gains maintained at 12-month follow-up.
Stanley, Hopko, et al., 2003	*N* = 12; *M* age = 71; met criteria for GAD	1. CBT with problem-solving skills training and sleep hygiene 2. Usual care	Stanley, Diefenbach, & Hopko, 2004	8 individual sessions	GADSS, PSWQ, BAI	CBT group showed significantly more improvement on GAD severity, worry, and depression ratings than usual care.
Wetherell et al., 2003	*N* = 75; *M* age = 67; met criteria for GAD	1. CBT 2. Discussion group (DG) focused on worry topics 3. WL	CBT based on Craske, Barlow & O'Leary, 1992	12 group sessions	GADSS, percent of day worrying, PSWQ, HAMA, BAI	CBT group showed significantly more improvement on GAD severity, worry, depression, and QOL than WL. CBT equivalent to DG on all but one measure of worry. Gains maintained at 6-month follow-up.

Note. GAD = generalized anxiety disorder; GADSS = Generalized Anxiety Disorder Severity Scale; CBT = cognitive behavioral therapy; CBT-MM = cognitive behavioral therapy plus medical management for medication taper; MM = medical management; ST = supportive therapy; BAI = Beck Anxiety Inventory; BDI–II = Beck Depression Inventory—II; HAMA = Hamilton Anxiety Rating Scale; SF-12 (MCS, PCS) = Short Form Health Survey (Mental Component scale, Physical Component scale); SIGH-A = Structured Interview Guide for the Hamilton Anxiety Scale; STAI-T = State–Trait Anxiety Inventory–Trait; EF = executive function; EUC = enhanced usual care; PCS = physical component summary; MCS = mental component summary; WL = waiting list; STAI-S = State–Trait Anxiety Inventory–State; CT = cognitive therapy; SCL-90 = Symptom Checklist-90; PSWQ = Penn State Worry Questionnaire; WS = Worry scale; HAMA = Hamilton Anxiety Rating Scale; FQ = Fear Questionnaire; QOL = Quality of life.
[a]Note that Keller et al., 1975, is CT only.

both medication and CBT. They found greater improvement in the latter group for phobic anxiety and obsessive–compulsiveness, although there were no significant differences between groups for worry, state, or trait anxiety levels.

Several studies examined patients with GAD alone. The most recent large-scale study provided some support for the efficacy of CBT for GAD with older primary care patients (Stanley et al., 2009). Although CBT was not more effective than treatment as usual on interviewer-rated measures of somatic anxiety symptoms or GAD severity, it was superior on self-reported symptoms of worry, depression, and QOL.

Mohlman et al. (2003) conducted two studies in which an enhanced form of CBT was compared with a wait-list control group. In the first study, CBT included teaching problem-solving skills, structuring daily activities, and sleep hygiene, and this group showed significant improvements in GAD symptoms 6 months after treatment versus no improvements in the control group. In the second study, enhanced CBT included teaching memory aids, and this group showed improvements in anxiety and worry and overall anxiety symptoms as compared with the wait-list control group. In a similar study, Stanley, Hopko, et al. (2003) compared GAD patients in a usual care control group with a group of patients who received CBT and training in problem-solving skills and sleep hygiene, and the latter group showed significantly lower worry, depression, and GAD symptom ratings than controls. Mohlman and Gorman (2005) conducted a follow-up study that examined patients based on executive functioning status (i.e., intact, improved, impaired). In this study, the intact and improved groups reported less worry, and the improved group reported less anxiety (trait) relative to the impaired and wait-list control groups. Stanley et al. (1996) showed that patients who received either CBT or supportive therapy improved in terms of anxiety, worry, and depression scores, and these improvements were maintained at the 6-month follow-up point. In a subsequent study conducted by Stanley, Beck, et al. (2003), patients who received CBT (compared with a minimal contact control group) showed less anxiety and worry and better QOL. Furthermore, these improvements were evident 12 months following treatment. Finally, Wetherell et al. (2003) compared three groups (i.e., CBT, worry discussion group, wait list) and found reduced GAD, worry, and depressive symptoms, and increased QOL for CBT patients versus wait-list patients. In addition, similar improvements were seen in the worry discussion group, and for both groups these improvements were maintained 6 months posttreatment.

Cognitive Therapy

Ayers et al. (2007) identified three studies that examined cognitive therapy (i.e., one type of CBT focusing primarily on thoughts and feelings) for anxiety; however, only one of these studies (i.e., Keller et al., 1975) provided support for its effectiveness in the geriatric population (see Table 2.1).

In this study, patients who received cognitive therapy were compared with patients on the wait list and showed significantly less state and trait anxiety and less irrational thinking than controls. The other two studies provided more support for the use of relaxation training and supportive therapy over cognitive therapy (DeBerry, Davis, & Reinhard, 1989; Sallis, Lichstein, Clarkson, Stalgaitis, & Campbell, 1983). In a study that compared three treatment groups (i.e., relaxation training, cognitive therapy with pleasant events scheduling, supportive therapy), patients who received cognitive therapy showed significantly lower heart rates.

Relaxation Training

Relaxation training, usually involving breathing and meditation and some form of progressive muscle relaxation (PMR), was shown to be effective in reducing anxiety in four out of five studies investigated (De Berry, 1981–1982, 1982; De Berry et al., 1989; Scogin et al., 1992; see Table 2.2). De Berry (1981–1982, 1982) compared patients who received PMR with patients who received pseudorelaxation and found that PMR patients reported significantly less state anxiety, muscle tension, sleep latency, nocturnal awakenings, and headaches, and these improvements were maintained 10 weeks following treatment. De Berry (1981–1982, 1982) emphasized the importance of practicing these skills to sustain long-term benefits from treatment. PMR was also more effective than cognitive therapy in reducing state anxiety, and these results were also maintained at the 10-week follow-up point (De Berry, 1989). In addition, Scogin et al. (1992) showed that patients who received PMR or imaginal relaxation training were significantly less anxious (state) than wait-list patients, and improvements were still evident 1 month after treatment. Rickard, Scogin, and Keith (1994) demonstrated that treatment benefits were evident 1 year following treatment-relaxation training for anxiety.

Thorp et al. (2009) conducted a meta-analysis that compared different behavioral treatments for geriatric anxiety. As expected, results of the meta-analysis indicated that some form of behavioral treatment was more effective than no treatment (i.e., control conditions). Interestingly, the study also suggested that CBT and relaxation training were comparable, and CBT plus relaxation training was not superior to relaxation techniques alone. This provides further support for the benefits of teaching basic relaxation skills to older patients with anxiety.

Supportive Therapy

Supportive therapy refers to an eclectic approach in which therapy is patient driven and strives to maintain well-being and reduce distress in the context of a supportive therapist–patient relationship (see Appendix 2.1 for

TABLE 2.2
Relaxation Training for Late-Life Anxiety

Authors	Sample	Conditions	Manual	Length of treatment	Outcome measures	Findings
De Berry, 1981–1982	N = 10; M age range = 69–84; recent widows with subjective reports of anxiety	1. PMR 2. Pseudorelaxation	Relaxation based on Wolpe, 1969; and Lazarus, 1966	Ten 1-hour group sessions	STAI-S, STAI-T	PMR group showed significant improvement on state anxiety, muscle tension, sleep latency, nocturnal awakenings, and headaches, whereas pseudorelaxation did not. At 10-week follow-up, PMR showed gains on state anxiety.
De Berry, 1982	N = 36; M age range = 63–79; mostly recent widows with subjective reports of anxiety	1. PMR and imagery with follow-up 2. PMR and imagery without follow-up 3. Pseudorelaxation	Relaxation based on Wolpe, 1969; and Lazarus, 1972	Ten 30-minute group sessions	STAI-S, STAI-T	Both PMR groups showed significant improvement on state and trait anxiety whereas pseudorelaxation did not. Gains maintained at 10-week follow-up.
De Berry et al., 1989	N = 32; M age = 69; subjective reports of anxiety	1. PMR and imagery 2. CT with assertiveness training 3. Pseudorelaxation	PMR and imagery based on Wolpe, 1969; Lazarus, 1972; and DeBerry 1982	Twenty 45-minute group sessions	STAI-S, STAI-T	PMR group demonstrated significant decrease in state anxiety, whereas pseudorelaxation and CT did not. Gains maintained at 10-week follow-up.
Rickard, Scogin, & Keith, 1994 (1-year follow-up from Scogin et al. [1992] study)	N = 27; M age = 68; subjective reports of anxiety	1. PMR 2. Imaginal relaxation 3. WL	Relaxation based on Bernstein & Borkovec, 1973; and Crist, 1986	4 individual sessions	Relaxation scale, SCL-90-R, STAI-S, STAI-T	Reduction in state and trait anxiety and significant decrease in psychological symptoms 1 year after treatment.
Scogin et al., 1992	N = 71; M age = 68; subjective reports of anxiety	1. PMR 2. Imaginal relaxation 3. WL	Relaxation based on Bernstein & Borkovec, 1973; and Crist, 1986	4 individual sessions	STAI-S, STAI-T, SCL-90	PMR and imaginal relaxation groups significantly reduced state anxiety relative to WL. Gains maintained at 1-month follow-up.

Note. PMR = progressive muscle relaxation; STAI-S = State–Trait Anxiety Inventory–State; STAI-T = State–Trait Anxiety Inventory–Trait; CT = cognitive therapy; WL = waiting list; SCL-90 = Symptom Checklist-90; SCL-90-R = Symptom Checklist-90-Revised.

reference: Novalis, Rojcewicz, & Peele, 1993). In three studies, Ayers et al. (2007) found some support for the use of supportive therapy, although data are inconsistent. Sallis et al. (1983) compared three groups of patients (i.e., relaxation training, cognitive therapy, supportive therapy) and found that patients who received supportive therapy had significantly less trait anxiety than the other two groups (see Table 2.3). Supportive therapy was compared with CBT in patients with several different anxiety disorders (i.e., GAD, panic disorder, social phobia, anxiety disorder not otherwise specified), and patients receiving CBT showed significantly more improvements in mood than those who received supportive therapy (Barrowclough et al., 2001). In contrast, Stanley et al. (1996) showed that patients who received either CBT or supportive therapy improved in terms of anxiety, worry, and depression scores, and these improvements were maintained at the 6-month follow-up point. Overall, however, supportive therapy has not been shown to be more effective than CBT or relaxation training.

Bibliotherapy

Bibliotherapy, often used as an adjunct to psychotherapy, integrates the use of books or other written materials to facilitate change. For subsyndromal anxiety, bibliotherapy may be a reasonable treatment approach. An investigation by van't Veer-Tazelaar et al. (2009) suggested that a stepped-care approach using bibliotherapy as the first-line treatment strategy was effective at preventing the onset of anxiety disorders and major depression among older adults with subsyndromal symptoms at baseline (see Table 2.4).

Individual Versus Group Therapy

Treatment for anxiety can be delivered in either individual or group formats. Research has provided support for the effectiveness of CBT for late-life anxiety in group settings (Stanley et al., 1996; Stanley, Beck, et al., 2003; Wetherell et al., 2003). Benefits to patients in group therapy include those commonly highlighted, such as normalization, the instillation of hope, altruism and information sharing, cohesiveness and catharsis, and opportunities to practice social skills and relate interpersonally to others (Yalom & Leszcz, 2005). Older adults are often more isolated and may have fewer relationships with people, having lost more friends to death and illness. Group therapy can provide a social outlet for these individuals. Individual therapy is typically preferable for individuals who are suicidal, homicidal, psychotic, or in crisis, as well as those who are cognitively impaired. Additionally, some individuals may have a strong preference for individual psychotherapy.

TABLE 2.3
Supportive Therapy for Late-Life Anxiety

Author	Sample	Conditions	Manual	Length of treatment	Outcome measures	Findings
Barrowclough et al., 2001	$N = 55$; met criteria for panic disorder (51%), social phobia (2%), GAD (19%), or anxiety disorder not otherwise specified (28%)	1. CBT 2. ST	ST based on Woolfe, 1989	8–12 sessions of individual home-delivered therapy	BAI, HAMA, STAI-T	CBT group reduced self-reports of anxiety and depression significantly more than ST immediately following treatment and during follow-up.
Sallis et al., 1983	$N = 38$; M age = 71; subjective reports of anxiety	1. Relaxation training 2. CT with pleasant events scheduling 3. ST	ST based on Johnson, 1972	Ten 60-min group sessions	STAI-T	ST group significantly reduced trait anxiety. CT with pleasant events significantly reduced heart rate.
Stanley et al., 1996	$N = 48$; M age = 68; met criteria for GAD	1. CBT 2. ST	ST based on Borkovec & Costello, 1993	14 group sessions	GADSS, percentage of day worrying, PSWQ, WS, STAI-T, HAMA, FQ	CBT and ST groups both significantly reduced worry, anxiety, and depression. Gains maintained at 6-month follow-up.

Note. CBT = cognitive behavioral therapy; ST = supportive therapy; BAI = Beck Anxiety Inventory; HAMA = Hamilton Anxiety Rating Scale; STAI-T = State–Trait Anxiety Inventory–Trait; CT = cognitive therapy; GADSS = Generalized Anxiety Disorder Severity Scale; PSWQ = Penn State Worry Questionnaire; WS = Worry scale; FQ = Fear Questionnaire.

TABLE 2.4
Bibliotherapy for Late-Life Anxiety

Author	Sample	Conditions	Manual	Length of treatment	Outcome measures	Findings
van't Veer-Tazelaar et al., 2009	$N = 170$; M age = 81; subjects with subthreshold symptoms of depression or anxiety but not meeting full diagnostic criteria	1. Intervention: Preventive stepped-care program[a] 2. Usual care program	Lewinsohn et al., 1984	Stepped care over 12 months (4 steps, 3 months per step)	MINI (6, 12 months), CES-D (3, 6, 9, 12 months)	Intervention decreased incidence rate of anxiety and depression disorders by half over 1 year, compared with usual care.

Note. CES-D = Center for Epidemiologic Studies Depression Scale; MINI = Mini International Neuropsychiatric Interview.
[a]Preventive stepped-care program included: (a) watchful waiting; (b) cognitive behavior therapy–based bibliotherapy; (c) brief cognitive behavior therapy–based problem-solving therapy; (d) referral to primary care. This is in comparison with the usual care program, which allowed unrestricted access to usual care for depression or anxiety concerns.

Cognitive Impairment

Patients with cognitive impairment may have difficulty with components of CBT that are more abstract or require more information or cognitive processing. As mentioned previously, strategies taught in some modules may be more accessible to such patients and should be included in their treatment programs. Thus, cognitively impaired adults with anxiety may benefit more from modules that are more personally relevant, concrete, and behaviorally focused. Relaxation techniques, which are highly effective for anxiety reduction, are well-defined and simple exercises that can be easily taught to cognitively impaired patients. Modules that consist of predominantly behavioral strategies (vs. cognitive processes), such as sleep hygiene guidelines, worry control exercises, and in vivo exposures, are also likely to be better used by these patients. Life review can be beneficial because remote personal historical memory may be intact.

Adapting EBT for the Real World
Shiva G. Ghaed

The purpose of this section is to provide a practical guide for the implementation of evidence-based treatment in your clinical practice. It should be noted that the treatment approach outlined in the subsequent sections of this chapter is adapted primarily to GAD and general anxiety symptoms. There are several ways in which treatment can be adjusted for a geriatric patient. First and foremost, caregivers and family members can be included in treatment planning and encouraged to accompany the patient to psychotherapy sessions. Depending on the stamina of the patient, sessions can be abbreviated, if necessary, decreasing patient burden. Also, if feasible, home visits can be made, which remedies problems related to transportation, medical issues, and lack of initiative, or avoidance.

It is important to recognize that older adults may be new to the psychotherapy process, and thus even prior to receiving psychoeducation about anxiety, they may need general information about the mechanics of psychotherapy itself. Establishing good rapport with these patients can be critical to subsequent adherence to the treatment program. It is my firm belief that one of the most effective techniques for establishing rapport early on and setting the stage for productive therapy is providing my patients validation for any reticence about beginning therapy and addressing any issues related to stigma associated with mental illness or fears about opening up to a stranger who they feel may not understand their perspective or life experiences.

As a therapist in the Veterans Affairs health care system, one becomes all too familiar with patients who present with numerous comorbidities and complex medical histories. With these and most medical patients, I like to provide an overview of the topography of anxiety in later life, including prevalence statistics, education about the most common anxiety disorders for the patient's relevant age group, and typical symptomatology of geriatric anxiety. In addition, my patients often find it helpful when I provide a description of current pharmacotherapy and psychotherapy approaches to treatment, as well a rationale for implementing evidence-based treatments. In addition to the treatment narrative that follows, I offer a listing of resources and suggested readings on anxiety and various clinical approaches in Appendix 2.1.

Once I have laid the groundwork for psychotherapy with my patient, I present a general definition and description of CBT. I describe the interrelationships among thoughts, emotions, and behaviors and those factors that serve to maintain them. I explain that one of my goals is to help the patient achieve a heightened awareness of any patterns that might be occurring within this triangle and that might be causing distress or negative outcomes (e.g., alienation, depression). I emphasize that therapy is a collaborative process, but also a didactic one, and my patients will be taught how to monitor internal processes and analyze them in methodical and rational ways. I teach my patients how cognitive processes can influence feelings by using relevant examples and then asking them to think of similar scenarios in their own daily lives. I reassure them that I will help them learn how to properly evaluate and replace self-defeating or maladaptive thought patterns, which in turn will likely alter the resulting emotions (i.e., more realistic thoughts lead to more balanced emotions).

One critical element of effective psychotherapy that I emphasize early on is the need for my patient to be engaged and responsive to homework assignments. Behavioral change is also a critical component of improving mood and reducing anxiety. I explain to my patients that in addition to cognitive restructuring, CBT targets maladaptive behaviors, such as avoidance, that are highly negatively reinforcing and ultimately exacerbate and perpetuate anxiety. I explain that techniques such as self-monitoring and the completion of at-home practice assignments in between sessions will help them accomplish this goal of behavioral change. It should be noted that homework assignments, in particular, are highly predictive of positive therapy outcomes. Furthermore, I find that using a Socratic, or open-ended questioning, approach is more effective than using a lecturing style.

For patients who are not already taking a psychotropic medication, I discuss with them that such medications may be more effective for many people than what I have to offer, at least as a first step. I encourage them to talk about medications with their doctor; I also provide referrals to psychiatrists with expertise in working with older adults if they are interested in getting the opinion of a specialist. Many patients come to therapy feeling better but not completely well after taking a medication, and I have had success in using psychotherapy as an adjunct for patients who still have anxiety or worry symptoms even with pharmacotherapy. For patients who do not respond to psychotherapy alone, I engage in motivational interviewing techniques to encourage a medication trial.

On a final note, ethical principles and standards dictate that professional psychologists practice within their range of competency, I encourage clinicians to obtain relevant training in evidence-based treatments prior to implementing psychotherapy with patients. Specialized training for anxiety disorders can be obtained at any stage of one's professional career and in a variety of ways. Health care providers are encouraged to attend professional conferences that are not only evidence based in their approach but also whose focus is on geropsychology. It is recommended that trainees new to this field join consultation groups or receive supervision from a licensed professional with expertise in delivering evidence-based treatments to late-life patients. In addition, there are many well-written manuals that outline evidence-based psychotherapy for each of the different anxiety disorders (e.g., the *Treatments That Work* series published by Oxford University Press; see Appendix 2.1), and therapists are encouraged to use a more manualized approach during early stages of learning these treatments. Finally, therapists can obtain multimedia (e.g., CDs, videotapes) that contain sample interviews with patients who are using specific psychotherapy modalities.

CASE EXAMPLE

The patient, "Helen," is a 75-year-old, widowed, Caucasian woman who presents with anxiety and depressive symptoms (i.e., referred to the clinic for GAD). Her medical problems include chronic pain, difficulty sleeping, and severe arthritis. She reports being overly worried about "everything" in her life, including her daughter's divorce, her son's financial troubles, health problems, and more recently, being asked to help care for her grandchildren. She is not able to leave her home because she is afraid that her arthritis will flare up and she will not have a place to rest or that she might injure herself. She refuses to consider a psychotropic medication but agrees to a brief course of psychotherapy (i.e., approximately 20 sessions) to help her learn new ways to cope with her anxiety and the stress of uncontrollable events around her. As her therapist, I begin a collaborative approach with her to create a treatment plan that focuses on the most relevant and distressing presenting issues. Appendix 2.2 presents sample outlines for a course of 20 CBT sessions.

Presession 1: Assessment

In the waiting room, Helen is asked to complete a "problem list" (see Appendix 2.3) to identify sources and levels of distress over the past month. This will aid me in planning the CBT intervention and identifying the most relevant problem areas on which to focus most efforts. Patients should also be asked to complete a measure of anxiety or worry at this time and every few sessions to track progress. In this case, Helen is provided the eight-item short form of the Penn State Worry Questionnaire (Meyer, Miller, Metzger, & Borkovec, 1990), which was developed for older adults and is frequently used with geriatric GAD patients (see Appendix 2.4). It should be noted that there are other measures available for use, for example, the GAD-7 (Spitzer, Kroenke, Williams, & Lowe, 2006), the Geriatric Anxiety Inventory (Pachana et al., 2007), and the well-known Beck Anxiety Inventory (Beck, Epstein, Brown, & Steer, 1988). Assessment results indicated difficulties with sleep, uncontrollable worry, and difficulties solving real-life problems. As such, a main focus of the intervention included relaxation training, problem solving, sleep hygiene, and controlling worry. Other interventions (assertive communication, pleasant activities, acceptance and mindfulness, and time management) also assisted with Helen's distressing anxiety symptoms as well as supported the use of the main strategies listed above.

Sessions 1–2: Building Rapport and Psychoeducation

During the first session, Helen is provided validation for her problems, positive feedback for seeking help, and encouragement about the benefits of therapy, as well as reassurance that this process will be a collaborative and supportive one. An introduction to therapy includes psychoeducation to help her recognize the effects of anxiety on her QOL and assess her current level of functioning. Together we review her problem list and identify the most currently impactful issues—her isolation due to multiple medical problems, difficulty with establishing boundaries with family members, and coping effectively with events that are out of her control. I supply Helen with take-home reading, as I do for all of my patients, which includes information on the prevalence and physiology of anxiety and a description of anxiety disorders. Finally, I emphasize the importance of self-monitoring and at-home practice. We agree that our next few sessions will focus on basic lifestyle habits that might help to alleviate anxiety, beginning with relaxation training.

I also discuss with Helen the major components of anxiety that will be the targets of treatment—physical sensations, thoughts–feelings, and behaviors. I ask Helen to describe her subjective experience of anxiety and provide examples of situations in which she has felt anxious or worried in the recent past. Normalizing anxiety and discussing its adaptive purpose, as well as offering a general description of the physiological response to anxiety and fear (i.e., "fight or flight"), can be helpful for patients. I introduce the idea of anxiety and worry as parts of a vicious cycle that can be broken, and I emphasize to Helen that anxiety is not dangerous despite subjective experience, and that it is also time limited. At the close of the therapy session, I raise the issue of at-home practice, allowing Helen to direct and determine the negotiation of this critical therapy component with the hope of increased adherence. Homework for the remainder of therapy will include thought-tracking forms, which ask the patient to identify the activating event, automatic thought, resulting emotions, and any behavioral consequences of the thoughts and feelings, as well as an anxiety rating (0–10).

Note to therapist: When patients have supportive family members living in the area, I always invite family members to attend one of the first few sessions. Family members can play an important role in treatment and can also provide useful information about the ways in which anxiety is affecting the patient's life.

Sessions 3–5: Relaxation Training

These sessions are devoted to providing Helen with relaxation training to help her recognize levels of tension in her body when she is feeling anxious and to allow her an opportunity to gain the maximum benefit from the process. Imagery and guided relaxation are preferable for Helen because of her chronic severe arthritis, which makes PMR a less feasible option. Imagery provides another effective technique for patients to relax by offering an opportunity to daydream or remember pleasant or peaceful places or experiences. Realism and elaboration are encouraged, and patients are asked to use all of their senses when engaging in imagery. I provided Helen with an audiotape of a guided relaxation exercise to help her with at-home practice, in addition to a sample script (see Appendix 2.5).

Note to therapist: Adequate time should be allotted for relaxation training given its more immediate effects on anxiety. It is typically taught during earlier stages of treatment and typically includes teaching techniques such as diaphragmatic (or deep) breathing, PMR, and guided imagery.

Relaxation training is the most effective component of CBT for geriatric anxiety (Thorp et al., 2009). For this reason, I usually spend several sessions on this component and carefully assess changes in anxiety levels during the weeks devoted to relaxation practice. With patients who do not achieve substantial benefit, I problem solve; often they are not spending enough time practicing, and I will use motivational interviewing techniques to increase their at-home practice. Even with consistent practice, however, some patients do not respond. For patients in this category who are not currently taking anxiolytic medication, I initiate another discussion about the benefits of pharmacotherapy before attempting additional psychotherapeutic techniques.

In Helen's case, she has some success practicing her newly acquired relaxation techniques. She provides positive feedback about its effectiveness, although she did not practice as much as she had originally intended. We briefly discuss what might be hindering her from practicing relaxation more often (e.g., twice daily), and I emphasize the importance of practice in order to establish a new habit in one's life.

Sessions 6–8: Problem Solving

Next, Helen is introduced to the idea of problem solving as an integral part of daily functioning. She learns that her anxiety is a barrier to effective problem solving not only because anxiety depletes her of energy required to reason through problems but also because it increases the likelihood of her engaging in unproductive worry. Using personal examples she has shared, I point out that she worries about unlikely and catastrophic events and then engages in unwanted or undesirable behaviors (e.g., worst-case scenarios about the possibility of injury prevent her from leaving her home).

Note to therapist: The SOLVE approach is an easily recalled and useful technique that can be presented to the patient (Wetherell, Ayers, et al., 2009). SOLVE stands for the following steps for problem solving: Select a Specific problem (i.e., one that can be solved and is not too large or vague), Outline possible solutions (i.e., brainstorm all possible solutions), List pros–cons of the two best solutions, Visualize a plan for the best solution (i.e., consider timeline, resources needed), and Evaluate the outcome of the solution chosen. (See Appendix 2.6 for a sample worksheet.)

I typically introduce problem solving right after relaxation and continue to include problem-solving homework assignments through the entire course of therapy. I also encourage patients to continue their relaxation practice.

Session 9: Sleep Hygiene

We move on to the next basic lifestyle issue—sleep—and we evaluate Helen's current sleep habits. I instruct her on basic sleep hygiene techniques to alleviate sleep-related problems. One set of basic guidelines for sleep that can be easily recalled uses the acronym DROWSE (Wetherell, Ayers, et al., 2009). These important rules are as follows: *D*on't nap during the day; *R*estrict awake time in bed to 15 minutes (i.e., if patient is not asleep after 15 minutes of lying in bed, encourage the patient to get up and engage in a relaxing activity until the onset of sleepiness); *O*utdoor light (i.e., getting outside in the afternoon) can help regulate the sleep–wake cycle; *W*ithin 3 hours of bedtime, refrain from the use of alcohol, caffeine, heavy meals, or exercise; *S*leep and sex should be the only activities done in bed; and *E*stablish a sleep–wake schedule (anchoring sleep by consistent morning-awakening time). Helen is asked to begin self-monitoring and a self-evaluation of her actual sleep habits so that we might be able to identify and change current problem behaviors that are likely contributing to her sleep difficulties.

Note to therapist: Sleep-related issues are common and should be given adequate attention with late-life anxiety patients. Patients should be taught that sleep deprivation is not dangerous despite how distressing it can be, and most of our "lost" sleep can be made up later. In addition, they should be informed that performance and cognitive abilities are not as greatly affected as they might be led to believe by their own subjective assessment. For additional information on sleep-related issues, please refer to Chapter 3, this volume.

Session 10: Controlling Worry

Every session from here on out begins with a check-in in regard to Helen's at-home practices of relaxation, problem solving, and sleep hygiene. In this session, we discuss how Helen can learn to control her worry through thought-stopping and stimulus-control techniques. Helen has some difficulty doing this because she sees her life stressors, not her worry, as the problem. She learns stimulus control by identifying what she worries about and when she tends to worry about it. She is also encouraged and agrees to schedule "worry time" (e.g., 30 minutes) at a consistent time and daily. I encourage her to commit to a specific location in her home for this daily worry exercise (e.g., designated "worry chair") to make it more likely that she engages in the exercise.

Sessions 11–12: Assertiveness and Effective Communication

At this point, Helen shows a comfortable understanding of how her thoughts, feelings, and behaviors are related. Thus, we move ahead to focus on other relevant problem areas, specifically assertiveness and effective communication techniques. Helen agrees that this discussion may benefit her because she has never felt comfortable establishing boundaries that protect her time or health. We spent ample time in session role playing so that we can identify aspects of communicating with close family and friends that might be most challenging to her. We agree on homework for her that includes practicing her assertiveness skills with a close friend (e.g., saying no to her daughter when she cannot take care of her grandchildren) and eventually assertively communicating her needs directly to her daughter.

Note to therapist: Often, older adults with anxiety may communicate more passively because it enables them to avoid confrontation, and thus they experience anxiety in social situations. However, the consequences of passivity can include feelings of low self-esteem and worthlessness and overall dissatisfaction due to not being able to voice one's needs or desires. Patients should be taught the main styles of communication (i.e., passive, aggressive, assertive), using examples that are personally relevant. Whereas passivity can lead to withdrawal, aggression can lead to alienation, and both are related to anxiety. Assertive communication is encouraged as a means for healthier social interactions in which patients can establish their own needs while also respecting the needs of others. Use of the SAS technique can help patients practice assertiveness by: Stating the problem and its consequences (without judgment or assumptions), Asking for what is needed clearly and directly, and Spelling out the benefits to the other person of cooperation (Wetherell, Ayers, et al., 2009).

Sessions 13–14: Increasing Pleasant Activities

The focus of this session is on encouraging Helen to increase the number of pleasurable activities in her life, which will not only likely improve her mood but also distract her from her current focus on somatic symptoms and chronic pain. First, we create a list of pleasant activities that she has enjoyed in the past or would like to enjoy currently. Second, we discuss what might be the reasons that she is not engaging in these activities. Finally, we discuss how her anxiety and fears might be contributing to her diminished involvement in pleasant activities. I emphasize to Helen that another advantage of engaging in pleasant activities is that it will help disconfirm irrational thoughts that may be leading to her avoidance of leaving the home or being more active.

Note to therapist: It can be particularly beneficial to educate patients who have comorbid depression about the importance of engaging in life more actively. Patients should be provided psychoeducation on the frequent comorbidity of anxiety and depression and the similarity in how they function cognitively and behaviorally. Remind your patient that engaging in pleasant activities offers opportunities for positive reinforcement and provides them with reward, pleasure, social support, and improved self-esteem. It is important to note that involvement in a pleasurable activity is more likely to occur when an individual commits to a clear plan and schedules the activity. Work with your patients in session to identify activities that they might find pleasurable, make a plan and set an obtainable goal, and follow through on that plan.

Sessions 15–16: Acceptance and Mindfulness

One of the areas of distress for Helen is feeling that she has no control over the events around her. The goal of these sessions is to teach her mindfulness strategies that may help her process the idea of acceptance of her current life circumstances as well as increased tolerance of the uncontrollable events in her life. Our discussion of greater acceptance includes all the major topics in her life: her chronic health conditions, interpersonal problems or problems that her children are experiencing in their lives, and stage-of-life transition issues.

Note to therapist: This can be a more intense topic to process with patients, and for this reason it is recommended for use in the latter sessions of therapy. Acceptance can also be introduced as an alternative to other more traditional coping techniques (e.g., relaxation) that can enable an individual to feel a greater sense of control and comfort with challenging situations or realities. Patients learn the five main components of awareness, which are: (a) awareness of the positive aspects of one's experiences (vs. getting caught up in the suffering), (b) acknowledgment of the face value of experiences (vs. associations with past and interpretations about meaning of events), (c) broader focus (i.e., seeing the big picture vs. focusing on distress and fears; recognizing values and priorities; setting short- and long-term goals), (d) distress tolerance (i.e., through distraction, self-soothing, self-care), and (e) ongoing nature of acceptance process (i.e., requiring commitment to daily practice of skills; Wetherell, Ayers, et al., 2009).

Session 17: Managing Time

Anxiety can result from poor time management, and a large part of one's ability to function efficiently and effectively from day to day relies on the ability to manage daily tasks in a timely fashion. Patients should be provided basic skills and strategies for time management and encouraged to know their limits (i.e., how much can be handled in one day or at one time) and to say no when necessary (i.e., assertive communication). Prioritizing and delegating (when possible) tasks, as well as planning ahead (i.e., overestimating vs. underestimating time needed to accomplish a task) and being flexible (i.e., eliminating perfectionistic tendencies), can aid in reducing stress and anxiety.

Sessions 18–20: Maintaining Progress

In Helen's final therapy sessions, we discuss the great progress she has made, areas for continued effort, and ways in which she can maintain her newly acquired coping skills. We carefully review the concepts and strategies she has learned over the duration of therapy. One of the most beneficial aspects of this phase of therapy is to allow Helen to articulate her perceptions of therapy progress as well as her specific challenges. Together, we discuss and ascertain what skills or techniques were least and most used or useful for her, including how often, when, and where she actually implemented these techniques. In the final session, Helen and I focus on relapse prevention, reviewing some of her known triggers, vulnerabilities, and new ways of coping in these times of crisis. Although she will no longer have homework assigned to her, I emphasize the importance of solidifying a new healthy habit through daily practice.

APPENDIX 2.1: RESOURCES AND SUGGESTIONS
FOR FURTHER READING

Antony, M., & Roemer, L. (2011). *Theories of psychotherapy series: Behavior therapy.* Washington, DC: American Psychological Association.

Craske, G. M. (2010). *Theories of psychotherapy series: Cognitive-behavioral therapy.* Washington, DC: American Psychological Association.

Craske, G. M., & Barlow, D. H. (2006). *Treatments that work series: Mastery of your anxiety and worry* (2nd ed.). New York, NY: Oxford University Press.

Davis, M., McKay, M., & Eshelman, E. R. (2008). *The relaxation & stress reduction workbook* (6th ed.). Oakland, CA: New Harbinger.

Dobson, K. (2011). *Theories of psychotherapy series: Cognitive therapy.* Washington, DC: American Psychological Association.

D'Zurilla, T., & Nezu, A. M. (2006). *Problem-solving therapy: A positive approach to clinical intervention* (3rd ed.). New York, NY: Springer.

Laidlaw, K., Thompson, L. W., Gallagher-Thompson, D., & Dick-Siskin, L. (2003). *Cognitive behaviour therapy with older people.* Hoboken, NJ: Wiley.

Novalis, P. N., Rojcewicz, S. J., & Peele, R. (1993). *Clinical manual of supportive psychotherapy.* Washington, DC: American Psychiatric Press.

Sorocco, K. H., & Lauderdale, S. (in press). *Implementing CBT for older adults: Interdisciplinary guide.* New York, NY: Springer.

Stanley, M. A., Diefenbach, G. J., & Hopko, D. R. (2004). Cognitive behavioral treatment for older adults with generalized anxiety disorder: A therapist manual for primary care settings. *Behavior Modification, 28,* 73–117.

University of Washington, Advancing Integrated Mental Health Solutions. (n.d.) *Impact: Evidence-based depression care.* Retrieved from http://impact-uw.org/

General Assessment Instruments

Beck Anxiety Inventory (Beck & Steer, 1993): 21 items, somatic emphasis; Geriatric Anxiety Inventory (Pachana, Byrne, Siddle, Koloski, Harley, & Arnold, 2007): 20 items, yes/no format may be helpful for cognitively impaired, newly developed

State–Trait Anxiety Inventory (Spielberger, Gorsuch, & Lushene, 1970): 20 items each subscale, may measure neuroticism more than anxiety

Anxiety and Depression Assessment Instruments

Brief Symptom Inventory-18 (Derogatis, 2001): 6 items each for depression, anxiety, somatic symptoms on separate subscale

Hospital Anxiety and Depression Scale (Zigmond & Snaith, 1983): 7 items each subscale, somatic items omitted

Specialized Assessment Instruments

PTSD Checklist (Blanchard, Jones-Alexander, Buckley, & Forneris, 1996): 17 items, 6-item short form

GAD-7 (Spitzer, Kroenke, Williams, & Bernd Löwe, 2006): 7 items, assesses worry plus some associated symptoms

Penn State Worry Questionnaire (Meyer, Miller, Metzger, & Borkovec, 1990): 16- and 8-item forms, measures pathological worry rather than GAD, per se, heavily used in research

Fear Questionnaire (Marks & Mathews, 1979): 5 items per subscale, agoraphobia, blood-injury phobia, social phobia

Obsessive-Compulsive Inventory–Revised (Foa, 2002): 16 items, OCD symptoms

Savings Inventory–Revised (Frost, Steketee, & Grisham, 2004): 23 items, 3 subscales for clutter, acquisition, and ability to discard

Organizational Websites

Anxiety Disorders Association of America: http://www.adaa.org
Association for Behavioral and Cognitive Therapies: http://www.abct.org
International OCD Foundation: http://www.ocdfoundation.org

Research and Training Sites

Late-life anxiety research program: Melinda Stanley, PhD, Menninger Department of Psychiatry and Behavioral Sciences, Baylor College of Medicine, http://www.bcm.edu/psychiatry/anxietycare/

Late-life compulsive hoarding: Catherine Ayers, PhD, ABPP, VA San Diego Healthcare System/University of California, San Diego, cayers@ucsd.edu

Late-life generalized anxiety and stress: Julie Wetherell, PhD, VA San Diego Healthcare System/University of California, San Diego, jwetherell@ucsd.edu

Late-life posttraumatic stress disorder: Steven Thorp, PhD, VA San Diego Healthcare System/University of California, San Diego, sthorp@ucsd.edu

APPENDIX 2.2: SAMPLE COGNITIVE BEHAVIORAL THERAPY SESSION OUTLINES

Sessions 1–2

Establish rapport; provide validation and reassurance.
Review problem list; identify areas of most distress.
Provide psychoeducation about anxiety disorders and treatment.
Provide general outline for therapy process.
Emphasize importance of self-monitoring and at-home practice.
Invite family member to one session if possible.
Elicit reactions to sessions.

Sessions 3–5

Provide relaxation training.
Address issues related to not completing home assignments.
Elicit reactions to sessions.

Sessions 6–8

Review homework (i.e., relaxation techniques, thought–mood tracking).
Teach strategies for problem solving.
Elicit reactions to sessions.

Session 9

Review homework (i.e., relaxation techniques, problem solving).
Address issues related to not practicing new skills at home.
Teach patient sleep hygiene strategies.
Elicit reaction to session.

Session 10

Review homework (i.e., relaxation techniques, problem solving, sleep guidelines).
Address issues related to not completing home assignments.
Instruct patient on methods for thought stopping and stimulus control.
Help patient schedule "worry" time.
Elicit reaction to session.

Sessions 11–12

Review homework (i.e., relaxation techniques, worry time, problem solving).
Address issues related to not completing home assignments.
Teach assertiveness and communication skills.
Role play with patient and assign homework to practice in real life.
Elicit reactions to sessions.

Sessions 13–14

Review homework (i.e., relaxation techniques, worry time, problem solving, assertiveness skills).
Address issues related to not completing home assignments.
Discuss how to increase pleasant activity scheduling.
Elicit reactions to sessions.

Sessions 15–16

Review homework (i.e., relaxation techniques, thought–mood tracking, worry time, problem solving, assertiveness skills, pleasant activities).
Address issues related to not completing home assignments.
Discuss mindfulness and acceptance of uncontrollable events.
Elicit reactions to sessions.

Session 17

Discuss importance of using all skills learned thus far to manage time.
Move toward termination.
Elicit reaction to session.

Sessions 18–20

Review all skills–techniques–strategies learned to date.
Discuss progress made in therapy, areas of continued effort, ongoing challenges.
Elicit reaction to therapy process.
Final session—termination.

APPENDIX 2.3: PROBLEM LIST QUESTIONNAIRE

The following is a list of problems that some older people have. Please indicate *how much each problem has bothered you over the past month*, using the following 0–10 scale:

0	1	2	3	4	5	6	7	8	9	10
Not at all		*A little*			*Somewhat*			*Quite a bit*		*A lot*

_____ 1. Feeling tense or unable to relax.

_____ 2. Insomnia or trouble sleeping.

_____ 3. Difficulty making decisions.

_____ 4. Serious life problems (including medical conditions or disability).

_____ 5. Physical pain.

_____ 6. Time-consuming, unproductive worry.

_____ 7. Expecting the worst or thinking you can't cope with things.

_____ 8. Problems with anxiety or depression for many years (or all your life).

_____ 9. Feeling depressed or not interested in your usual activities.

_____ 10. Phobias or fears.

_____ 11. Not being assertive enough.

_____ 12. Not having enough time to get things done.

_____ 13. Other: _____

_____ 14. Other: _____

_____ 15. Other: _____

APPENDIX 2.4: PENN STATE WORRY QUESTIONNAIRE (ABBREVIATED)

Rate each of the following statements on a scale of 1 (*"not at all typical of me"*) to 5 (*"very typical of me"*). Please do not leave any items blank.

Not at all typical of me				Very typical of me
1	2	3	4	5

	1	2	3	4	5
1. My worries overwhelm me.	1	2	3	4	5
2. Many situations make me worry.	1	2	3	4	5
3. I know I should not worry about things, but I just cannot help it.	1	2	3	4	5
4. When I am under pressure I worry a lot.	1	2	3	4	5
5. I am always worrying about something	1	2	3	4	5
6. As soon as I finish one task, I start to worry about everything else I have to do.	1	2	3	4	5
7. I have been a worrier all my life.	1	2	3	4	5
8. I notice that I have been worrying about things.	1	2	3	4	5

From "Development and Validation of the Penn State Worry Questionnaire," by T. J. Meyer, M. L. Miller, R. L. Metzger, and T. D. Borkovec, 1990, *Behaviour Research and Therapy, 28*, pp. 487–495. Copyright 1990 by Elsevier. Reprinted with permission.

APPENDIX 2.5: RELAXATION SCRIPT

As you settle into relaxation pose, relax the weight of your body into the support of the floor. Notice how the body makes contact with the support of the floor. Relax the back of your legs . . . the back of your hips . . . your lower back, middle back and upper back. Relax the back of your shoulders . . . the back of your arms . . . the back of your neck . . . and the back of your head. Make any adjustments you need to, to relax the body into the ground more fully. Relax into the support of floor, completely.

Relax the muscles of your face. Relax your eyes and your forehead. Relax your temples and cheeks. Relax you mouth and jaw. Relax your whole face. Place your hands on your belly. Feel the rise and fall of your belly as you breathe. Notice each inhalation as it enters the body, and each exhalation as it exits the body. Let your breathing be soft, full and easy. No effort. Let the body be breathed. As you inhale, say silently in your mind, "Let." As you exhale, silently say "Go." Inhale, "Let." Exhale, "Go."

Continue to observe the breath, letting the body sink deeper and deeper into relaxation. Let your arms rest by your side. As you exhale, make a soft fist with each hand. As you inhale, relax the fist, and let your hands remain softly curled and relaxed. Let the body sink deeper and deeper into the support of the floor.

Now, bring your awareness to your feet. Feel the soles of your feet, and all 10 toes. Imagine that you could inhale and exhale through the soles of your feet. Imagine the breath entering the body through the soles of the feet, and exiting the body through the soles of the feet. Inhale. Exhale.

Now, bring your awareness to your hands. Feel the backs of the hands, the palms of the hands and all 10 fingers. Imagine that you could inhale and exhale through the palms of your hands. Imagine the breath entering the body through the palms of your hands, and exiting the body through the palms of your hands. Inhale. Exhale.

Now, bring your awareness to your belly. Feel the belly rise and fall as you breathe. Imagine that you could inhale and exhale through the navel. Imagine the breath entering the body through the navel and filling the belly. Imagine the breath exiting the body through the navel. Inhale. Exhale.

Now, let your mind relax deeper, below awareness of the breath. Let the mind relax below the level of concentration on anything, including the breath. Let the body and mind let go. Let go, completely.

[Let students or client relax. When you are ready, continue.]

Notice your breathing. Notice each inhalation as it enters the body and each exhalation as it exits the body. Bring your hands back to the belly, and feel the belly rise and fall. Let your breathing be soft, full and easy. Notice the whole body. Notice the whole body supported by the floor. Notice how easy it is to be in *your* body, in *this* moment. Feeling fully supported, in this pose, and in all areas of your life.

When you're ready to begin moving out of relaxation, gently move the fingers and toes. Let some sensation spread into the hands and feet. Stretch or move in any way that feels good. Then roll onto your right side, and rest there. Breathe easily. Take the best feeling of this relaxation with you.

APPENDIX 2.6: SOLVE WORKSHEET

Anxiety (circle a number):

0	1	2	3	4	5	6	7	8	9	10
None		Mild			Moderate		Strong			Extreme

Symptoms:
[   ] Worried, nervous, or fearful
[   ] Restlessness/keyed up/on edge
[   ] Fatigue
[   ] Difficulty concentrating
[   ] Irritability
[   ] Muscle tension
[   ] Trouble sleeping
[   ] Pounding or racing heart
[   ] Shortness of breath
[   ] Trembling or shaking
[   ] Nausea/diarrhea/upset stomach
[   ] Numbness or tingling
[   ] Faintness or dizzy spells
[   ] Hot or cold flashes

Use the "SOLVE" technique:

Specific problem:

_____

_____

_____

Outline all possible solutions:

_____

_____

_____

List the advantages and disadvantages of the two best solutions:

_____

_____

_____

Visualize a plan for the best solution, including resources and date:

_____

_____

_____

Evaluate the results: Do it and see how it worked.

_____

_____

_____

REFERENCES

Ayers, C. R., Sorrell, J. T., Thorp, S. R., & Wetherell, J. L. (2007). Evidence-based psychological treatments for late-life anxiety. *Psychology and Aging, 22*, 8–17. doi:10.1037/0882-7974.22.1.8

Barrowclough, C., King, P., Colville, J., Russell, E., Burns, A., & Tarrier, N. (2001). A randomized trial of the effectiveness of cognitive-behavioral therapy and supportive counseling for anxiety symptoms in older adults. *Journal of Consulting and Clinical Psychology, 69*, 756–762. doi:10.1037/0022-006X.69.5.756

Beck, A. T., Epstein, N., Brown, G., & Steer, R. A. (1988). An inventory for measuring clinical anxiety: Psychometric properties. *Journal of Consulting and Clinical Psychology, 56*, 893–897. doi:10.1037/0022-006X.56.6.893

Beck, A. T., & Steer, R. A. (1993). *Manual for the Beck Depression Inventory*. San Antonio, TX: The Psychological Corporation.

Beekman, A. T., Bremmer, M. A., Deeg, D. J. H., Van Balkom, A. J. L. M., Smit, J. H., De Beurs, E., . . . Van Tilberg, W. (1998). Anxiety disorders in later life: A report from the Longitudinal Aging Study Amsterdam. *International Journal of Geriatric Psychiatry, 13*, 717–726. doi:10.1002/(SICI)1099-1166(1998100)13:10<717::AID-GPS857>3.0.CO;2-M

Beekman, A. T., De Beurs, E., Van Balkom, A. M., Deeg, D. H., Van Dyck, R., & Van Tilburg, W. (2000). Anxiety and depression in later life: Co-occurrence and communality of risk factors. *American Journal of Psychiatry, 157*, 89–95.

Blanchard, E. B., Jones-Alexander, J., Buckley, T. C., & Forneris, C. A. (1996). Psychometric properties of the PTSD checklist (PCL). *Behavioral Research & Therapy, 34*, 669–673. doi:10.1016/0005-7967(96)00033-2

Brenes, G. A., Guralnik, J. M., Williamson, J., Fried, L. P., & Penninx, B. H. (2005). Correlates of anxiety symptoms in physically disabled older women. *American Journal of Geriatric Psychiatry, 13*, 15–22.

Brenes, G. A., Guralnik, J. M., Williamson, J. D., Fried, L. P., Simpson, C., Simonsick, E. M., & Penninx, B. W. J. H. (2005). The influence of anxiety on the progression of disability. *Journal of the American Geriatrics Society, 53*, 34–39. doi:10.1111/j.1532-5415.2005.53007.x

De Berry, S. (1981–1982). An evaluation of progressive muscle relaxation on stress related symptoms in a geriatric population. *International Journal of Aging & Human Development, 14*, 255–269. doi:10.2190/5C1R-9D61-YG2N-A7LV

De Berry, S. (1982). The effects of meditation-relaxation on anxiety and depression in a geriatric population. *Psychotherapy: Theory, Research & Practice, 19*, 512–521. doi:10.1037/h0088465

De Berry, S., Davis, S., & Reinhard, K. E. (1989). A comparison of meditation-relaxation and cognitive/behavioral techniques for reducing anxiety and depression in a geriatric population. *Journal of Geriatric Psychiatry, 22*, 231–247.

de Beurs, E., Beekman, A. T. F., van Balkom, A. M., Deeg, D. H., van Dyck, R., & van Tilburg, W. (1999). Consequences of anxiety in older persons: Its effect on disability, well-being and use health services. *Psychological Medicine, 29*, 583–593. doi:10.1017/S0033291799008351

Derogatis, L. R. (2001). *Brief Symptom Inventory 18: Administration, Scoring, and Procedures Manual.* Minneapolis, MN: NCS Pearson Inc.

Diem, S. J., Blackwell, T. L., Stone, K. L., Yaffe, K., Haney, E. M., Bliziotes, M. M., & Ensrud, K. E. (2007). Use of antidepressants and rates of hip bone loss in older women: The study of osteoporotic fractures. *Archives of Internal Medicine, 167*, 1240–1245. doi:10.1001/archinte.167.12.1240

Eckhardt-Henn, A., Breuer, P., Thomalske, C., Hoffmann, S. O., & Hopf, H. C. (2003). Anxiety disorders and other psychiatric subgroups in patients complaining of dizziness. *Journal of Anxiety Disorders, 17*, 369–388. doi:10.1016/S0887-6185(02)00226-8

Flint, A. J. (1994). Epidemiology and comorbidity of anxiety disorders in the elderly. *American Journal of Psychiatry, 151*, 640–649.

Foa, E. B., Huppert, J. D., Leiberg, S., Langner, R., Kichic, R., Hajcak, G., & Salkovskis, P. M. (2002). The obsessive-compulsive inventory: Development and validation of a short version. *Psychological Assessment, 14*, 485–496. doi:10.1037/1040-3590.14.4.485

Frost, R. O., Steketee, G., & Grisham, J. (2004). Measurement of compulsive hoarding: saving inventory-revised. *Behaviour Research and Therapy, 42*, 1163–1182. doi:10.1016/j.brat.2003.07.006

Golden, A. G., Preston, R. A., Barnett, S. D., Llorente, M., Hamdan, K., & Silverman, M. A. (1999). Inappropriate medication prescribing in homebound older adults. *Journal of the American Geriatrics Society, 47*, 948–953.

Gorenstein, E. E., Kleber, M. S., Mohlman, J., DeJesus, M., Gorman, J. M., & Papp, L. A. (2005). Cognitive-behavioral therapy for management of anxiety and medication taper in older adults. *American Journal of Geriatric Psychiatry, 13*, 901–909.

Gurian, B. S., & Minor, J. H. (1991). Anxiety in the elderly: Treatment and research. In C. Salzman & B. D. Lebowitz (Eds.), *Clinical presentation of anxiety in the elderly* (pp. 31–44). New York, NY: Springer.

Haug, T. T., Mykletun, A., & Dahl, A. A. (2002). Are anxiety and depression related to gastrointestinal symptoms in the general population? *Scandinavian Journal of Gastroenterology, 37*, 294–298. doi:10.1080/003655202317284192

Hendriks, G. J., Oude Voshaar, R. C., Keijsers, G. P. J., Hoogduin, C. A. L., & van Balkom, A. J. L. M. (2008). Cognitive-behavioural therapy for late-life anxiety disorders: A meta-analysis. *Acta Psychiatrica Scandinavica, 117*, 403–411. doi:10.1111/j.1600-0447.2008.01190.x

Himmelfarb, S., & Murrell, S. A. (1984). The prevalence and correlates of anxiety symptoms in older adults. *Journal of Psychology, 116*, 159–167. doi:10.1080/00223980.1984.9923632

Kawachi, I., Sparrow, D., Vokonas, P. S., & Weiss, S. T. (1994). Symptoms of anxiety and risk of coronary heart disease. *Circulation, 90,* 2225–2229.

Keller, J. F., Croake, J. W., & Brooking, J. Y. (1975). Effects of a program in rational thinking on anxieties in older persons. *Journal of Counseling Psychology, 22,* 54–57. doi:10.1037/h0076144

Kessler, R. C., Berglund, P., Demler, O., Jin, R., Merikangas, K. R., & Walters, E. E. (2005). Lifetime prevalence and age-of-onset distributions of *DSM-IV* disorders in the National Comorbidity Survey Replication. *Archives of General Psychiatry, 62,* 593–602. doi:10.1001/archpsyc.62.6.593

Khan, A., Leventhal, R. M., Khan, S., & Brown, W. A. (2002). Severity of depression and response to antidepressants and placebo: An analysis of the Food and Drug Administration database. *Journal of Clinical Psychopharmacology, 22,* 40–45. doi:10.1097/00004714-200202000-00007

Klap, R., Unroe, K. T., & Unutzer, J. (2003). Caring for mental illness in the United States: A focus on older adults. *American Journal of Geriatric Psychiatry, 11,* 517–524. doi:10.1176/appi.ajgp.11.5.517

Lenze, E. J., Mulsant, B. H., Mohlman, J., Shear, M. K., Dew, M. A., Schulz, R., . . . Reynolds, C. F., III (2005). Generalized anxiety disorder in late life: Lifetime course and comorbidity with major depressive disorder. *American Journal of Geriatric Psychiatry, 13,* 77–80. doi:10.1176/appi.ajgp.13.1.77

Lenze, E. J., Mulsant, B. H., Shear, M. K., Schulberg, H. C., Dew, M. A., Begley, A. E., . . . Reynolds, C. F., III (2000). Comorbid anxiety disorders in depressed elderly patients. *American Journal of Psychiatry, 157,* 722–728. doi:10.1176/appi.ajp.157.5.722

Lenze, E. J., Rogers, J. C., Martire, L. M., Mulsant, B. H., Rollman, B. L., Dew, M. A., . . . Reynolds, C. F., III (2001). The association of late-life depression and anxiety with physical disability: A review of the literature and prospectus for future research. *American Journal of Geriatric Psychiatry, 9,* 113–135. doi:10.1176/appi.ajgp.9.2.113

Lenze, E. J., Rollman, B. L., Shear, M. K., Dew, M. A., Pollock, B. G., Ciliberti, C., . . . Reynolds, C. F., III (2009). Escitalopram for older adults with generalized anxiety disorder: A randomized controlled trial. *JAMA, 301,* 295–303. doi:10.1001/jama.2008.977

Lenze, E. J., & Wetherell, J. L. (2009). Bringing the bedside to the bench, and then to the community: A prospectus for intervention research in late-life anxiety disorders. *International Journal of Geriatric Psychiatry, 24,* 1–14. doi:10.1002/gps.2074

Lewinsohn, P. M., Antonuccio, D. O., Steinmetz, J. L., & Teri, L. (1984). *The coping with depression course: A psychoeducational intervention for unipolar depression.* Eugene, OR: Castalia.

Marks, I. M., & Mathews, A. M. (1979). Brief standard self-rating for phobic patients. *Behaviour Research & Therapy, 17,* 263–267. doi:10.1016/0005-7967(79)90041-X

Mamdani, M., Rapoport, M., Shulman, K. I., Herrmann, N., & Rochon, P. A. (2005). Mental health-related drug utilization among older adults: Prevalence, trends, and costs. *American Journal of Geriatric Psychiatry, 13,* 892–900.

Meyer, T. J., Miller, M. L., Metzger, R. L., & Borkovec, T. D. (1990). Development and validation of the Penn State Worry Questionnaire. *Behaviour Research and Therapy, 28*, 487–495. doi:10.1016/0005-7967(90)90135-6

Mohlman, J., Gorenstein, E. E., Kleber, M., DeJesus, M., Gorman, J. M., & Papp, L. A. (2003). Standard and enhanced cognitive-behavioral therapy for late-life generalized anxiety disorder. *American Journal of Geriatric Psychiatry, 11*, 24–32.

Mohlman, J., & Gorman, J. M. (2005). The role of executive functioning in CBT: A pilot study with anxious older adults. *Behaviour Research and Therapy, 43*, 447–465. doi:10.1016/j.brat.2004.03.007

Novalis, P. N., Rojcewicz, S. J., & Peele, R. (1993). *Clinical manual of supportive psychotherapy*. Washington, DC: American Psychiatric Press.

Pachana, N. A., Byrne, G. J., Siddle, H., Koloski, N., Harley, E., & Arnold, E. (2007). Development and validation of the Geriatric Anxiety Inventory. *International Psychogeriatrics, 19*, 103–114. doi:10.1017/S1041610206003504

Paterniti, S., Dufouil, C., & Alperovitch, A. (2002). Long-term benzodiazepine use and cognitive decline in the elderly: The epidemiology of vascular aging study. *Journal of Clinical Psychopharmacology, 22*, 285–293. doi:10.1097/00004714-200206000-00009

Pearson, J. L., & Brown, G. K. (2000). Suicide prevention in late life: Directions for science and practice. *Clinical Psychology Review, 20*, 685–705. doi:10.1016/S0272-7358(99)00066-5

Pinquart, M., & Duberstein, P. R. (2007). Treatment of anxiety in older adults: A meta-analytic comparison of behavioral and pharmacological interventions. *American Journal of Geriatric Psychiatry, 15*, 639–651.

Poikolainen, K. (2000). Risk factors for alcohol dependence: A case-control study. *Alcohol and Alcoholism, 35*, 190–196. doi:10.1093/alcalc/35.2.190

Rickard, H. C., Scogin, F., & Keith, S. (1994). A one-year follow-up of relaxation training for elders with subjective anxiety. *The Gerontologist, 34*, 121–122. doi:10.1093/geront/34.1.121

Sallis, J. F., Lichstein, K. L., Clarkson, A. D., Stalgaitis, S., & Campbell, M. (1983). Anxiety and depression management for the elderly. *International Journal of Behavioral Geriatrics, 1*, 3–12.

Schuurmans, J., Comijs, H., Emmelkamp, P. M., Gundy, C. M., Weijnen, I., van den Hout, M., & van Dyck, R. (2006). A randomized, controlled trial of the effectiveness of cognitive-behavioral therapy and sertraline versus a waitlist control group for anxiety disorders in older adults. *American Journal of Geriatric Psychiatry, 14*, 255–263.

Schuurmans, J., Comijs, H., Emmelkamp, P. M., Weijnen, I. J., van den Hout, M., & van Dyck, R. (2009). Long-term effectiveness and prediction of treatment outcome in cognitive behavioral therapy and sertraline for late-life anxiety disorders. *International Psychogeriatrics, 21*, 1148–1159.

Scogin, F., Rickard, H. C., Keith, S., Wilson, J., & McElreath, L. (1992). Progressive and imaginal relaxation training for elderly persons with subjective anxiety. *Psychology and Aging, 7*, 419–424. doi:10.1037/0882-7974.7.3.419

Spielberger, C. D., Gorsuch, R. L., & Lushene, R. E. (1970). *Manual for the State-Trait Anxiety Inventory*. Palo Alto, CA: Consulting Psychologists Press.

Spitzer, R. L., Kroenke, K., Williams, J. B., & Lowe, B. (2006). A brief measure for assessing generalized anxiety disorder: The GAD-7. *Archives of Internal Medicine, 166*, 1092–1097.

Stanley, M. A., Beck, J. G., & Glassco, J. D. (1996). Treatment of generalized anxiety in older adults: A preliminary comparison of cognitive-behavioral and supportive approaches. *Behavior Therapy, 27*, 565–581. doi:10.1016/S0005-7894 (96)80044-X

Stanley, M. A., Beck, J. G., Novy, D. M., Averill, P. M., Swann, G. J., Diefenbach, G. J., & Hopko, D. R. (2003). Cognitive-behavioral treatment of late-life generalized anxiety disorder. *Journal of Consulting and Clinical Psychology, 71*, 309–319. doi:10.1037/0022-006X.71.2.309

Stanley, M. A., Hopko, D. R., Diefenbach, G. J., Bourland, S. L., Rodriquez, H., & Wagener, P. (2003). Cognitive-behavioral therapy for late-life generalized anxiety disorder in primary care. *American Journal of Geriatric Psychiatry, 11*, 92–96.

Stanley, M. A., Roberts, R. E., Bourland, S. L., & Novy, D. M. (2001). Anxiety disorders among older primary care patients. *Journal of Clinical Geropsychology, 7*, 105–116. doi:10.1023/A:1009533621832

Stanley, M. A., Wilson, N. L., Novy, D. M., Rhoades, H. M., Wagener, P. D., Greisinger, A. J., . . . Kunik, M. E. (2009). Cognitive behavior therapy for generalized anxiety disorder among older adults in primary care: A randomized clinical trial. *JAMA, 301*, 1460–1467. doi:10.1001/jama.2009.458

Szanto, K., Prigerson, H., Houck, P., Ehrenpreis, L., & Reynolds, C. F., III (1997). Suicidal ideation in elderly bereaved: The role of complication grief. *Suicide & Life-Threatening Behavior, 27*, 194–207.

Thorp, S. R., Ayers, C. R., Nuevo, R., Stoddard, J. A., Sorrell, J. T., & Wetherell, J. L. (2009). Meta-analysis comparing different behavioral treatments for late-life anxiety. *American Journal of Geriatric Psychiatry, 17*, 105–115. doi:10.1097/ JGP.0b013e31818b3f7e

Van Hout, H. P., Beekman, A. F., De Beurs, E., Comijs, H., Van Marwijk, H., De Haan, M., . . . Deeg, D. J. H. (2004). Anxiety and the risk of death in older men and women. *The British Journal of Psychiatry, 185*, 399–404. doi:10.1192/ bjp.185.5.399

van't Veer-Tazelaar, P. J., van Marwijk, H. W. J., van Oppen, P., van Hout, H. P. J., van der Horst, H. E., Cuijpers, P., . . . Beekman, A. T. F. (2009). Stepped-care prevention of anxiety and depression in late life: A randomized controlled trial. *Archives of General Psychiatry, 66*, 297–304. doi:10.1001/archgenpsychiatry.2008.555

Wetherell, J. L., Ayers, C. R., Sorrell, J. T., Thorp, S. R., Nuevo, R., Belding, W., . . . Patterson, T. L. (2009). Modular treatment for anxiety in older primary care patients. *American Journal of Geriatric Psychiatry, 17*, 483–492. doi:10.1097/ JGP.0b013e3181a31fb5

Wetherell, J. L., Gatz, M., & Craske, M. G. (2003). Treatment of generalized anxiety disorder in older adults. *Journal of Consulting and Clinical Psychology, 71*, 31–40. doi:10.1037/0022-006X.71.1.31

Wetherell, J. L., Kaplan, R. M., Kallenberg, G., Dresselhaus, T. R., Sieber, W. J., & Lang, A. J. (2004). Mental health treatment preferences of older and younger primary care patients. *International Journal of Psychiatry in Medicine, 34*, 219–233. doi:10.2190/QA7Y-TX1Y-WM45-KGV7

Wetherell, J. L., Petkus, A. J., McChesney, K., Stein, M. B., Judd, P. H., Rockwell, E., . . . Patterson, T. L. (2009). Older adults are less accurate than younger adults at identifying symptoms of anxiety and depression. *Journal of Nervous and Mental Disease, 197*, 623–626. doi:10.1097/NMD.0b013e3181b0c081

Wetherell, J. L., Sorrell, J. T., Thorp, S. R., & Patterson, T. L. (2005). Psychological interventions for late-life anxiety: A review and early lessons from the CALM Study. *Journal of Geriatric Psychiatry and Neurology, 18*, 72–82. doi:10.1177/0891988705276058

Wetherell, J. L., Thorp, S. R., Patterson, T. L., Golshan, S., Jeste, D. V., & Gatz, M. (2004). Quality of life in geriatric generalized anxiety disorder: A preliminary investigation. *Journal of Psychiatric Research, 38*, 305–312. doi:10.1016/j.jpsychires.2003.09.003

Yalom, I. D., & Leszcz, M. (2005). *The theory and practice of group psychotherapy* (5th ed.). New York, NY: Basic Books.

Zigmond, A. S., & Snaith, R. P. (1983). The Hospital Anxiety and Depression Scale. *Acta Psychiatrica Scandinavica, 67*, 361–370. doi:10.1111/j.1600-0447.1983.tb09716.x

Zwart, J.-A., Dyb, G., Hagen, K., Ødegard, K. J., Dahl, A. A., Bovim, G., & Stovner, L. J. (2003). Depression and anxiety disorders associated with headache frequency. The Nord-Trøndelag Health Study. *European Journal of Neurology, 10*, 147–152. doi:10.1046/j.1468-1331.2003.00551.x

3

EVIDENCE-BASED TREATMENTS FOR INSOMNIA IN OLDER ADULTS

HALEY R. DILLON, RYAN G. WETZLER, AND KENNETH L. LICHSTEIN

Insomnia is the most common sleep problem in the general population, with chronic insomnia being most prevalent in older adults (Foley et al., 1995; Lichstein, Durrence, Riedel, Taylor, & Bush, 2004; Morphy, Dunn, Lewis, Boardman, & Croft, 2007; Ohayon, 2002). *Insomnia* is defined as a complaint of difficulty falling asleep, difficulty staying asleep, early morning awakenings, and/or nonrestorative sleep, which results in daytime consequences (*Diagnostic and Statistical Manual of Mental Disorders,* 4th ed., text revision; *DSM–IV–TR;* American Psychiatric Association, 2000). Particularly in older adults, consequences of insomnia can include increased risk for the onset of depression and anxiety, substance abuse, cognitive decline, falls, and reduced quality of life (Jelicic et al., 2002; Perlis et al., 2006; Stone, Ensrud, & Ancoli-Israel, 2008; Taylor, Lichstein, & Durrence, 2003; Zammit, Weiner, Damato, Sillup, & McMillan, 1999).

Although insomnia is generally more prevalent, more chronic, and more impairing in older adults, poor sleep is not an inevitable result of aging. Instead, sleep disturbances in older adults are associated with high levels of medical and psychiatric comorbidities (Foley, Ancoli-Israel, Britz, & Walsh, 2004; Foley, Monjan, Simonsick, Wallace, & Blazer, 1999; Taylor et al., 2007; Vitiello, Moe, & Prinz, 2002). Medications used to treat these concurrent health problems can further impair sleep in older adults, as can circadian rhythm disturbances and other primary sleep disorders (i.e., obstructive sleep apnea, periodic leg movement disorder) that are more common with increasing age (Ancoli-Israel & Cooke, 2005; Vaz Fragoso & Gill, 2007).

Normal age-related changes in sleep structure and pattern can also render an individual more susceptible to sleep disturbance (Morgan, 2000). Sleep becomes lighter with age, as the amount of time spent in Stages 1 and 2 sleep increases and deep slow-wave sleep (Stages 3–4) decreases. The shifts between sleep stages are more frequent, and combined with the greater propensity for light sleep, this leads older adults to experience more nighttime awakenings and arousals. Average duration of nighttime sleep is reduced in older adults, although their sleep need has typically not changed. Finally, circadian rhythm changes can affect the timing and resilience of the 24-hour sleep–wake cycle. For example, the sleep phase of older adults tends to advance, with typical sleep onset and wake-up times that are several hours earlier than desired. Changes in activity level, napping behavior, and light exposure can also influence the sleep–wake cycle. As a result, older adults may need to adjust their expectations and habits to continue obtaining the sleep they need.

Over the past 2 decades, psychological treatments for sleep disturbances have increasingly focused on older adults, with several reviews and meta-analyses reporting beneficial effects of cognitive behavioral treatments for late-life insomnia (e.g., Irwin, Cole, & Nicassio, 2006; Montgomery & Dennis, 2004; Nau, McCrae, Cook, & Lichstein, 2005). In spite of this progress, however, sleep disorders remain a significant public health concern (Colten & Altevogt, 2006). In addition, there is often a gap between research and actual clinical practice (Persons, 1995). To address these concerns, McCurry, Logsdon, Teri, and Vitiello (2007) conducted a review of the insomnia treatment literature to identify the most efficacious psychological treatments for older adults. Following the criteria specified by the American Psychological Association's (APA) Committee on Science and Practice for Clinical Psychology (Weisz & Hawley, 2001), McCurry et al. identified two evidence-based treatments (EBTs) for insomnia in older adults; sleep restriction-compression therapy and multicomponent cognitive behavioral therapy for insomnia (CBT-I). A third treatment, stimulus control therapy, was partially supported as an EBT for insomnia in older adults.

This chapter aims to facilitate the implementation of EBTs for insomnia in older adults by reviewing both research and clinical application. The first part of the chapter presents the identified EBTs for late-life insomnia and summarizes current research support. The remainder of the chapter addresses the application of these psychological treatments in clinical settings. A certified behavioral sleep medicine (BSM) specialist shares his experiences as a clinician and presents a case example to illustrate how EBTs can be provided in clinical practice. Finally, the chapter concludes with sample treatment materials and patient handouts.

The Evidence

Haley R. Dillon and Kenneth L. Lichstein

This section describes the EBTs for sleep disturbances in older adults that were identified in the original article by McCurry et al. (2007). In addition, we review the most recent evidence from an updated literature search (from January 2006 through December 2008).

SLEEP RESTRICTION—SLEEP COMPRESSION THERAPY

Sleep restriction therapy (Spielman, Saskin, & Thorpy, 1987) is a behavioral treatment for insomnia designed to improve sleep consolidation. Many people with insomnia spend too much time in bed in an effort to recover lost sleep. However, this practice often leads to an increase in sleep fragmentation and time spent awake in bed, which can heighten sleep performance anxiety and perpetuate the sleep difficulty. The goal of sleep restriction therapy is to maximize *sleep efficiency* (SE; ratio of time spent asleep to time spent in bed × 100), by limiting the time spent in bed to match the actual or estimated amount of sleep reported by the client. Any mild sleep deprivation that is experienced by restricting time in bed will increase homeostatic drive and make it easier to fall asleep and stay asleep during the allotted time period in bed, thus consolidating sleep.

Sleep restriction therapy begins with having clients complete 2 to 3 weeks of sleep diaries (see the example diary in Appendix 3.1), which provides a daily record of the client's self-reported sleep. The initial time in bed (TIB) prescription is then set to be roughly equal to the average total sleep time (TST) calculated from the baseline sleep diaries. On the basis of the prescribed amount of TIB, a sleep schedule with a fixed bedtime and arise time is set for the following week. The client continues to keep sleep diaries throughout the course of treatment, and the amount of time allowed in bed is subsequently increased or decreased based on the client's reported sleep efficiencies, until an optimal sleep schedule is reached. (See Wohlgemuth

& Edinger, 2000, for detailed instructions on implementing sleep restriction therapy.)

Sleep compression therapy is a modified version of sleep restriction that gradually restricts TIB to match TST instead of making this change immediately. In sleep compression (Lichstein, Thomas, & McCurry, 2010; Riedel, Lichstein, & Dwyer, 1995), the client's self-reported average TST and average TIB are calculated from 2 weeks of baseline sleep diaries. The difference between the average TIB and average TST is then divided equally among a prespecified number of sessions to gradually reach the same goal as sleep restriction therapy, where TIB matches TST.

McCurry et al. (2007) identified three studies that provide evidence-based support for sleep restriction–compression therapy in older adults with insomnia. One study used sleep restriction (Friedman et al., 2000), whereas the other two studies used sleep compression (Lichstein, Riedel, Wilson, Lester, & Aguillard, 2001; Riedel et al., 1995). The mean effect size (ES) relative to controls across the three studies was 0.77. No new studies meeting EBT criteria have tested sleep restriction–compression as a stand-alone treatment for insomnia in older adults.

MULTICOMPONENT CBT

As noted in another review of psychological treatments for insomnia, there is a growing trend for combining two or more individual therapies into a single package treatment (Morin et al., 2006). Multicomponent CBT-I is a popular combination treatment that meets evidence-based criteria for treating late-life insomnia. Although specific techniques can vary, CBT-I typically includes sleep hygiene education, stimulus control, sleep restriction–compression, relaxation training, and cognitive therapy.

Sleep hygiene is a standard component of multicomponent CBT-I that refers to a set of behaviors and lifestyle practices that can affect sleep. Examples include avoiding caffeine and/or alcohol use near bedtime and keeping a comfortable sleep environment (i.e., dark room, cool temperature, reduced noise). There is not a standard set of recommendations for good sleep hygiene, but a sample patient handout of common guidelines is included in Appendix 3.2.

Behavioral interventions such as sleep restriction–compression and stimulus control therapy are the mainstay of CBT-I. Stimulus control therapy (Bootzin, 1977; Bootzin & Epstein, 2000) is based on the idea that the bed and bedroom can become associated with states of wakefulness (e.g., tossing and turning, watching television, reading, worrying). Over time, the bed and bedroom can become conditioned cues for arousal and wakefulness instead of sleep. Stimulus control therapy includes a set of behavioral instructions (see Appendix 3.3) designed to break these maladaptive associations between the bed and sleep-incompatible behaviors, and strengthen the bed and bedroom as discriminative stimuli for sleep.

Relaxation training is often included as a way to help reduce physiological and/or cognitive arousal that may interfere with sleep. A variety of relaxation procedures have been used in CBT-I, including progressive muscle relaxation, passive relaxation, guided imagery, autogenic training, meditation, and biofeedback (Manber & Kuo, 2002). A verbatim script for a hybrid relaxation procedure that involves passive relaxation and autogenic phrases can be found in Lichstein (2000).

Finally, most CBT-I treatment packages include a cognitive or educational component that addresses sleep-related beliefs and attitudes, as well as treatment motivation and compliance. People with insomnia often hold dysfunctional beliefs and unrealistic expectations about their sleep that can lead to sleep-incompatible behaviors (e.g., spending excessive time in bed, increased arousal and bedtime worry about sleep loss) that maintain the sleep disturbance. Formal cognitive restructuring therapy (described in Morin, Savard, & Blais, 2000) helps clients identify, challenge, and replace dysfunctional cognitions with a more realistic and rational view. The degree of sleep education that is shared with clients can aid in this goal. Particularly with older adult populations, information about normal age-related changes is essential.

The original review of EBTs for late-life insomnia identified seven studies that support CBT-I in older adults (Hoelscher & Edinger, 1988; Lichstein, Wilson, & Johnson, 2000; McCurry, Logsdon, Vitiello, & Teri, 1998; Morin, Colecchi, Stone, Sood, & Brink, 1999; Morin, Kowatch, Barry, & Walton, 1993; Rybarczyk et al., 2005; Rybarczyk, Lopez, Benson, Alsten, & Stepanski, 2002). An updated literature search identified one additional study that contributed to the evidence base for CBT-I (Sivertsen et al., 2006). Table 3.1 lists treatment components and between-group ESs at posttreatment for all eight trials that support CBT-I. Across the eight studies, the mean ES for CBT relative to control was large at 1.03.

In the newly added study, Sivertsen et al. (2006) found beneficial effects for CBT-I when comparing it with pharmacotherapy and placebo treatment in 46 older adults. At 6 weeks posttreatment, objective measures of sleep (polysomnography) showed that the CBT-I group had significantly less total wake time at night than both the pharmacotherapy (ES = 1.23) and placebo (ES = 1.61) groups and had a significantly better sleep efficiency than the placebo group (ES = 1.32). An important finding to note is that beneficial effects in the CBT-I group were actually stronger at the 6-month follow-up than at posttreatment.

TABLE 3.1
Studies That Contribute to the Evidence-Based Status of Multicomponent Cognitive Behavioral Therapy for Insomnia in Older Adults

Study	Treatment conditions	Length and format	M ES
Hoelscher & Edinger, 1988	Multicomponent (SC, SR, education) (multiple baseline design)	4 individual sessions	1.12
Lichstein, Wilson, & Johnson, 2000	Multicomponent (SH, SC, RE) vs. wait-list control	4 individual sessions	0.76
McCurry, Logsdon, Vitiello, & Teri, 1998	Multicomponent (SH, SC, SCO, RE) vs. wait-list control	4–6 sessions (4 individual, 6 group)	0.74
Morin, Kowatch, Barry, & Walton, 1993	CBT (SH, SC, SR, CT) vs. wait-list control	8 group sessions	1.01
Morin, Colecchi, Stone, Sood, & Brink, 1999	CBT (SH, SC, SR, CT) vs. medication vs. combination CBT–medication vs. placebo	8 group sessions	1.07
Rybarczyk, Lopez, Benson, Alsten, & Stepanski, 2002	CBT (SH, SC, SR, CT, RE) vs. HART vs. wait-list control	8 group sessions	1.36
Rybarczyk et al., 2005	CBT (SH, SC, SR, CT, RE) vs. SMW–placebo	8 group sessions	0.76
Sivertsen et al., 2006	CBT (SH, SC, SR, CT, RE) vs. medication vs. placebo	6 individual sessions	1.39

Note. ES = effect size; SC = stimulus control therapy; SR = sleep restriction therapy; SH = sleep hygiene; RE = relaxation therapy; SCO = sleep compression therapy; CT = cognitive therapy; CBT = cognitive behavior therapy; HART = home audiotape relaxation therapy; SMW = stress management and wellness.

The new search also yielded two studies testing abbreviated versions of CBT-I in older adults. According to the APA coding manual, two versions of a treatment program are considered to be the same treatment if study authors judge the treatment to be essentially the same and treatment duration is at least 75% of the longer version. Because of the much shorter duration of the abbreviated version, it will be considered a separate treatment from the four- or eight-session CBT-I previously described.

Abbreviated CBT-I could not be classified as a separate EBT because there was not a minimum of 30 participants who represented the active treatment across the two studies. However, both studies found the brief multicomponent treatment to be superior to sleep hygiene education–information-only control groups. Germain et al. (2006) delivered a combination of sleep restriction, stimulus control, and sleep hygiene education (n = 17) in one initial treatment session that was followed up 2 weeks later with a 30-minute "booster session." McCrae et al. (2007) used two in-person treatment sessions and two follow-up phone calls to administer a multicomponent treatment composed of sleep restriction, stimulus control, and relaxation training (n = 11). Corroborating evidence is needed to provide further support for the use of abbreviated CBT-I in older adults. Future studies should also explore whether variations in the length–duration of CBT-I affect treatment outcome.

TREATMENTS REQUIRING ADDITIONAL EVIDENCE

Stimulus control therapy, as previously described, is a behavioral intervention for insomnia that can be used in combination with other techniques or as a standalone treatment. McCurry et al. (2007) identified two studies (Morin & Azrin, 1988; Puder, Lacks, Bertelson, & Storandt, 1983) that revealed group stimulus control therapy with older adults to be superior to wait-list/delayed-treatment control conditions, but the number of participants across studies that received stimulus control did not meet evidence-based criteria of 30 participants in the active treatment condition. An updated search of the literature did not yield additional studies by using stimulus control as an individual treatment, so it remains a partially supported treatment. However, the lack of evidence for classifying stimulus control therapy as an EBT for late-life insomnia is likely due in part to the growing popularity of combination treatments for insomnia. It should be noted that stimulus control is considered an empirically supported treatment for younger adults (Morin et al., 2006) and was included in all eight of the studies supporting CBT-I as an evidence-based treatment (EBT) for older adults.

MULTICOMPONENT TREATMENTS
WITH SPECIAL POPULATIONS

There is substantial heterogeneity across the older adult population with the increasing prevalence of chronic diseases, medical comorbidity, and cognitive impairment. This section discusses variations of multicomponent CBT-I that have been studied in special populations of older adults. Because the following studies tailored treatment implementation and outcomes to meet the unique needs of their target population, these studies were not included in the formal evidence-based review. However, they provide further support for the use of multicomponent CBT-I in older adults and should be considered worthy of further investigation.

Older adults with insomnia are more likely than other age groups to be prescribed benzodiazepine hypnotics (Stewart et al., 2006), which increase the risk of falls and other adverse effects and can lead to hypnotic-dependent insomnia. As a result, several treatment studies have targeted sleep interventions at chronic users of sleep medications. Morgan et al. (2003) found that hypnotic-dependant older adults treated with CBT-I in a primary care setting had greater reductions in medication use and greater sleep improvements than those who received usual care. Two studies found that adding CBT-I to a benzodiazepine-tapering program facilitated medication withdrawal in older adults with insomnia (Baillargeon et al., 2003; Morin et al., 2004). Further support for the efficacy of psychological treatments for late-life insomnia comes from a recent study that indicated that CBT-I leads to sleep improvements in hypnotic-dependant older adults even when sleep medication consumption is held constant (Soeffing et al., 2008).

Researchers have also adapted CBT interventions to address sleep–wake disturbances in older adults with dementia. Treatments for this population are usually multidimensional, involving a variety of behavioral and nonpharmacological techniques aimed at increasing social and physical activity and decreasing daytime sleep. For example, Alessi et al. (2005) used a combination of behavioral activation, daytime light exposure, reduced daytime spent in bed, and basic sleep hygiene (i.e., structured bedtime routine, reduction of nighttime noise and light) in a randomized controlled trial with nursing home residents. In comparison with residents who received usual care ($n = 56$), the 5-day intervention led to modest improvements in sleep–wake rhythms and wakefulness during the night for the intervention group ($n = 58$).

Treatment setting is of particular importance with this population, as many older adults with dementia reside in nursing homes or long-term-care facilities that can present additional challenges (e.g., nighttime noise). To our knowledge, only one study has been conducted outside of an inpatient setting. McCurry et al. (2005) administered a multicomponent treatment for insomnia to community-dwelling older adults with Alzheimer's disease and their family caregivers. The 8-week intervention (consisting of daily physical activity, daily light therapy, and sleep hygiene education for participants and their caregivers) led to reductions in both the frequency and duration of nighttime awakenings.

OTHER PSYCHOLOGICAL TREATMENTS

Three other psychological interventions (i.e., relaxation training, biofeedback, and paradoxical intention) have been shown to be effective stand-alone treatments for adults with chronic insomnia (Morin et al., 2006). However, because of the lack of research on these treatments in older insomnia populations, they were not included in the current evidence-based review. Similarly, other nonpharmacological treatments for insomnia that were excluded from this review may hold promise for treating late-life insomnia. Most complementary and alternative medicine (CAM) treatments were not reviewed here because they do not meet the definition for "psychological treatments" that was put forth by APA's 2005 Presidential Task Force on Evidence-Based Practice. However, there is a growing literature on using CAM to treat sleep disturbances in older adults, including techniques such as bright-light therapy, exercise and physical activity, massage, acupressure, and tai chi (see Gooneratne, 2008, for a review). The evidence supporting these types of treatments, however, is still too preliminary to yield conclusions about their efficacy.

For treatment providers interested in more information and details on implementing specific treatment components, we recommend the following books:

1. *Treatment of Late-Life Insomnia* (Lichstein & Morin, 2000)
2. *Insomnia: Psychological Assessment and Management* (Morin, 1993)

Adapting EBT for Clinical Settings

Ryan G. Wetzler

Before discussing specific strategies and challenges to implementing EBTs, it may be helpful to know a bit about my practice setting and training. I am currently a full-time clinician, working in an independent sleep disorders center in Louisville, Kentucky. Our group has three sleep labs, eight physicians, and currently one psychologist. The group is highly specialized, with our physicians being board certified in internal medicine, pulmonary and critical care medicine, as well as sleep medicine. My particular area of focus is on applying psychological principles to the evaluation and treatment of the full spectrum of sleep disorders, including insomnia, circadian rhythm sleep disorders, narcolepsy–hypersomnia, nightmares–parasomnias, and other sleep-related difficulties (i.e., difficulty adhering to continuous positive airway pressure for treating sleep apnea).

I was originally trained in health psychology and completed a fellowship in sleep medicine–BSM, leading up to certification in the practice of BSM. As such, my clinical perspective is very much informed by a health psychology perspective, and my treatment focus is typically on the patient's sleep problems. In addition, most of my training and experience occurred within medical settings, and hence I hope to share the challenges I experienced when integrating a psychological approach in an established medical setting.

I realize that other chapters have focused on challenges to adapting EBT protocols–manuals to clinical practice settings, and I do plan to discuss this in brief. However, before we jump into the nuts and bolts of this, I believe we need to first consider the bigger picture. The bigger picture is one in which very few psychologists are integrated into settings where they can even have an opportunity to practice in this way. I have the luxury of being able to apply such strategies due at least in part to the specialized nature of my treatment setting. In my opinion, the only way to proliferate the practice of EBTs is to develop opportunities for psychology to work in specialized clinics, which are most commonly medically based. As such, the following review first addresses issues related to practice opportunity and only then discusses the practice itself. Significant challenges we have encountered include

- limited community understanding of evidence-based psychological intervention,
- difficulty in establishing consistent referral sources,
- reimbursement challenges, and
- difficulty in applying a research model of treatment to complex clinical populations.

Following is a more detailed discussion of these challenges and adaptations we found successful in managing them.

LIMITED COMMUNITY UNDERSTANDING

Until its establishment as a subspecialty of health psychology and clinical sleep medicine in 2003, BSM was not a term familiar to many. Even with the decades of research support for cognitive behavioral intervention strategies for insomnia, far too few recognize the value of a BSM specialist. The challenge of disseminating the value of evidence-based behavioral interventions for sleep disorders remains decades behind their availability to the public. The problem of dissemination runs deep and is a frequently discussed topic. The challenge is multifaceted and includes misinformation and limited understanding amongst medical providers, the general public, and even fellow mental health providers. There is often a lack of awareness that EBTs for insomnia even exist. In my experience, several strategies have positively impacted the challenge of dissemination. These efforts have included developing patient brochures, presenting at local conferences, publishing in local journals, and most important, having face-to-face discussions with health care providers. Taking a proactive stance on community education can go a long way in increasing the sustainability of an empirically based practice and can have a positive impact on establishing consistent referrals.

DIFFICULTY ESTABLISHING REFERRAL SOURCES

Establishing a new business is never easy and is no different than establishing a new service line highlighting empirically supported treatments. As much as we might like to ignore the financial realities of clinical practice, the bottom line in the success of any service is profitability. To put this in perspective, the first BSM program I was involved in failed within 2 years due to lack of funding. The program was staffed by a practicum student, and it was discontinued because the hospital was not willing to pay the $2,000 per year for supervision of the student to maintain the program. Lesson learned: No matter how valuable and effective a treatment may be, if the service cannot financially sustain itself, it is sure to perish. As such, an important step in establishing a successful BSM practice is to develop consistent referral sources. Developing consistent referral sources can be challenging, and it hinges on (a) choosing the correct location to set up a practice and (b) marketing of the service.

The first step in establishing a referral basis is deciding where to establish the practice. This decision is made on a variety of factors, and for BSM the most logical place would seem to be the sleep disorders center or through affiliation with a sleep disorders center. Because few are familiar with CBT-I or other BSM services, it may be difficult to establish a practice outside of the environment in which many with sleep problems would seek help. Although it may appear equally logical to set up shop in a primary care office, psychologists in such settings typically serve more as generalists than specialists, and financial barriers continue to exist that may interfere with the financial sustainability of a primary care–based practice. In an established specialty clinic, it is more likely that the other health care providers will have an understanding of the services being provided and may even seek out such professionals to round out their practices. In addition, being located in such a setting may legitimize the service in the eyes of those who would otherwise be unlikely to follow through on a referral to a BSM specialist. Setting up shop in an established specialty clinic also has a proven track record with success in a variety of other health psychology subspecialties, including chronic pain, headaches, and weight loss.

The second and most challenging aspect of developing consistent referral sources is marketing. Historically, marketing has been a dirty word in the field of psychology due at least in part to traditional psychology practices really not needing to market their services. As such, many involved in traditional psychological practice continue to frown on the marketing of psychologically based treatments. It must be recognized that the practice of clinical health psychology specialties is different from traditional practice in a variety of ways. Intervention strategies are brief and effective, and, hence, turnover is great. Because BSM providers do not hold onto patients for years, open spots are frequent. To sustain such a practice, a consistent number of referrals (at least 15 per month) is needed. As such, it becomes increasingly important to get out of the office and discuss BSM services in the community. The most effective strategy we have found is to use the same tactics that have been developed and proven by the pharmaceutical industry. This includes staff lunches and individualized discussion with community primary care and specialty health care providers. Our experience has been that we are welcomed into such practices and our message is received very well. Such providers seem hungry for a different message than are given by drug reps and see BSM services as a highly valued community resource.

REIMBURSEMENT CHALLENGES

Many trailblazers in the practice of health psychology have encountered significant obstacles in getting paid by insurance for the services they provide. This challenge continues, yet it has been offset slightly by the advent of the health and behavior codes. Although far from perfect, these codes have enabled psychologists to provide empirically supported psychological intervention strategies to many with debilitating medical conditions. Of course, there are downsides to these codes. The first is that they are not consistently reimbursed as well as traditional psychological practice codes. Second, there continues to be mass confusion in regard to their use, both among insurance carriers as well as psychologists and health care systems. For the past 5 years we have grappled with the most appropriate manner to bill for BSM services and have concluded that there is no single best method.

FROM THE BENCH TO THE BEDSIDE

The final and perhaps most daunting obstacle to the proliferation of BSM and other EBTs is clinician resistance. This resistance takes many forms. Common themes of this resistance include (a) the practicality of developing such services, (b) difficulties adapting the research-based treatment protocols to clinical practice, and (c) concerns regarding the applicability of such protocols to complex clinical cases. Some may find it difficult to devote the countless hours it takes to develop and implement such programs. As a now-established EBT provider, I can reflect with certainty that the preliminary time spent in program development was well worth a few sleepless nights along the way. The good news is that once the initial time investment is made, maintaining and expanding the program become much easier. Incidentally, since we developed our initial insomnia treatment program 6 years ago, it has been completely overhauled three times.

ADAPTING BSM TO CLINICAL SETTINGS

Most of the evidence available in regard to psychological treatments comes in the form of efficacy trials. Such trials are conducted on highly specific populations and highly specific problems. With regard to the insomnia literature, many of the studies are on primary insomnia, a condition infrequently encountered in clinical practice. The most common patient in our clinic presents with chronic insomnia as well as a myriad of coexisting health conditions. Unfortunately, the efficacy literature does not necessarily speak to this more complex presentation. The way in which we have adapted these protocols was through first understanding our population. This may be done through discussions with others who are practicing in the area, or in our case through formal program evaluation procedures. What we found in our patients were high rates of depression, anxiety, chronic pain, and other stress-related medical problems.

The treatment protocols used in efficacy studies of multicomponent CBT-I typically focus on sleep hygiene education, sleep restriction therapy, and stimulus control therapy. In adapting this to our clinical population, we added more in-depth cognitive therapy, relaxation training, and mindfulness training to our clinical treatment protocol. We also added supplemental EBT's to address specific coexisting conditions that we encounter frequently, such as behavior activation therapy for depression, disrupted homeostatic sleep drive, or both; interoceptive desensitization for panic disorder; cognitive therapy for generalized anxiety disorder; prolonged exposure therapy for posttraumatic stress disorder; activity–rest–pacing for chronic pain; and a variety of others. Finally, we developed complementary programs for other commonly encountered sleep disorders, including programs for continuous positive airway pressure adherence, narcolepsy–hypersomnia, and circadian rhythm sleep disorders.

Other adaptations involve the way in which EBTs are administered. Treatment protocols used in research studies are highly standardized, with little flexibility in procedures or treatment timeline. In clinical settings, it is nearly impossible to move at the same pace with every patient. For example, we occasionally see highly motivated and well-educated patients who quickly grasp the treatment concepts and readily comply with our instructions. After the first few sessions with these patients, they need little guidance from us, and remaining sessions can be spread out over time. However, most of our patients, particularly those with more complex presentations and comorbidities, have difficulty with treatment adherence and need a higher level of support and accountability.

Treatment resistance and noncompliance often stem from the patient's lack of understanding as to why he or she is being asked to follow certain instructions. For this reason, we spend a lot of time explaining the rationale behind each intervention that is presented. We encourage patient questions, which aid in identifying and troubleshooting potential problem areas. Common issues with older adults include difficulties staying awake until the prescribed bedtime and unintentional napping during the day due to lack of activity. Additionally, older adults may be resistant to following a strict sleep schedule because they no longer have to wake up to get to work on time or take care of children. Many older adults we see are adjusting to recent life changes, such as retirement or loss of a spouse. In these cases, we frequently use complementary treatment strategies, such as behavioral activation, to help increase patient's activity level and amount of social interaction. As you will see in the case example, compromise is often necessary to get the patient on board with even attempting to follow treatment recommendations.

Sleep logs are a final issue to mention. Although sleep logs are the primary way in which we track treatment adherence and progress, patients are not always compliant. Commonly encountered problems include patients not understanding how to fill out the sleep logs, as well as patients having concerns about filling the logs out "accurately." To combat these issues, I spend a significant amount of time upfront with the patient, explaining the purpose of the sleep diaries and the correct way to fill them out. I emphasize that the logs are designed to capture the patient's perception of their sleep and that we want the patient's best estimate of their sleep pattern the night before, not the specific clock times.

When a patient fails to bring in a completed sleep log or complains that it made her or his sleep "worse," I probe the patient's approach. With forgetful patients, simple strategies such as leaving the sleep log and a pencil by the bed or on the breakfast table can help them be more consistent. I have also found that most patients who report that keeping the sleep log is interfering with their sleep are overly concerned with recording exact times and are filling it out incorrectly. For example, patients may be fixating on the clock in an attempt to record their exact bedtime or getting up during every nighttime awakening to record it on the sleep log. Redirecting the patient's approach to the sleep logs and reassuring them that we do not expect perfection can often resolve the issue. However, we still have to make compromises with many patients. Instead of keeping ongoing sleep logs throughout the duration of treatment, we may have patients record their sleep every other week or every other session. When patients are greatly opposed to keeping sleep logs, we have devised other ways to track their compliance, such as short daily checklists of the most important treatment goals (e.g., patients check yes or no as to whether they actually got up at their prescribed wake-up time, whether they napped during the day).

In the next section, we describe a prototypical case example of an older woman being treated for chronic insomnia in our BSM clinic.

CASE EXAMPLE

"Ms. Insomnia" is a 70-year-old, African American woman who completed our multicomponent CBT-I program in 2008. Her case represents a prototypical case seen in our clinic.

Presenting Complaint and Sleep History

Ms. Insomnia presents with reports of not being able to sleep at night, feeling her sleep is "restless," and waking up approximately every 2 hours with difficulty getting back to sleep. She describes "anxiety" that causes her to have to go to the hospital. She explains that during these experiences she has an increasing heart rate, sweating, feelings of the "chills," and feeling dizzy. She has experienced this difficulty for the past 2 years, having presented multiple times to the hospital with what appears to be panic attacks. She describes trouble getting to sleep and staying asleep for at least the past 3 months.

Ms. Insomnia reports a history of using lorazepam to help her sleep. She describes the medication as having minimal impact on her ability to sleep at night, which resulted in her discontinuing its use against medical advice. She is currently taking Tylenol PM on a nightly basis with minimal efficacy.

Family and Social History

Ms. Insomnia currently resides in Louisville, Kentucky, and has been living by herself for the past couple of years. She worked for 35 years as a nursing assistant and has been on Social Security disability for the past 9 years secondary to cardiovascular disease and cancer. She completed 9 years of education. She is currently separated and reports two previous marriages that ended in divorce. She has five children and 12 grandchildren. She reports that relations with family members are generally "good" with no ongoing problems or conflicts mentioned. When asked about her social life, she states, "I go to church and do not go out anywhere else."

Medical and Psychiatric History (as Reported by the Client)

- Surgical history: Cardiac bypass in 2005, mastectomy in 2006
- Medical conditions: Allergies or asthma, arthritis in her shoulder and both knees, history of breast cancer, hypertension, and ongoing pain condition rated as an 8 on a scale from 0 to 10, with 10 indicating the most severe pain she could imagine
- Current medications: Metformin, Crestor, warfarin, aspirin, diltiazem, isosorbide, sotalol, potassium, metoclopramide, and over-the-counter medication (e.g., acetaminophen)
- Psychiatric history: She reports a history of some depression and anxiety following divorce from her first husband in 1978. At that point, she saw a psychiatrist and was prescribed antidepressant medication. She denies any other history of psychiatric treatment. However, she had presented to the emergency room approximately 12 times over the past 2 years for panic symptoms.

Mental Status Exam

Ms. Insomnia presented for the evaluation as oriented × 3. Her interactional style was pleasant and cooperative. Eye contact was good. Speech was relevant and organized. Affect appeared within normal limits. She denies significant memory problems or problems with concentration or attention. She describes a recent decrease in appetite. Ms. Insomnia denies current suicidal or homicidal ideation or intent.

Summary of Results From Assessment Measures

Sleep History Questionnaire (see Appendix 3.4)

Currently, Ms. Insomnia reports taking 4 hours to fall asleep most nights. She reports an average of six awakenings per night, with approximately 5 hours spent awake during the night. She estimates her average TST is 3 hours per night, but she feels like she needs at least 6 hours of sleep to feel rested the next day.

Ms. Insomnia reports signs and symptoms suggestive of possible obstructive sleep apnea syndrome, insomnia, restless legs syndrome, and circadian rhythm sleep disorder. She denies signs or symptoms suggestive of narcolepsy, significant parasomnia, or bruxism. Review of sleep-scheduling practice suggests that she does not maintain a regular sleep–wake schedule and has a tendency to sleep in approximately 2 hours on weekends.

Sleep Hygiene Practice Scale (Lacks, 1987)

Ms. Insomnia reports engaging in five of seven counterproductive conditioning behaviors, six of 10 general sleep hygiene practices, and experiencing one of four interfering environmental factors. Results suggest that poor sleep hygiene practices may be having an impact on her ability to sleep at night.

Insomnia Severity Index (Morin, 1993)

Total score = 20, suggestive of moderate insomnia.

Pre-Sleep Arousal Scale (Nicassio, Mendlowitz, Fussell, & Petras, 1985)

Total cognitive arousal score = 25, suggestive of conditioned cognitive arousal to her bedroom. Total somatic arousal score = 22, suggestive of conditioned somatic arousal to her bedroom as well. Overall results suggest conditioning factors may be a playing a major role in her ongoing difficulty sleeping.

Daytime Alertness (Regestein Hyperarousal) Scale (Regestein, Dambrosia, Hallett, Murawski, & Paine, 1993)

Total score = 39, suggestive of mild physiologic hyperarousal.

Epworth Sleepiness Scale (Johns, 1991)

Total score (0–24) = 13, suggestive of excessive daytime sleepiness, which is likely associated with sleep deprivation. However, this score also may suggest a need for an overnight sleep study to rule out obstructive sleep apnea syndrome if she does not respond to treatment for insomnia.

Dysfunctional Beliefs and Attitudes About Sleep Questionnaire (Morin, 1993)

Total score = 28, suggestive of sleep-related worry and maladaptive sleep-related beliefs, which are likely contributing to her ongoing sleep disturbance.

Motivation for Change Index[1]

Review suggests adequate motivation for change, and, thus, it is believed that Ms. Insomnia would likely benefit from cognitive behavioral intervention for her insomnia.

Personality Assessment Inventory (Morey, 1991)

Validity of test results: questionable. Results should be viewed with caution. Ms. Insomnia's profile showed clinical elevations on the Depression scale, Paranoia scale, and Schizophrenia scale. Subclinical elevations were found on the Somatization scale, Anxiety scale, Anxiety-Related Disorder scale, and Borderline Personality scale.

Case Conceptualization

Overall results of Ms. Insomnia's evaluation suggest severe sleep onset and sleep maintenance insomnia, with sleep state misperception. Our clinic conceptualizes insomnia cases according to the behavioral model of insomnia. According to this model, insomnia is viewed as a function of three interconnected factors; predisposing, precipitating, and perpetuating factors. These factors are summarized for Ms. Insomnia as follows.

Predisposing Factors

Ms. Insomnia presents reporting a strong worry proneness and ruminative tendency. She also reports being more of a lark versus an owl, suggesting a natural propensity for circadian phase advance. Factors such as these frequently render individuals vulnerable to the experience of insomnia.

Precipitating Factors

Ms. Insomnia describes the onset of significant anxiety and panic approximately 2 years ago, which coincides with her mastectomy and cardiac

---

[1]Contact author R.W. for scale information.

bypass. At the same point, Ms. Insomnia's children moved out of the home, leaving her with few social supports.

Perpetuating–Maintaining Factors

A review of assessment results suggests a variety of factors involved in her ongoing sleep disturbance, including poor sleep hygiene practices, mild physiologic hyperarousal, severe cognitive arousal, severe conditioned cognitive and somatic arousal, circadian disruption, limited social support, moderate-to-severe anxiety, and possible underlying sleep disorders.

Treatment Plan

We plan to meet with Ms. Insomnia in 1 to 2 weeks to review and discuss all assessment results in detail. At that time, we will discuss treatment options, including both pharmacologic and psychological treatment approaches. If she is interested in cognitive behavioral intervention, we will initiate the treatment process at that time. We will then see this patient two to 10 times on a weekly or biweekly basis and provide her with our empirically supported, multicomponent, cognitive behavioral treatment process. Specific intervention strategies will include a combination of some or all of the following interventions based on her particular needs: sleep hygiene education, sleep restriction therapy, stimulus control therapy, sleep specific cognitive therapy, relaxation training, thermal biofeedback, bright-light therapy, and others as clinically indicated. We will monitor treatment progress using sleep logs on a session-by-session basis.

Other Treatment Considerations

1. Although the patient's primary complaint is insomnia, she also reports possible symptoms of sleep apnea. If Ms. Insomnia does not respond to insomnia treatment, or if she continues to report poor sleep and excessive daytime sleepiness despite improvements in her sleep quantity, we will consider the need for an overnight sleep study to rule out underlying or co-occurring sleep disorders.
2. We will continue to evaluate Ms. Insomnia's anxiety and depression during the course of treatment. We plan to focus more attention in the treatment process for her insomnia on stress management and may add interoceptive desensitization for panic as clinically indicated. If adequate treatment gains are not forthcoming and her anxiety and depression symptoms persist or worsen, we will consider referral for assessment and treatment of a possible anxiety–mood disorder.

3. Throughout treatment, we will encourage Ms. Insomnia to begin increasing her level of social activity and social interaction. We will explore the potential benefits of her getting involved at her local senior center.

Session-by-Session Outline

Treatment sessions were conducted with Ms. Insomnia on a biweekly basis, and treatment outcomes were tracked by using weekly sleep logs with ratings of daytime stress and sadness. In the sections below, we present an overview of each treatment session and a brief rationale for the interventions used. Each session overview is followed by a synopsis of the sleep log scores for that visit. For clarification, *sleep-onset latency* refers to the average amount of time it took to initiate sleep, with anything less than 30 minutes being normal. *Nightly awakenings* refer to the average number of times the individual was aware of waking up throughout the night. *Wake time after sleep onset* refers to the average amount of time a person spent awake in the night following awakenings, with anything less than 30 minutes being normal. *Total sleep time* refers to the average amount of time the patient reports sleeping each night. Finally, *sleep efficiency percentage* is a calculation of the amount of time an individual reports sleeping divided by the amount of time they spent in bed, with greater than 85% being normal. To monitor Ms. Insomnia's mood, her sleep log included daily ratings of daytime stress and sadness (ratings from 0–10, with 10 = *severe*).

Session 1: Diagnostic Interview and Psychological Testing

During this initial visit the goal is to establish rapport with the patient and determine whether he or she would be likely to benefit from BSM services. In this visit, we review all of our intake questionnaires and have the patient complete all psychological testing procedures. You may have noticed that our evaluation process is highly specialized and makes use of a number of assessment materials. The rationale for this comprehensive approach is multifaceted. The first reason is that many patients we see have had sleep problems for a long time and had their sleep problems dismissed on multiple occasions. We do not want the patient to feel as though we are minimizing his or her difficulty; instead, we want patients to see that we have thoroughly evaluated their sleep problem and understand it inside and out. The extensive evaluation process is the first step in this direction. Second, psychological testing procedures serve to identify specific social, cognitive, behavioral, and psychophysiological factors involved in perpetuating, maintaining, or exacerbating the presenting problem. These factors represent modifiable therapeutic targets for cognitive and behavioral intervention. Testing also specifies other potential contributors, including comorbid psychiatric disturbances, that may warrant clinical attention. Third, and perhaps most important, the testing enables the clinician to communicate in a direct and comprehensive fashion the reasons why an individual is not sleeping and thereby the rationale for cognitive behavioral intervention. On the basis of Ms. Insomnia's assessment results (discussed previously), she appears to be a reasonable candidate for cognitive behavioral intervention for insomnia.

Sleep Log Data From Session 1:

Sleep-onset latency = 274 minutes

Wake time after sleep onset = 80 minutes

Nightly awakenings = 4.6

Estimated total sleep time = 2.6 hours

Sleep efficiency (%) = 21

Daytime stress rating* = 7.5

Daytime sadness rating* = 6.5

---

*Daytime ratings on scale from 0 to 10, with 10 being *severe*.

Session 2: Evaluation Feedback and Treatment Initiation

The goal of this visit is to establish the rationale for the intervention strategy. Here we review all psychological assessment results in detail. As mentioned earlier, the goal is to let the individual know that we were comprehensive in our approach and understand what is going on. In addition, we hope reviewing the material will help the patient to gain insight into contributors to their sleep problem. Feedback is commonly provided in a manner consistent with motivational interviewing.

My general approach to treatment is to provide a clear rationale for an intervention strategy before suggesting anything. In this case, we set Ms. Insomnia on a regular sleep–wake schedule to reentrain her circadian rhythm. It was suspected her circadian rhythm was delayed because of her tendency to "sleep in" 2 hours on the weekend. Prior to setting her on a schedule, I discussed with her how the circadian timing system works and how sleeping in as a means to catch up on sleep would not work and could just make things worse. Then we collaboratively set her on a slightly restricted sleep schedule from 12:30 a.m. to 7 a.m. The rationale for prescribing only 6.5 hours in bed is that she had previously been spending 8.5 hours in bed but only sleeping 2.6 hours of this. Ideally, we would restrict the allowable time in bed further, because she reports less than 3 hours of sleep a night. However, the patient stated she could not remain awake until 2 a.m.; therefore, we compromised by choosing a 12:30 a.m. bedtime (using sleep compression instead of sleep restriction). We also provided a handout on general sleep information and good sleep hygiene practices because of evidence from the evaluation that suggested poor sleep hygiene practices.

Sleep Log Data From Session 2:

Sleep-onset latency = 171 minutes

Wake time after sleep onset = 86 minutes

Nightly awakenings = 2.6

Estimated total sleep time = 3.3 hours

Sleep efficiency (%) = 32

Daytime stress rating = 3

Daytime sadness rating = 3

Session 3: Sleep Restriction Therapy

Review of Ms. Insomnia's recent sleep diaries showed a decrease in time to fall asleep and an increase in sleep efficiency. Because of the patient's success with the slight sleep compression implemented at the last visit and her tolerance of having a later bedtime, we introduced textbook sleep restriction therapy. More or less, she saw the impact of the strategy on her sleep and was now willing to go forth and take it to the next level. We limited her time in bed to 5.5 hours and discussed the rationale behind sleep restriction therapy, which is to increase drive toward sleep and increase confidence in her ability to fall asleep.

Sleep Log Data From Session 3:

Sleep-onset latency = 77 minutes

Wake time after sleep onset = 13 minutes

Nightly awakenings = 2.6

Estimated total sleep time = 4.1 hours

Sleep efficiency (%) = 51

Daytime stress rating = 1.5

Daytime sadness rating = 1.5

Session 4: Stimulus Control Therapy

The rationale for stimulus control therapy is to promote healthy responses to difficulty getting to sleep or getting back to sleep. As a core component of multicomponent CBT-I, it was implemented because of the patient's self-reported experience of conditioned wakefulness, as well as scores from the Pre-Sleep Arousal Scale, suggesting counterproductive experiences in bed. Frequently, those with insomnia will spend excessive amounts of time in bed awake, which over time contributes to "conditioned wakefulness" or the bed becoming a stronger cue for worry, stress, and anxiety versus sleep. Such patients will frequently report falling asleep on the couch, but being wide awake as soon as they lie down in bed. In addition, the strategy provides guidance for the patient on how to respond to a bad night to prevent relapse.

The rationale and instructions for stimulus control therapy (see Appendix 3.3) were discussed in great detail with Ms. Insomnia to ensure understanding and some level of commitment. We emphasize to our patients that stimulus control therapy is only effective when it is followed consistently over a course of several weeks. We also remind patients that psychological treatments for insomnia do not show immediate results, as do medications. Preparing the patient for what he or she can expect over the course of treatment will help to avoid unnecessary discouragement and premature termination of treatment.

Sleep Log Data From Session 4:

Sleep-onset latency = 31 minutes

Wake time after sleep onset = 57 minutes

Nightly awakenings = 1.7

Estimated total sleep time = 4.9 hours

Sleep efficiency (%) = 63

Daytime stress rating = 1.5

Daytime sadness rating = 1

Session 5: Relaxation Training With Focus on Identifying and Coping with Panic

Relaxation training was introduced because of the patient's self-reported history of panic attacks and her assessment results (she exhibited a general vulnerability to anxiety on the Daytime Alertness Scale and had a moderate elevation on the anxiety scale of the Personality Assessment Inventory). In addition, the goal of CBT-I is not only to get people sleeping but also to keep them sleeping. As such, relaxation strategies could potentially prevent relapse because it is typically stressors that trigger bouts of insomnia.

> *Sleep Log Data From Session 5:*
>
> Sleep-onset latency = 20 minutes
>
> Wake time after sleep onset = 13 minutes
>
> Nightly awakenings = 1
>
> Estimated total sleep time = 5 hours
>
> Sleep efficiency (%) = 75
>
> Daytime stress rating = 1
>
> Daytime sadness rating = 1

Session 6: Introduction to Cognitive Therapy for Insomnia

Cognitive therapy for insomnia was initiated because of Ms. Insomnia's responses on the Dysfunctional Beliefs and Attitudes About Sleep Questionnaire. What this instrument suggested is that a number of ways in which the patient was thinking about sleep were just getting in the way. Education about sleep and normal age-related changes in sleep was presented to help Ms. Insomnia identify unrealistic expectations and beliefs she had about her sleep. Cognitive restructuring was introduced as a means to correct these beliefs to both decrease current worry about sleep and to promote healthy coping with sleep disturbance in the future.

> *Sleep Log Data From Session 6:*
>
> Sleep-onset latency = 8 minutes
>
> Wake time after sleep onset = 6 minutes
>
> Nightly awakenings = 1
>
> Estimated total sleep time = 6.1 hours
>
> Sleep efficiency (%) = 72
>
> Daytime stress rating = 0.5
>
> Daytime sadness rating = 1

On examining the sleep logs Ms. Insomnia brought into Sessions 5 and 6, we see that the amount of time spent awake in bed (i.e., sleep-onset latency and wake time after sleep onset) has markedly decreased since she began treatment. However, her sleep-efficiency percentages remain lower than we would expect with the corresponding reductions in wake time. This issue is likely due to *sleep-state misperception*, which is the tendency to misperceive one's sleep.

Specifically, Ms. Insomnia perceives that she is sleeping far less than she is actually sleeping, which results in inaccurate estimates of TST. The educational material and cognitive therapy techniques used with Ms. Insomnia in Session 6 are also aimed at recognizing and reducing possible sleep-state misperception.

Session 7: Introduction to Mindfulness

The rationale for including mindfulness was based on the patient's history of anxiety and her current depression. In a way, we conceptualized her case as an anxiety-based depression. We thought being introduced to the concept of mindfulness might instill a perspective that would insulate her from future episodes of worry and anxiety. Mindfulness is also a nice way to integrate the relaxation therapies and cognitive therapies. Mindfulness has been found in some studies to prevent relapse of depression. Perhaps it can do the same for insomnia. (See Kabat-Zinn, 1990, and Ong & Sholtes, 2010, for more information on mindfulness.)

<u>*Sleep Log Data From Session 7:*</u>

Sleep-onset latency = 8 minutes

Wake time after sleep onset = 8 minutes

Nightly awakenings = 0.9

Estimated total sleep time = 7.7 hours

Sleep efficiency (%) = 89

Daytime stress rating = 0.25

Daytime sadness rating = 0.10

Review of Ms. Insomnia's most recent sleep log (from Session 7, above) shows no changes in sleep-onset latency or wake time after sleep onset but notable increases in TST and sleep efficiency. Following the cognitive therapy session (Session 6), Ms. Insomnia began resolving her tendency toward misperceiving her sleep. The jump in sleep efficiency in Session 7 likely reflects her more-accurate estimate of TST.

Session 8: 1-Month Follow-Up Visit

At her 1-month follow-up visit, Ms. Insomnia's sleep logs showed continued improvement in her sleep. She also reported that her mood and stress levels were more stable than before treatment. We briefly reviewed her progress and encouraged her to continue following all treatment recommendations. The rest of the session was spent discussing applications of mindfulness to everyday life circumstances. She was encouraged to contact our office should she experience relapse of symptoms.

> *Sleep Log Data From Session 8:*
>
> Sleep-onset latency = 6 minutes
>
> Wake time after sleep onset = 6 minutes
>
> Nightly awakenings = 0.4
>
> Estimated total sleep time = 7.6 hours
>
> Sleep efficiency (%) = 94
>
> Daytime stress rating = 0.10
>
> Daytime sadness rating = 0.25

Overall Outcomes

In summary, Ms. Insomnia experienced significant improvement in her sleep and also experienced significant improvements in self-reported levels of daily anxiety and depression. Her sleep log data are presented in Table 3.2.

TABLE 3.2
Ms. Insomnia's Sleep Log Data

CBT treatment outcomes	Sleep-onset latency (in minutes)	Wake time after sleep onset (in minutes)	Estimated total sleep time (hours/night)	Sleep efficiency (%)
Pretreatment	274	80	2.6	21
Posttreatment	8	8	7.7	89
1-month follow-up	6	6	7.6	94

Note. CBT = cognitive behavioral therapy.

APPENDIX 3.1: SLEEP DIARY

Please answer the following questionnaire **WHEN YOU AWAKE IN THE MORNING**. Enter yesterday's day and date and provide the information to describe your sleep the night before. Definitions explaining each line of the questionnaire are given below.

Item Definitions

1. If you napped yesterday, enter total time napping in *minutes*.
2. What time did you enter bed for the purpose of going to sleep (not for reading or other activities)?
3. Counting from the time you wished to fall asleep, how many *minutes* did it take you to fall asleep?
4. How many times did you awaken during the night?
5. What is the total time (# *minutes*) you were awake during the middle of the night? This does <u>not include</u> time to fall asleep at the beginning of the night. It also does <u>not include</u> awake time in bed before the final morning arising.
6. What time did you wake up for the last time this morning?
7. What time did you actually get out of bed this morning?
8. Pick <u>one</u> number below to indicate your overall QUALITY RATING or satisfaction with your sleep.

   1 = very poor   2 = poor   3 = fair   4 = good   5 = excellent

9. List any sleep medication or alcohol taken at or near bedtime, and give the amount and time taken.

Example

Yesterday's day ⇒ Yesterday's date ⇒	Tuesday 10/14/97	Day 1	Day 2	Day 3	Day 4	Day 5	Day 6	Day 7
1. NAP (yesterday)	70 min							
2. BEDTIME (last night)	10:55 p.m.							
3. TIME TO FALL ASLEEP	65 min							
4. # OF AWAKENINGS	4							
5. WAKE TIME in middle of night (# of minutes)	110 min							
6. FINAL WAKE-UP	6:05 a.m.							
7. OUT OF BED	7:10 a.m.							
8. QUALITY RATING	2							
9. BEDTIME MEDICATIONS (include amount & time)	Ambien 10 mg 10:40 p.m.							

APPENDIX 3.2: SLEEP HYGIENE INSTRUCTIONS

Sleep hygiene identifies everyday behaviors that may help or hurt sleep. Following the instructions below increases the likelihood that you will sleep well. Failing to follow any of these instructions may lead to sleep disruption.

1. Avoid caffeine after noon: Caffeine is a stimulant that can lead to increased arousal and difficulty falling and staying asleep. Some people are very sensitive to the effects of caffeine, and use of caffeine after noon may disrupt sleep.
2. Avoid exercise within 2 hours of bedtime: Exercising too close to bedtime may put your body in an aroused state when you need to be relaxing. However, participation in regular exercise that occurs earlier in the day is healthy and may even improve sleep.
3. Avoid nicotine within 2 hours of bedtime: Nicotine, like caffeine, is a stimulant that can make falling and staying asleep difficult.
4. Avoid alcohol within 2 hours of bedtime: Although you may initially feel sleepy after drinking alcohol, alcohol use near bedtime usually leads to more awake time during the night.
5. Avoid heavy meals within 2 hours of bedtime: Heavy meals close to bedtime put a strain on your digestive system while you are trying to sleep. Heavy meals may produce physical discomfort or metabolic changes that interfere with sleep.
6. Avoid napping: Napping during the day may disrupt sleep or make it harder to fall asleep at night. If you must nap, keep it short (less than half an hour) and do it early in the day (before 3 p.m.).

APPENDIX 3.3: STIMULUS CONTROL INSTRUCTIONS

A person's body should automatically associate getting into bed with going to sleep. Sometimes people develop habits that may make the bedroom a nonsleep promoting environment. Using the bed or bedroom for other activities (e.g., reading or watching TV, planning what needs to be done the next day), may cause a person's body to associate getting into bed with being awake; this may interfere with sleep. Stimulus control helps break this association and reestablish the bed and bedroom as a sleep-promoting place. Follow all six instructions to increase the likelihood that you will sleep well.

1. **Don't use your bed or bedroom for anything (any time of the day) but sleep (or sex).** Doing other things in bed is "misusing" the bed. There is an appropriate time and place for everything. Doing other things reinforces the notion that a variety of actions are appropriate in that setting (e.g., if you often watch television in bed, going to bed will become a cue to begin thinking about things related to what you have seen on television). If the bed is reserved for sleep alone, then climbing into bed will be a strong cue for you to fall asleep.

2. **Lie down in bed intending to go to sleep *only when you are very sleepy*.** Don't let the clock dictate when you go to bed. By staying up until you have a strong urge to sleep, you will be more likely to fall asleep quickly, reinforcing the association between bed and sleep. If you go to bed when you are not sleepy, you might toss and turn, begin to think and get mentally and physically aroused. That would only reinforce the old habit patterns we are trying to eliminate. By establishing a fixed time for getting up and allowing your bedtime to vary, your body can determine how much sleep you need to function well. Your body will let you know this by getting sleepy when it is time for you to go to bed.

3. **Get out of bed if you do not initially fall asleep within 15–20 minutes, and go to another room to do a relaxing activity (e.g., reading or watching TV in a dimly lit room). Go back to bed only when you feel extremely sleepy again. If you do not fall asleep within 20 minutes upon returning to bed, repeat this instruction as many times as needed.** Although the idea of getting out of bed to promote better sleep might seem counterintuitive or strange, the reason for doing this is to strengthen the association of the bed and bedroom with sleep. By getting out of bed when you have not fallen asleep after 15–20 minutes, you

can promote this association. (Clock watching for this rule is not recommended. Get out of bed when you *feel* it has been about 15 to 20 minutes.)

4. **If you wake up during the night and do not fall back to sleep within 15–20 minutes, follow rule # 3 again.** New habits come only with repeated practice. When first beginning this treatment, it is common to have to get up many times each night before falling asleep.

5. **Use your alarm to leave bed at the _same time every morning_ regardless of the amount of sleep obtained.** This will help your body acquire a constant sleep rhythm. By varying the time you get up you are shifting your rhythm each day so that it is not in stable harmony with clock time.

6. **Avoid napping.** Naps meet some of your sleep need and make it less likely that you will fall asleep quickly. By not napping, you also help to ensure that any sleep deprivation you feel from last night will increase your likelihood of falling asleep quickly tonight. If you must nap, do not nap past 3 p.m. Napping throws your body rhythm off schedule and makes it more difficult for you to sleep at night.

APPENDIX 3.4: SLEEP HISTORY QUESTIONNAIRE

Name _____

Age_____   Race/Ethnicity_____   Date_____

Name of Primary Physician: _____

Name of Referring Physician (*if not your primary physician*): _____

Briefly describe the problem(s) you are experiencing with your sleep or the reason you were referred to our sleep center. _____
_____
_____

When did you first notice your sleep problem? What may have contributed to the onset of your difficulty sleeping (i.e., birth of a child, death of a loved one, traumatic event)? _____
_____
_____

What do you feel are the major contributors to your sleep problem at this time? _____
_____
_____

What medications and other treatments have you tried for your sleep problem to date? _____
_____
_____

What medication(s) are you currently taking for sleep? And how many times per week? _____
_____
_____

How long (on average) does it take you to get to sleep? _____

How many times do you wake up in an average night? _____

How long on average do you remain awake during these awakenings (in total)? _____

How much sleep do you get in total in an average night? _____hours/night

How much sleep do you feel you need each night to feel well rested and able to function? _____hours/night

| | | Does a poor night's sleep make you | | | Does a poor night's sleep negatively affect your |

Does a poor night's sleep make you

	YES	NO
Depressed	☐	☐
Anxious	☐	☐
Irritable	☐	☐
Fatigued	☐	☐

Does a poor night's sleep negatively affect your

	YES	NO
Ability to concentrate	☐	☐
Memory	☐	☐
Ability to work	☐	☐
Mood	☐	☐

Other (please describe): _____

Sleep Symptoms:

	YES	NO
Has anyone told you that you snore loudly?	☐	☐
Has your family told you that you quit breathing at night?	☐	☐
Have you ever awakened gasping for breath?	☐	☐
Have you ever awakened at night with a sour taste in your mouth, or a burning sensation in your chest?	☐	☐
Do you have morning headaches?	☐	☐
Are you sleepy even when you increase your sleep time?	☐	☐

	YES	NO
Do you have trouble getting to sleep at night?	☐	☐
Do you have trouble staying asleep at night?	☐	☐
Do you have frequent awakenings and/or restless sleep?	☐	☐

	YES	NO
Do you frequently kick and jerk your legs at night while trying to fall asleep?	☐	☐
Do you have discomfort in your legs while trying to fall asleep?	☐	☐
If YES to previous question, does moving your legs give you relief of discomfort?	☐	☐
Do you have tingling or discomfort in your legs during the day?	☐	☐
Do you have discomfort in your legs when sitting for long periods?	☐	☐

	YES	NO
Do you have sudden episodes of sleep during the day?	☐	☐
Have you ever experienced periods in which you feel paralyzed while going to sleep, or waking up?	☐	☐

Have you ever had visual hallucinations or dream-like
    mental images when falling to sleep? . . . . ☐ ☐
Have you ever experienced sudden physical weakness
    during strong emotions? (such as your mouth dropping
    open or legs going limp, during laughter or anger). . . . . . . ☐ ☐
Were you excessively sleepy as a teenager or
    young adult? . . . . ☐ ☐

	YES	NO
Do you sleep walk?	☐	☐
Do you talk in your sleep?	☐	☐
Do you have frequent nightmares?	☐	☐
Do you ever wake up screaming at night?	☐	☐
Do you eat in the middle of the night?	☐	☐
Do you physically act out your dreams at night?	☐	☐

	YES	NO
Do you grind your teeth in your sleep?	☐	☐
Have you or your dentist noticed your teeth		
being worn down?	☐	☐
Have you noticed that your teeth hurt?	☐	☐
Do you experience pain in your jaw muscles?	☐	☐
Has anyone told you that you make sounds with		
your teeth or jaw during sleep?	☐	☐

	YES	NO
Do you have rotating or night shift work?	☐	☐
Have you ever worked shift work or had an		
on-call schedule?	☐	☐
Do you have difficulty getting to sleep at your		
desired time?	☐	☐
Do you wake up in the morning prior to your		
desired time?	☐	☐
Do you find that your present sleep schedule is		
inconvenient, inappropriate, or unsatisfactory?	☐	☐

Sleep Schedule

	Weekday	Weekend
Time you go to bed	_____	_____
Time you get up	_____	_____
Average amount of sleep per night	_____	_____

REFERENCES

Alessi, C. A., Martin, J. L., Webber, A. P., Cynthia Kim, E., Harker, J. O., & Joseph-son, K. R. (2005). Randomized, controlled trial of a nonpharmacological inter-vention to improve abnormal sleep/wake patterns in nursing home residents. *Journal of the American Geriatrics Society, 53*, 803–810. doi:10.1111/j.1532-5415.2005.53251.x

American Psychiatric Association. (2000). *Diagnostic and statistical manual of mental disorders* (4th ed., text rev.). Washington, DC: Author.

Ancoli-Israel, S., & Cooke, J. R. (2005). Prevalence and comorbidity of insomnia and effect on functioning in elderly populations. *Journal of the American Geri-atrics Society, 53*(Suppl. 7), S264–S271. doi:10.1111/j.1532-5415.2005.53392.x

Baillargeon, L., Landreville, P., Verreault, R., Beauchemin, J. P., Gregoire, J. P., & Morin, C. M. (2003). Discontinuation of benzodiazepines among older insomniac adults treated with cognitive-behavioural therapy combined with gradual taper-ing: A randomized trial. *Canadian Medical Association Journal, 169*, 1015–1020.

Bootzin, R. (1977). Effects of self-control procedures for insomnia. In R. B. Stuart (Ed.), *Behavioral self-management: Strategies, techniques and outcomes* (pp. 176–195). New York, NY: Brunner/Mazel.

Bootzin, R. R., & Epstein, D. R. (2000). Stimulus control. In K. L. Lichstein & C. M. Morin (Eds.), *Treatment of late-life insomnia* (pp. 167–184). Thousand Oaks, CA: Sage.

Colten, H. R., & Altevogt, B. M. (Eds.). (2006). *Sleep disorders and sleep deprivation: An unmet public health problem*. Washington, DC: National Academies Press.

Foley, D., Ancoli-Israel, S., Britz, P., & Walsh, J. (2004). Sleep disturbances and chronic disease in older adults: Results of the 2003 National Sleep Founda-tion Sleep in America survey. *Journal of Psychosomatic Research, 56*, 497–502. doi:10.1016/j.jpsychores.2004.02.010

Foley, D. J., Monjan, A. A., Brown, S. L., Simonsick, E. M., Wallace, R. B., & Blazer, D. G. (1995). Sleep complaints among elderly persons: An epidemiologic study of three communities. *Sleep, 18*, 425–432.

Foley, D. J., Monjan, A., Simonsick, E. M., Wallace, R. B., & Blazer, D. G. (1999). Incidence and remission of insomnia among elderly adults: An epidemiologic study of 6,800 persons over three years. *Sleep, 22*(Suppl. 2), 366–372.

Friedman, L., Benson, K., Noda, A., Zarcone, V., Wicks, D. A., O'Connell, K., . . . Yesavage, J. A. (2000). An actigraphic comparison of sleep restriction and sleep hygiene treatments for insomnia in older adults. *Journal of Geriatric Psychiatry and Neurology, 13*, 17–27. doi:10.1177/089198870001300103

Germain, A., Moul, D. E., Franzen, P. L., Miewald, J. M., Reynolds, C. F., III, Monk, T. H., & Buysse, D. J. (2006). Effects of a brief behavioral treatment for late-life insomnia: Preliminary findings. *Journal of Clinical Sleep Medicine, 2*, 403–406.

Gooneratne, N. S. (2008). Complementary and alternative medicine for sleep disturbances in older adults. *Clinics in Geriatric Medicine, 24*, 121–138. doi:10.1016/j.
cger.2007.08.002

Hoelscher, T. J., & Edinger, J. D. (1988). Treatment of sleep maintenance insomnia
in older adults: Sleep period reduction, sleep education, and modified stimulus
control. *Psychology and Aging, 3*, 258–263. doi:10.1037/0882-7974.3.3.258

Irwin, M. R., Cole, J. C., & Nicassio, P. M. (2006). Comparative meta-analysis
of behavioral interventions for insomnia and their efficacy in middle-aged
adults and in older adults 55+ years of age. *Health Psychology, 25*, 3–14.
doi:10.1037/0278-6133.25.1.3

Jelicic, M., Bosma, H., Ponds, R. W. H. M., van Boxtel, M. P. J., Hous, P. J., &
Jolles, J. (2002). Subjective sleep problems in later life as predictors of cogni-
tive decline. Report from the Maastricht Ageing Study (MAAS). *International
Journal of Geriatric Psychiatry, 17*, 73–77. doi:10.1002/gps.529

Johns, M. W. (1991). A new method for measuring daytime sleepiness: The Epworth
Sleepiness Scale. *Sleep, 14*, 540–545.

Kabat-Zinn, J. (1990). *Full catastrophe living: Using the wisdom of your body and mind
to face stress, pain and illness.* New York, NY: Delacorte Press.

Lacks, P. (1987). *Behavioral treatment for persistent insomnia.* New York, NY: Pergamon Press.

Lichstein, K. L. (2000). Relaxation. In K. L. Lichstein & C. M. Morin (Eds.), *Treatment of late-life insomnia* (pp. 185–206). Thousand Oaks, CA: Sage.

Lichstein, K. L., Durrence, H. H., Riedel, B. W., Taylor, D. J., & Bush, A. J. (2004).
Epidemiology of sleep: Age, gender, and ethnicity. Mahwah, NJ: Erlbaum.

Lichstein, K. L., & Morin, C. M. (Eds.). (2000). *Treatment of late-life insomnia.* Thousand Oaks, CA: Sage.

Lichstein, K. L., Riedel, B. W., Wilson, N. M., Lester, K. W., & Aguillard, R. N.
(2001). Relaxation and sleep compression for late-life insomnia: A placebo-
controlled trial. *Journal of Consulting and Clinical Psychology, 69*, 227–239.
doi:10.1037/0022-006X.69.2.227

Lichstein, K. L., Thomas, S. J., & McCurry, S. M. (2010). Sleep compression. In
M. Perlis, M. Aloia, & B. Kuhn (Eds.), *Behavioral treatments for sleep disorders:
A comprehensive primer of behavioral sleep medicine interventions* (pp. 55–59). New
York, NY: Academic Press.

Lichstein, K. L., Wilson, N. M., & Johnson, C. T. (2000). Psychological treatment
of secondary insomnia. *Psychology and Aging, 15*, 232–240. doi:10.1037/0882-
7974.15.2.232

Manber, R., & Kuo, T. F. (2002). Cognitive–behavioral therapies for insomnia.
In T. L. Lee-Chiong, M. J. Sateia, & M. A. Carskadon (Eds.), *Sleep medicine*
(pp. 177–185). Philadelphia, PA: Hanley & Belfus.

McCrae, C. S., McGovern, R., Lukefahr, R., & Stripling, A. M. (2007). Research
Evaluating Brief Behavioral Sleep Treatments for Rural Elderly (RESTORE):

A preliminary examination of effectiveness. *The American Journal of Geriatric Psychiatry, 15,* 979–982. doi:10.1097/JGP.0b013e31813547e6

McCurry, S. M., Gibbons, L. E., Logsdon, R. G., Vitiello, M. V., & Teri, L. (2005). Nighttime insomnia treatment and education for Alzheimer's disease: A randomized, controlled trial. *Journal of the American Geriatrics Society, 53,* 793–802. doi:10.1111/j.1532-5415.2005.53252.x

McCurry, S. M., Logsdon, R. G., Teri, L., & Vitiello, M. V. (2007). Evidence-based psychological treatments for insomnia in older adults. *Psychology and Aging, 22,* 18–27. doi:10.1037/0882-7974.22.1.18

Montgomery, P., & Dennis, J. (2004). A systematic review of non-pharmacological therapies for sleep problems in later life. *Sleep Medicine Reviews, 8,* 47–62. doi:10.1016/S1087-0792(03)00026-1

Morey, L. C. (1991). *The Personality Assessment Inventory: Professional manual.* Odessa, FL: Psychological Assessment Resources.

Morgan, K. (2000). Sleep and aging. In K. L. Lichstein & C. M. Morin (Eds.), *Treatment of late-life insomnia* (pp. 3–36). Thousand Oaks, CA: Sage.

Morgan, K., Dixon, S., Mathers, N., Thompson, J., & Tomeny, M. (2003). Psychological treatment for insomnia in the management of long-term hypnotic drug use: A pragmatic randomised controlled trial. *The British Journal of General Practice, 53,* 923–928.

Morin, C. M. (1993). *Insomnia: Psychological assessment and management.* New York, NY: Guilford Press.

Morin, C. M., & Azrin, N. H. (1988). Behavioral and cognitive treatments of geriatric insomnia. *Journal of Consulting and Clinical Psychology, 56,* 748–753. doi:10.1037/0022-006X.56.5.748

Morin, C. M., Bastien, C., Guay, B., Radouco-Thomas, M., Leblanc, J., & Vallieres, A. (2004). Randomized clinical trial of supervised tapering and cognitive behavior therapy to facilitate benzodiazepine discontinuation in older adults with chronic insomnia. *The American Journal of Psychiatry, 161,* 332–342. doi:10.1176/appi.ajp.161.2.332

Morin, C. M., Bootzin, R. R., Buysse, D. J., Edinger, J. D., Espie, C. A., & Lichstein, K. L. (2006). Psychological and behavioral treatment of insomnia: Update of the recent evidence (1998–2004). *Sleep, 29,* 1398–1414.

Morin, C. M., Colecchi, C., Stone, J., Sood, R., & Brink, D. (1999). Behavioral and pharmacological therapies for late-life insomnia: A randomized controlled trial. *JAMA, 281,* 991–999. doi:10.1001/jama.281.11.991

Morin, C. M., Kowatch, R. A., Barry, T., & Walton, E. (1993). Cognitive-behavior therapy for late-life insomnia. *Journal of Consulting and Clinical Psychology, 61,* 137–146. doi:10.1037/0022-006X.61.1.137

Morin, C. M., Savard, J., & Blais, F. C. (2000). Cognitive therapy. In K. L. Lichstein & C. M. Morin (Eds.), *Treatment of late-life insomnia* (pp. 207–230). Thousand Oaks, CA: Sage.

Morphy, H., Dunn, K. M., Lewis, M., Boardman, H. F., & Croft, P. R. (2007). Epidemiology of insomnia: A longitudinal study in a UK population. *Sleep, 30,* 274–280.

Nau, S. D., McCrae, C. S., Cook, K. G., & Lichstein, K. L. (2005). Treatment of insomnia in older adults. *Clinical Psychology Review, 25,* 645–672. doi:10.1016/j.cpr.2005.04.008

Nicassio, P. M., Mendlowitz, D. R., Fussell, J. J., & Petras, L. (1985). The phenomenology of the pre-sleep state: The development of the pre-sleep arousal scale. *Behaviour Research and Therapy, 23,* 263–271. doi:10.1016/0005-7967(85)90004-X

Ohayon, M. M. (2002). Epidemiology of insomnia: What we know and what we still need to learn. *Sleep Medicine Reviews, 6,* 97–111. doi:10.1053/smrv.2002.0186

Ong, J., & Sholtes, D. (2010). A mindfulness-based approach to the treatment of insomnia. *Journal of Clinical Psychology, 66,* 1175–1184. doi:10.1002/jclp.20736

Perlis, M. L., Smith, L. J., Lyness, J. M., Matteson, S. R., Pigeon, W. R., Jungquist, C. R., & Tu, X. (2006). Insomnia as a risk factor for onset of depression in the elderly. *Behavioral Sleep Medicine, 4,* 104–113. doi:10.1207/s15402010bsm0402_3

Persons, J. B. (1995). Why practicing psychologists are slow to adopt empirically-validated treatments. In S. C. Hayes, V. M. Follette, R. M. Dawes, & K. E. Grady (Eds.), *Scientific standards of psychological practice: Issues and recommendations* (pp. 141–157). Reno, NV: Context Press.

Puder, R., Lacks, P., Bertelson, A. D., & Storandt, M. (1983). Short-term stimulus control treatment of insomnia in older adults. *Behavior Therapy, 14,* 424–429. doi:10.1016/S0005-7894(83)80104-X

Regestein, Q. R., Dambrosia, J., Hallett, M., Murawski, B., & Paine, M. (1993). Daytime alertness in patients with primary insomnia. *The American Journal of Psychiatry, 150,* 1529–1534.

Riedel, B. W., Lichstein, K. L., & Dwyer, W. O. (1995). Sleep compression and sleep education for older insomniacs: Self-help versus therapist guidance. *Psychology and Aging, 10,* 54–63. doi:10.1037/0882-7974.10.1.54

Rybarczyk, B., Lopez, M., Benson, R., Alsten, C., & Stepanski, E. (2002). Efficacy of two behavioral treatment programs for comorbid geriatric insomnia. *Psychology and Aging, 17,* 288–298. doi:10.1037/0882-7974.17.2.288

Rybarczyk, B., Stepanski, E., Fogg, L., Barry, P., Lopez, M., & Davis, A. (2005). A placebo-controlled test of cognitive-behavioral therapy for comorbid insomnia in older adults. *Journal of Consulting and Clinical Psychology, 73,* 1164–1174. doi:10.1037/0022-006X.73.6.1164

Sivertsen, B., Omvik, S., Pallesen, S., Bjorvatn, B., Havik, O. E., Kvale, G., . . . Nordhus, I. H. (2006). Cognitive behavioral therapy vs zopiclone for treatment of chronic primary insomnia in older adults: A randomized controlled trial. *JAMA, 295,* 2851–2858. doi:10.1001/jama.295.24.2851

Soeffing, J. P., Lichstein, K. L., Nau, S. D., McCrae, C. S., Wilson, N. M., Aguillard, R. N., . . . Bush, A. J. (2008). Psychological treatment of insomnia in hypnotic-dependant older adults. *Sleep Medicine, 9,* 165–171. doi:10.1016/j.sleep.2007.02.009

Spielman, A. J., Saskin, P., & Thorpy, M. J. (1987). Treatment of chronic insomnia by restriction of time in bed. *Sleep, 10,* 45–56.

Stewart, R., Besset, A., Bebbington, P., Brugha, T., Lindesay, J., Jenkins, R., . . . Meltzer, H. (2006). Insomnia comorbidity and impact and hypnotic use by age group in a national survey population aged 16 to 74 years. *Sleep, 29,* 1391–1397.

Stone, K. L., Ensrud, K. E., & Ancoli-Israel, S. (2008). Sleep, insomnia and falls in elderly patients. *Sleep Medicine, 9*(Suppl. 1), 18–22. doi:10.1016/S1389-9457(08)70012-1

Taylor, D. J., Lichstein, K. L., & Durrence, H. H. (2003). Insomnia as a health risk factor. *Behavioral Sleep Medicine, 1,* 227–247. doi:10.1207/S15402010BSM0104_5

Taylor, D. J., Mallory, L. J., Lichstein, K. L., Durrence, H. H., Riedel, B. W., & Bush, A. J. (2007). Comorbidity of chronic insomnia with medical problems. *Sleep, 30,* 213–218.

Vaz Fragoso, C. A., & Gill, T. M. (2007). Sleep complaints in community-living older persons: A multifactorial geriatric syndrome. *Journal of the American Geriatrics Society, 55,* 1853–1866. doi:10.1111/j.1532-5415.2007.01399.x

Vitiello, M. V., Moe, K. E., & Prinz, P. N. (2002). Sleep complaints cosegregate with illness in older adults: Clinical research informed by and informing epidemiological studies of sleep. *Journal of Psychosomatic Research, 53,* 555–559. doi:10.1016/S0022-3999(02)00435-X

Weisz, J. R., & Hawley, K. M. (2001). *Procedural and coding manual for identification of evidence-based treatments.* Los Angeles: University of California.

Wohlgemuth, W. K., & Edinger, J. D. (2000). Sleep restriction therapy. In K. L. Lichstein & C. M. Morin (Eds.), *Treatment of late-life insomnia* (pp. 147–166). Thousand Oaks, CA: Sage.

Zammit, G. K., Weiner, J., Damato, N., Sillup, G. P., & McMillan, C. A. (1999). Quality of life in people with insomnia. *Sleep, 22*(Suppl. 2), S379–S385.

4

EVIDENCE-BASED PSYCHOLOGICAL TREATMENTS FOR GERIATRIC DEPRESSION

AVANI SHAH, FORREST SCOGIN, AND MARK FLOYD

Depression is one of the most common and debilitating psychological disorders experienced in late life, with prevalence rates of significant depressive symptoms in community-dwelling older adults as high as 25% (Koenig & Blazer, 1992), resulting in mortality, disability, and health decline. Unfortunately, older adults face a number of challenges in obtaining adequate depression treatment. Geriatric depression is often complicated by the presence of medical conditions (Katon & Ciechanowski, 2002) and polypharmacy (Pollock, 1999), requiring more specialized care. Other barriers to adequate depression treatment for older adults include underrecognition of depression (Cole & Yaffe, 1996; Mulsant & Ganguli, 1999), lack of transportation and mobility limitations (Bruce, Citters, & Bartels, 2005), and stigma (Sirey et al., 2001). Older adults also wait longer before they seek treatment, with an average delay of 6 to 8 years (P. S. Wang et al., 2005). Moreover, the lack of professionals who specialize in mental health and aging (LaMascus, Bernard, Barry, Salerno, & Weiss, 2005) creates a gap in treatment availability for older adults and signals a significant problem, especially with the expected growth of this population from 2010 to 2030.

With these factors as a backdrop, in this chapter, we first provide an overview of evidence-based psychological treatments (EBTs) for depression. Psychological treatments are an important aspect of health care for older adults, especially with respect to depression. Because our overarching goal in this chapter is to help bridge the research-to-practice translation, coauthor Mark Floyd then shares his perspective on implementing such treatments in nonacademically based practice settings. This we hope will illuminate some of the strengths and weaknesses of providing services informed by an evidence-based perspective. There are undoubtedly many challenges to the use of protocol-driven psychological interventions, yet our belief is that practice guided by evidence is optimal. We conclude the chapter by providing information on resources that can aid the implementation of evidence-based practice with depressed older adults.

The Evidence

Avani Shah and Forrest Scogin

In this section, we overview the evidence base for psychological treatments for depression experienced by older adults. This section builds on the work of our team (Scogin, Welsh, Hanson, Stump, & Coates, 2005) undertaken as part of the Society of Clinical Geropsychology's effort to identify EBTs for older adults. At that time, we conducted an exhaustive review of the literature on psychological treatments for geriatric depression. A more thorough description of the methods used to identify EBTs is provided in the introductory chapter of this book. In simplified terms, it was necessary to have two controlled trials of the same treatment in which significant reductions in depressive symptoms were found. It is impressive that six approaches were identified as EBTs for geriatric depression: behavior therapy, cognitive behavioral therapy (CBT), cognitive bibliotherapy, problem-solving therapy (PST), brief psychodynamic therapy, and reminiscence therapy (RT). In that approximately 5 years has passed since the publication of this review, our first task for this chapter was to review the literature to determine whether work published between 2005 and 2008 had altered the list of EBTs. Whereas several noteworthy publications on psychological treatment of depression appeared during this interval, and are noted in this review of the evidence, there were no changes to the list of EBTs for late-life depression. A brief overview of the six approaches and the research support follows.

BEHAVIOR THERAPY

Behavior therapy for depression has great promise for application in a variety of settings and aging populations. The major premise of the treatment is easily understood by most older adult clients, and the application of the protocol is arguably less technically demanding for clinicians. Much of the work in the area stems from the contributions of Lewinsohn and colleagues (Lewinsohn, 1974; Lewinsohn, Biglan, & Zeiss, 1976). They observed that depressed individuals tended to participate in fewer and at times less satisfying pleasant activities and experienced a higher number of negative events. From these findings, behavioral therapy for depression emerged in which the connection between mood and behaviors was central. One of the goals of behavior therapy is to teach clients to observe the mood–behavior relation by recording their mood and activity patterns. Subsequently, clients learn to identify pleasant activities through activity checklists and eventually to increase the frequency and quality of their pleasant activities. According to the behavioral theory, depression will improve when clients engage more often in satisfying pleasant activities.

Behavior therapy with depressed older adults has been reasonably well-researched. Six out of seven studies support behavior therapy as an EBT for depression in older adults (Gallagher & Thompson, 1982; Haringsma, Engels, Cuijpers, & Spinhoven, 2006; Lichtenberg, Kimbarow, Morris, & Vangel, 1996; Rokke, Tomhave, & Jocic, 1999; Teri, Logsdon, Uomoto, & McCurry, 1997; Thompson, Gallagher, & Breckenridge, 1987). Behavior therapy was superior to a control condition in five of the studies (Gallagher & Thompson, 1982; Lichtenberg et al., 1996; Rokke et al., 1999; Teri et al., 1997; Thompson et al., 1987). In one of the studies, behavior therapy was found to be nonsignificantly different in efficacy from other EBTs, psychodynamic therapy, and CBT (Gallagher & Thompson, 1982). The results of one pilot study also suggest that behavior therapy could possibly be beneficial for older adults in nursing home settings, but not enough information was provided to determine whether this study contributes to the evidence-based status of this treatment (Meeks, Looney, Haitsma, & Teri, 2008).

The versatility of behavior therapy can be ascertained by examining the varying contexts in which it has been successful. For example, behavior therapy has been effective with lower levels of depressive symptomatology as well as for those meeting criteria for major depressive disorder. Across the five studies, behavior therapy has also improved depressive symptoms with differing session number and length, with as few as six 30-minute sessions (Lichtenberg et al., 1996). Moreover, behavior therapy has the potential to be administered by professionals other than mental health clinicians, as indicated by the Lichtenberg et al. (1996) study in which occupational therapists delivered the treatment.

Behavioral activation (Jacobson et al., 1996) is a promising variant of this approach that presents a simplified approach that can be appealing for use with older adults who are evidencing cognitive impairment. It has not currently received EBT status with older adults, although our group has conducted several pilot investigations (e.g., Snarski et al., 2011).

Resources are provided in Appendix 4.1 to assist those who may be interested in using behavior therapy techniques with depressed older adults. Refer to Table 4.1 for a list of studies contributing to the EBT status of behavior therapy for older adults.

COGNITIVE BEHAVIORAL THERAPY

CBT, as exemplified by Beck et al. (1979), blends behavioral techniques such as behavioral activation, relaxation training, and assertiveness skills with cognitive techniques that identify, challenge, and change maladaptive thoughts. The primary goal of the treatment is to target and change both the depressogenic thinking and the behavioral patterns that lead to and maintain depression.

We located eight studies that provide support for CBT as a beneficial treatment for late-life depression (Campbell, 1992; Floyd, Scogin, McKendree-Smith, Floyd, & Rokke, 2004; Fry, 1984; Gallagher & Thompson, 1982; Gallagher-Thompson & Steffen, 1994; Laidlaw et al., 2008; Rokke et al., 1999; Thompson et al., 1987). In these studies, CBT was found to be either superior to a control condition or nonsignificantly different from another EBT (behavioral therapy or brief psychodynamic therapy). On the basis of the coding criteria, only one of the located CBT studies did not show evidence for significantly reduced depressive symptomatology (De Berry, Davis, & Reinhard, 1989). Thus, the majority of studies reviewed supported CBT.

In these studies, the average session length was 60 minutes, and the number of treatment sessions varied between 10 and 18. A lengthier version of CBT (Steuer et al., 1984) had 46 sessions and was efficacious when compared with psychodynamic therapy; however, it was coded as a different treatment because it was much longer than the other CBT protocols. Another study was coded as a variant of CBT (Hyer et al., 2008) because the intervention was delivered in blended group (13 sessions), individual (two sessions), and staff-aided (two sessions) formats. In this randomized study, CBT was shown to be more effective than treatment as usual.

Clinicians may be concerned that older adults will find CBT too challenging. CBT does make demands on working memory capacity, but with usually minor adaptations this form of treatment can be beneficial for most older adults. CBT has been adapted by Thompson and colleagues

TABLE 4.1
Research Contributing to the Evidence-Based Psychological Treatment Status of Behavioral Therapy

Authors	Sample	Conditions	Length of treatment	Outcome measures	Findings
Gallagher & Thompson, 1982	$N = 30$; 55 years and older; BDI > 17, HRSD > 14	1. Behavioral therapy ($n = 10$) 2. CBT ($n = 10$) 3. Brief–relational insight therapy ($n = 10$)	16 sess., 90-min sess.	BDI, HRSD, SADS-C, SRS, SDS	Significant and comparable initial improvement for all groups; cognitive and behavioral groups maintained gains longer than those in brief–relational group
Haringsma, Engels, Cuijpers, & Spinhoven, 2006	$N = 119$; 55 years and older; Presence of prior depressive symptoms	1. Coping with depression ($n = 61$) 2. Wait-list control ($n = 58$)	11 group sess., 2-hr sess.	CES-D	Significant improvement in the intervention condition
Lichtenberg, Kimbarow, Morris, & Vangel, 1996	$N = 37$; 60 years and older; GDS > 10	1. Behavioral therapy by psycho-logists ($n = 13$) 2. Behavioral therapy by occupational therapists ($n = 13$) 3. No treatment control ($n = 11$)	6 sess., 30-min sess.	GDS	Significantly greater improvement in behavioral groups than in no-treatment control group
Meeks, Looney, Haitsma, & Teri, 2008	$N = 20$; 55 years and older; GDS > 11	1. Behavioral therapy ($n = 13$) 2. Control group ($n = 7$)	10 sess., 40-min sess.	GDS, HRSD	

(continues)

TABLE 4.1
Research Contributing to the Evidence-Based Psychological Treatment Status of Behavioral Therapy *(Continued)*

Authors	Sample	Conditions	Length of treatment	Outcome measures	Findings
Rokke, Tomhave, & Jocic, 1999	$N = 40$; 60 years of age or older; HRSD > 9, BDI > 9, GDS > 10	1. Behavioral therapy ($n = 8$) 2. CBT ($n = 9$) 3. Wait-list control ($n = 23$)	10 sess., 60-min sess.	BDI, GDS	Comparable improvement for CBT and BT; significantly greater improvement in CBT & BT compared with wait-list control group
Teri, Logsdon, Uomoto, & McCurry, 1997	$N = 72$; patient–caregiver dyads, GDS > 9, met RDC and *DSM–III–R* criteria for major or minor depressive disorder	1. Behavioral therapy ($n = 42$) 2. Typical care control ($n = 10$) 3. Wait-list condition ($n = 20$)	9 sess., 60-min sess.	BDI, CSDD	Significantly greater improvement in behavioral group than in typical care and wait-list control conditions
Thompson, Gallagher, & Breckinridge, 1987	$N = 95$; 60 years of age or older; met RDC criteria for MDD, BDI > 16, HRSD > 13	1. Behavioral therapy ($n = 25$) 2. Cognitive therapy ($n = 27$) 3. Brief psycho-dynamic therapy ($n = 24$) 4. Wait-list control ($n = 19$)	18 sess., 60-min sess.	BDI, BSI-D, GDS, HRSD	Comparable improvement for BT, CT, and BPT; control group did not improve

Note. sess. = session; CBT = cognitive behavioral therapy; BDI = Beck Depression Inventory; BSI-D = Brief Symptom Inventory–Depression subscale; CES-D = Center for Epidemiologic Studies Depression; CSDD = Cornell Scale for Depression in Dementia; *DSM–III–R = Diagnostic and Statistical Manual of Mental Disorders—Third Edition–Revised;* GDS = Geriatric Depression Scale; HRSD = Hamilton Rating Scale for Depression; MDD = major depressive disorder; RDC = Research Diagnostic Criteria; SADS-C = Schedule for Affective Disorders and Schizophrenia–Change Interview; SDS = Zung Self-Rating Depression Scale; SRS = Self-Rating Scale; BT = behavioral therapy; CT = cognitive therapy; BPT = brief psychodynamic therapy.

(Gallagher-Thompson & Thompson, 2010; Laidlaw, Thompson, Dick-Siskin, & Gallagher-Thompson, 2003) to meet the needs of older adults. The modifications needed for CBT have been identified in several articles (e.g., Rybarczyk, Gallagher-Thompson, Rodman, Zeiss, Gantz, & Yesavage, 1992). For example, age-related physical and cognitive declines for some older consumers may impede compliance with written homework assignments or other aspects of the treatment program. Specifically, modifications such as providing in-session memory aids (e.g., cue cards, written material on an easel), slowing down the pace of the therapy process, providing a recording of the session, and simplifying homework assignments can maximize fit between the treatment and the older adult. At this time, CBT is the most extensively researched psychological treatment for depressed older adults. Refer to Appendices 4.1 to 4.6 for additional resources in conducting CBT and to Table 4.2 for studies contributing to the EBT status of CBT.

COGNITIVE BIBLIOTHERAPY

Cognitive bibliotherapy, that is, cognitive therapy (CT) delivered through a book, is one of the most thoroughly researched self-help approaches. CT includes a number of psychoeducational components, such as reading and homework assignments. Thus, it is not surprising that CT has been developed for self-administration in book format. Because of the availability and low cost of cognitive bibliotherapy, it has the potential to be provided to older adults, who may otherwise encounter barriers to traditionally delivered psychotherapy because of mobility limitations, transportation difficulties, or financial concerns.

Four studies support cognitive bibliotherapy as an EBT for depression in older adults (Floyd et al., 2004; Landreville & Bissonnette, 1997; Scogin, Hamblin, & Beutler, 1987; Scogin, Jamison, & Gochneaur, 1989). All of the studies used the *Feeling Good* book (Burns, 1980), allowing participants to work through the book at their own pace over approximately a 4-week period. During this time, participants received only minimal brief weekly contacts. Refer to Table 4.3 for a list of studies that contribute to the EBT status of cognitive bibliotherapy.

PROBLEM-SOLVING THERAPY

PST (Nezu, Nezu, & Perri, 1989) has become a highly valued approach for treating depression in older adults. According to PST for depression (Arean et al., 1993), deficiencies in problem-solving skills prevent older

TABLE 4.2

Research Contributing to the Evidence-Based Psychological Treatment Status of Cognitive Behavioral Therapy

Authors	Sample	Conditions	Length of treatment	Outcome measures	Findings
Campbell, 1992	$N = 103$; aged 64–82; met *DSM–III–R* criteria for depression	1. CBT ($n = ?$) 2. Attention placebo ($n = ?$) 3. No treatment control ($n = ?$)	16 sess., 60-min sess.	SDS	Significantly greater improvement in CBT group as compared with the attention placebo and no treatment control groups
De Berry, Davis, & Reinhard, 1989	$N = 32$; aged 65–75	1. Relaxation–Meditation ($n = 13$) 2. CBT ($n = 10$) 3. Attention placebo ($n = 9$)	20 sess., 45-min sess.	BDI	RM group showed greater improvement than CBT and attention placebo, but not significantly so
Floyd, Scogin, McKendree-Smith, Floyd, & Rokke, 2004	$N = 35$, 60 years of age or older, HRSD > 9	1. CBT ($n = 8$) 2. Cognitive bibliotherapy ($n = 13$) 3. Wait-list control ($n = 14$)	16 sess., 50-min sess.	GDS, HRSD	Significantly greater improvement in CBT and CB than in the wait-list control group; CBT superior to CB on GDS
Fry, 1984	$N = 28$; aged 67–80	1. CBT ($n = 17$) 2. Wait-list control ($n = 11$)	12 sess., 60-min sess.	DEQ, MMPI-2	Significantly greater improvement in CBT group as compared with the wait-list control group
Gallagher & Thompson, 1982	$N = 30$; 55 years and older; BDI > 17, HRSD > 14	1. BT ($n = 10$) 2. CBT ($n = 10$) 3. Brief–relational insight therapy ($n = 10$)	16 sess., 90-min sess.	BDI, HRSD, SADS-C, SDS	Significant and comparable initial improvement for all groups; CBT and behavioral groups maintained gains longer than those in brief–relational group

Study	Sample/criteria	Treatment groups	Sessions	Measures	Results
Gallagher-Thompson & Steffen, 1994	N = 52; met RDC criteria for major, minor, or intermittent depressive disorder, BDI > 9	1. CBT (n = 31) 2. Brief psychodynamic therapy (n = 21)	18 sess., 60-min sess.	BDI, HRSD, GDS, SADS-C	Comparable improvement for both groups
Laidlaw et al., 2008	N = 40; HRSD > 7, BDI-II > 13	1. CBT (n = 21) 2. Treatment as usual (n = 23)	8 sess., 60-min sess.?	HRSD	Significantly greater improvement in CBT group as compared with treatment as usual group
Rokke, Tomhave, & Jocic, 1999	N = 40; 60 years of age or older; HRSD > 9, BDI > 9, GDS > 10	1. BT (n = 8) 2. CBT (n = 9) 3. Wait-list control (n = 23)	10 sess., 60-min sess.	BDI, GDS, HRSD	Comparable improvement for CBT and BT; significantly greater improvement in CBT and BT groups as compared with the wait-list control group
Steuer et al., 1984	N = 35; 55 years of age or older; met DSM-III criteria for major depressive disorder	1. Psychodynamic therapy (n = 10) 2. CBT (n = 10)	46 sess.	HAMD, SDS, BDI	Both groups improved significantly; significantly greater improvement in CBT group than PT
Thompson, Gallagher, & Breckinridge, 1987	N = 95; 60 years of age or older; met RDC criteria for MDD, BDI > 16, HRSD > 13	1. BT (n = 25) 2. Cognitive therapy (n = 27) 3. Brief psychodynamic therapy (n = 24) 4. Wait-list control (n = 19)	18 sess., 60-min sess.	BDI, BSI-D, GDS, HRSD	Comparable improvement for all treatment groups; control group did not improve

Note. sess. = session; ? = indicates sample size is unknown; BDI = Beck Depression Inventory; BSI-D = Brief Symptom Inventory–Depression subscale; BT = behavioral therapy; CB = cognitive bibliotherapy; CBT = cognitive behavioral therapy; DEQ = Depressive Experiences Questionnaire; *DSM–III–R* = *Diagnostic and Statistical Manual of Mental Disorders—Third Edition—Revised*; GDS = Geriatric Depression Scale; HAMD = Hamilton Depression Scale; HRSD = Hamilton Rating Scale for Depression; MMPI-2 = Minnesota Multiphasic Personality Inventory–2; PT = psychodynamic therapy; RDC = Research Diagnostic Criteria; SADS-C = Schedule for Affective Disorders and Schizophrenia–Change Interview; SDS = Zung Self-Rating Depression Scale.

TABLE 4.3
Research Contributing to the Evidence-Based Psychological Treatment Status of Cognitive Bibliotherapy

Authors	Sample	Conditions	Length of treatment	Outcome measures	Findings
Floyd, Scogin, McKendree-Smith, Floyd, & Rokke, 2004	$N = 35$; 60 years of age or older; HRSD > 9	1. CBT ($n = 8$) 2. CB ($n = 13$) 3. Wait-list control ($n = 14$)	4 weeks	GDS, HRSD	Significantly greater improvement in CBT and CB as compared with the wait-list control group; CBT superior to CB on GDS
Landreville & Bissonnette, 1997	$N = 23$; 55 years of age or older; diagnosed depressive disorder	1. CB ($n = 12$) 2. Wait-list control ($n = 11$)	4 weeks	GDS, HRSD	Significantly greater improvement in CB as compared with the wait-list control group
Scogin, Hamblin, & Beutler, 1987	$N = 20$; 60 years of age or older; HRSD > 9	1. CB ($n = 8$) 2. Attention placebo ($n = 6$) 3. Wait-list control ($n = 6$)	4 weeks	BDI, GDS, HRSD	Significantly greater improvement with CB as compared with the attention placebo and wait-list control group
Scogin, Jamison, & Gochneaur, 1989	$N = 44$; 60 years of age or older; HRSD > 9	1. CB ($n = 15$) 2. BB ($n = 14$) 3. Wait-list control ($n = 15$)	4 weeks	GDS, HRSD	Significantly greater improvement with CB and BB as compared with the wait-list control group; comparable efficacies between CB and BB

Note. CBT = cognitive behavioral therapy; BB = behavioral bibliotherapy; BDI = Beck Depression Inventory; CB = cognitive bibliotherapy; GDS = Geriatric Depression Scale; HRSD = Hamilton Rating Scale for Depression.

adults from successfully coping with routine problems as well as the challenges in late life (e.g., health, financial, loss, retirement), resulting in depression. The premise of PST is to teach clients the skills to address their own problems in an organized step-by-step fashion. This approach encourages clients to first identify their problems and then to formulate a number of potential solutions. Next, each solution is examined for feasibility, and the most suitable course of action is selected for implementation. Finally, the client is asked to evaluate the outcome after each solution is applied. In PST, the therapist serves as a coach in the problem-solving process, allowing each stage of the process to be primarily guided by the client to allow for the development of problem-solving skills that can be applied independently even after psychotherapy has ended.

Five studies have shown for support PST as an EBT for depression in older adults (Alexopoulos, Raue, & Arean, 2003; Arean et al., 1993; Gellis et al., 2008; Gellis, McGinty, Horowitz, Bruce, & Misener, 2007; Hussian & Lawrence, 1981). These studies speak to the flexibility of PST in being applied to different populations of older adults, including nursing home residents, home care recipients, and the community dwelling. Session number and length ranged from as few as five 30-minute sessions for nursing home patients to as many as 12 sessions, 90 minutes in length, for community-dwelling older adults. Fewer and shorter sessions were common in the nursing home and home-care settings. Refer to Appendix 4.1 for resources to assist in conducting PST. See Table 4.4 for a list of studies contributing to the EBT status of PST.

BRIEF PSYCHODYNAMIC THERAPY

The goal of brief psychodynamic therapy is to increase insight through the patterns observed in the therapeutic relationship, to examine areas of conflict, and to explore unconscious processes in a time-limited manner (Horowitz & Kaltreider, 1979). Two studies (Gallagher-Thompson & Steffen, 1994; Thompson et al., 1987) have examined the efficacy of brief psychodynamic therapy for older adults with depression, supporting the treatment as an EBT. Both studies involved 18 one-hour sessions. Refer to Table 4.5 to obtain additional information about these studies. A study with 46 sessions of short-term psychodynamic psychotherapy (Steuer et al., 1984) was coded as a distinct treatment because of its length. This study showed that a lengthier form of psychotherapy effectively treated depressive symptoms in older adults. Brief psychodynamic therapy is not to be confused with classic psychoanalysis, in which much longer treatment duration is typical and the goals of treatment tend to be more far-reaching. We did not

TABLE 4.4
Research Contributing to the Evidence-Based Psychological Treatment Status of Problem-Solving Therapy

Authors	Sample	Conditions	Length of treatment	Outcome measures	Findings
Alexopoulos, Raue, & Areán, 2003	$N = 25$; 65 years of age and older; HRSD > 17	1. PST ($n = 12$) 2. Supportive therapy ($n = 13$)	12 sess., 60-min sess.	HRSD	Significantly greater improvement in PST group as compared with the supportive therapy group
Areán, Perri, Nezu, Schein, Christopher, & Joseph, 1993	$N = 67$; aged 55–80; met RDC criteria for MDD; BDI > 20, HRSD > 18, GDS > 10	1. PST ($n = 19$) 2. RT ($n = 28$) 3. Wait-list control ($n = 20$)	12 sess., 90-min sess.	BDI, GDS, HRSD	Significantly greater improvement in PST & RT groups as compared with the wait-list control group; improvement significantly greater for PST than for RT
Gellis, McGinty, Horowitz, Bruce, & Misener, 2007	$N = 40$; 65 years of age or older; CES-D > 22	1. PST (home care; $n = 20$) 2. Usual care ($n = 20$)	6 weeks, 6 sess.	BDI, CES-D, GDS, QOLI	Significantly greater improvement in PST group as compared with the usual care
Gellis, McGinty, Tierney, Jordan, Burton, & Misener, 2008	$N = 62$; 65 years of age or older; CES-D sf > 15, HRSD sf >11	1. PST (home care; $n = 30$) 2. Usual care ($n = 32$)	6 weeks, 6 sess., 60-min sess.	GDS-15, HRSD sf, QOLI	Significantly greater improvement in PST group as compared with the usual care except on QOLI
Hussian & Lawrence, 1981	$N = 36$; nursing home residents	1. PST ($n = 12$) 2. SR ($n = 12$) 3. Wait-list control ($n = 12$)	5 sess., 30-min sess.	BDI, SRS	Significantly greater improvement in PST & SR as compared with the wait-list control group; PST showed greater improvement than SR on BDI

Note. sess. = session; BDI = Beck Depression Inventory; CES-D = Center for Epidemiologic Studies Depression Scale; GDS = Geriatric Depression Scale; HRSD = Hamilton Rating Scale for Depression; MDD = major depressive disorder; PST = problem-solving therapy; RDC = research diagnostic criteria; RT = reminiscence therapy; SR = social reinforcement; QOLI = Quality of Life Inventory; SRS = Self-Rating Scale.

TABLE 4.5

Research Contributing to the Evidence-Based Psychological Treatment Status of Brief Psychodynamic Therapy

Authors	Sample	Conditions	Length of treatment	Outcome measures	Findings
Gallagher-Thompson & Steffen, 1994	N = 52; met RDC criteria for major, minor, or intermittent depressive disorder; BDI > 9	1. CBT (n = 31) 2. Brief psychodynamic therapy (n = 21)	18 sess., 60-min sess.	BDI, GDS, HRSD, SADS-C	Comparable improvement for both groups
Thompson, Gallagher, & Breckinridge, 1987	N = 95; 60 years of age or older; met RDC criteria for MDD, BDI > 16, HRSD > 13	1. Behavioral therapy (n = 25) 2. Cognitive therapy (n = 27) 3. Brief psychodynamic therapy (n = 24) 4. Wait-list control (n = 19)	18 sess., 60-min sess.	BDI, BSI-D, GDS, HRSD	Comparable improvement for all three experimental groups; control group did not improve

Note. sess. = session; BDI = Beck Depression Inventory, BSI-D = Brief Symptom Inventory: Depression Subscale, CBT = cognitive behavioral therapy; GDS = Geriatric Depression Scale, HRSD = Hamilton Rating Scale for Depression, MDD = Major Depressive Disorder, RDC = Research Diagnostic Criteria, SADS-C = Schedule for Affective Disorders and Schizophrenia–Change Interview.

find any controlled studies of psychoanalysis for depression experienced by older adults. Consult Appendix 4.1 for additional resources on implementing psychodynamic psychotherapy.

REMINISCENCE THERAPY

RT is one of the only psychological therapies developed specifically for older adults. On the basis of Erickson's (1963) stages of psychosocial development, the primary developmental task in late life is reflecting on meaningful life events to achieve ego integrity and avoid despair. The rationale for RT is straightforward: focusing on the narration of significant positive and negative life events to achieve ego integrity and self-actualization (Birren & Deutchman, 1991). The opportunity to reflect on and integrate successes and failures at this stage in one's life can help resolve conflicts, develop a renewed sense of meaning, and even reshape identity. Many older adults find RT appealing because it tends to capitalize on well-preserved memories rather than on emphasizing working memory. Working memory tends to show age-related declines, and therapies that emphasize working memory, such as CBT, are sometimes challenging for older adults with mild and moderate cognitive impairment.

According to Webster, Bohlmeijer, and Westerhof (2010), three major types of reminiscence interventions are available: simple and unstructured; life review or structured reminiscence; and life review therapy, which is highly structured and frequently combined with other treatment modalities (e.g., CT, PST, narrative therapy). Six out of eight studies support RT as an EBT for late-life depression (Arean et al., 1993; Goldwasser, Auerbach, & Harkins, 1987; Serrano, Latorre, Gatz, & Montanes, 2004; J. J. Wang, 2005, 2007; Watt & Cappeliez, 2000). Most of these studies used life review therapy, which is highly structured. As few as four to as many as 12 session protocols were represented in the studies. Session lengths also varied, with some studies having sessions as short as 30 minutes and others using 90-minute sessions. An advantage of RT is its logical delivery in a group setting, which is cost-effective and a format favored in the EBT studies (e.g., Arean et al., 1993; Goldwasser et al., 1987; J. J. Wang, 2007). Three of the studies provided RT in long-term-care settings, suggesting the potential for application to a vulnerable subpopulation (Goldwasser et al., 1987; J. J. Wang, 2005, 2007). This approach could also be useful for those with memory impairments as two of these studies provided RT to depressed older adults with dementia (Goldwasser et al., 1987; J. J. Wang, 2007). Many long-term-care settings for older adults already incorporate elements of reminiscence into recreational activities (e.g., music from prior eras, discussion groups), which may make RT more acceptable to staff and therefore more likely to be implemented. Though RT has the potential to be delivered by social workers, nurses, occupational therapists, and recreational therapists, particularly in long-term settings, none of the EBT studies evaluated this. Stinson and Kirke (2006) examined the impact of nurse-delivered RT in an assisted living facility, but depressive symptoms did not significantly decrease following treatment compared with the control group. Refer to Appendix 4.1 for additional resources in implementing RT and to Table 4.6 for a list of studies contributing to the EBT status of RT.

INTERVENTIONS NEEDING FURTHER STUDY

Several other treatments for late-life depression did not meet EBT status because only one controlled study assessed was available. A list of the interventions is included in Table 4.7.

In these next sections, we hope to take this presentation on EBTs for depressed older adults to a more practical level. In the abstract, most psychologists would agree that the use of treatments with a solid record of effectiveness is the proper course of action. However, we do not practice in the abstract, and when it comes time to implement a treatment plan, issues arise. As clinical researchers, we encounter the same issues in clinical trials; rarely can a protocol be delivered with complete fidelity to depressed older adults even in the context of a carefully monitored efficacy investigation. Nonetheless, we believe that EBTs adapted to the context in which they are provided should be given first consideration by clinicians and consumers. In the paragraphs that follow, Mark Floyd discusses his conceptualization and implementation of evidence-based practice.

Adapting EBT for the Real World

Mark Floyd

I am currently a full-time clinician in the Veterans Affairs system, splitting my time between a 120-bed skilled nursing facility and home-based primary care. The patients in both locations are predominantly older adults and have a mixture of mental disorders (e.g., depression, anxiety disorders, psychotic disorders) and health problems (e.g., chronic pain, chronic illness, disability). I have participated in a randomized clinical trial using CBT, and I am a firm believer in using the science of psychotherapy to guide my work as a clinician. However, I find it difficult to follow treatment

TABLE 4.6
Research Contributing to the Evidence-Based Psychological Treatment Status of Reminiscence Therapy

Authors	Sample	Conditions	Length of treatment	Outcome measures	Findings
Areán et al., 1993	N = 67; aged 55–80; met RDC criteria for MDD; BDI > 20, HRSD > 18, GDS > 10	1. PST (n = 19) 2. RT (n = 28) 3. Wait-list control (n = 20)	12 sess., 90-min sess.	BDI, GDS, HRSD	Significantly greater improvement in PST and RT groups as compared with the wait-list control group; significantly greater improvement for PST than RT
Goldwasser, Auerbach, & Harkins, 1987	N = 30; demented nursing home residents	1. RT (n = 9) 2. Reality orientation (n = 9) 3. No treatment control (n = 9)	10 sess., 30-min sess.	BDI	Significantly greater improvement in RT as compared with other conditions
Klausner et al., 1998	N = 13; ages 55 and above; met criteria for MDD	1. RT (n = 4) 2. Goal-focused psycho-therapy (n = 4)	11 sess., 60-min sess.	BDI, HRSD, Montgomery-Asberg Scale for Depression	Improvement in both groups, but GFP improved more

Study	Sample	Groups	Sessions	Measures	Results
Serrano, Latorre, Gatz, & Montanes, 2004	N = 43; ages 60 years and above	1. Life review (n = 20) 2. Social services as usual (n = 23)	4 sess., 1/week	CES-D	Significantly greater improvement in LR
J. J. Wang, 2005	N = 48; 65 years of age or older; long-term-care facility	1. RT (n = 25) 2. Control group (n = 20)	4 months, 1/week, 30–45-min sess.	GDS-15, AER	Significantly greater improvement in RT group as compared with control group
J. J. Wang, 2007	N = 102; 65 years of age or older	1. Experimental (n = 51) 2. Control (n = 51)	8 sess., 1/week	GDS-15, CSDD	Significantly greater improvement in experimental group on CSDD than control group
Watt & Cappeliez, 2000	N = 40; ages 60 years and above; GDS > 13	1. Integrative reminiscence therapy (n = 16) 2. Instrumental reminiscence therapy (n = 12) 3. Attention placebo (n = 12)	6 sess., 90-min sess.	GDS, HRSD	Significantly greater improvement in RT

Note. sess. = session; AER = Apparent Emotion Rating Scale; BDI = Beck Depression Inventory; CES-D = Center for Epidemiological Studies Depression Scale; CSDD = Cornell Scale for Depression in Dementia; GDS = Geriatric Depression Scale; GFP = goal-focused psychotherapy; HRSD = Hamilton Rating Scale for Depression; MDD = major depressive disorder; LR = life review; PST = problem-solving therapy; RDC = research diagnostic criteria; RT = reminiscence therapy.

TABLE 4.7
Interventions Needing Further Study

Study	Modality	Outcome
Viney, Benjamin, & Preston, 1989	Personal construct therapy	Superior to no treatment control
Dhooper, Green, Huff, & Austin-Murphy, 1993	Coping together group therapy	Superior to no treatment control
Mossey, Knott, Higgins, & Talerico, 1996	Short-term inter-personal psycho-therapy	Superior to attention-placebo control
Scogin et al., 1989	Behavioral bibliotherapy	Comparable to cognitive bibliotherapy and superior to delayed treatment control
Gallagher & Thompson, 1982	Relational–insight therapy	Comparable to behavioral and CBT
Klausner et al., 1988	Goal-focused therapy	Superior to reminiscence therapy
Steuer et al., 1984	Psychodynamic therapy	Comparable to CBT
Hyer et al., 2008	Group, individual, and staff CBT	Superior to treatment as usual
Spek et al., 2008[a]	Internet-based CBT	Superior to a delayed treatment control
Van Schaik et al., 2005	Interpersonal psycho-therapy	Superior to care as usual

Note. CBT = cognitive behavioral therapy.
[a]Mean age of participants was 55.

manuals verbatim and frequently feel compelled to deviate from protocol. The guiding principles I follow are: (a) deliver as closely as is practicable, the treatments as outlined in the treatment manuals used in EBT research; (b) remain flexible and deviate from the treatment manual when it makes good clinical sense; and (c) approach each case from a scientist–practitioner viewpoint, using a hypothesis generation and testing methodology for each specific intervention. My orientation is primarily cognitive behavioral, but I also frequently use RT and motivational interviewing because these techniques work well with the home-based primary care population. Motivational interviewing is not an EBT for late-life depression, but it does have a strong track record with adult populations.

I start each case in hopes of following the CBT protocol verbatim. I begin the first therapy session with the treatment rationale. Most patients are active participants in this session and respond favorably to the rationale. The first problem I encounter in the home-based primary care population is a resistance to homework. This resistance is not specific to psychotherapy, but rather it is more of a general characteristic of the patient's problems. Many of the patients in home-based primary care have chronic health problems resulting from a lifetime of poor decision making, unhealthy lifestyle, and a refusal to follow the suggestions of health care providers. The patients are noncompliant with psychotherapy homework in the same way they are non-compliant with diet, exercise, and medication schedules. The compliance problems begin when I introduce activity recording and the patient balks at having to write something down. We discuss the reluctance and typically end the session with the patient making a commitment to attempt the home-work. At the start of the next session, the patient confesses to not doing the homework assignment. At this point, I must choose between sticking to the protocol and refusing to continue therapy if the patient is unwilling to do homework or accepting that the patient is not likely to ever do homework and proceeding as best we can. In most cases, I accept they will not do home-work on their own and never assign it again. We do all exercises together during the session. It is much less time efficient and possibly fosters more of a dependence on me in the beginning, but with repetition the patient learns the techniques and begins using them outside the session.

Elements of CBT that I almost always use include the three- and five-column techniques and collaborative empiricism. Whenever I hear a cogni-tive distortion, I ask whether the statement is indeed true or whether it is an exaggeration due to the influence of emotions. I summarize the treatment rationale again if necessary to reinforce how thoughts and emotions are con-nected. We examine the evidence and accordingly revise the thought. With repetition, the patient learns to recognize a cognitive distortion and how to use these cognitive behavioral techniques to reduce distress. We review the importance of identifying the specific words in their self-talk and stress the need to avoid exaggerations of distress.

Another CT technique I frequently use is described as "the downward arrow technique" in *Feeling Good* (Burns, 1980). This technique is well suited for dealing with situations that are a realistic problem (as opposed to a cogni-tive distortion) on the surface. For example, the downward arrow technique is useful in helping patients to accept the realities of such late-life situations as loss of independence, increased disability, and loss of loved ones. The technique teaches them how to drill down into their thought processes and identify cognitive distortions. It often exposes distorted thoughts, such as "I cannot be happy if I am disabled" or "my life is meaningless without my spouse," that coexist with what appears to be normal grief for the loss of mobility or the loss of a spouse. Loss is an inevitable consequence of aging, but loss does not mean everyone is doomed to unhappiness.

As mentioned previously, loss is a difficult part of aging and a recurrent issue in work with the older population. I find that everyone "knows" they will die, and in most cases they have no distress associated with the thought of death. However, they rarely consider how the aging process is a gradual progression toward disability, loss of independence, and the loss of loved ones, and when faced with these circumstances they often become depressed. Rather than focusing on what they have and making adjustments to enjoy life as much as possible, they focus on their losses and remain stuck in a rut of trying to continue their life as it was before the loss. Acceptance, or passive coping, is necessary when active coping fails, and I help them understand and apply both. I encourage the use of the serenity prayer as a general problem-solving model—to accept what they cannot change but to do as much as possible to make changes to match their wants and needs.

RT provides another path toward acceptance of events in life. Older adults frequently stray off topic into a review of the past, and when they do, I encourage them to elaborate on the events and the downstream effects. This gives me an opportunity to rid the patient of cognitive distortions associated with their past. When there are no distortions, I try to stress how mistakes can have positive effects later in life and that the nature of life is we are forced into making decisions between mutually exclusive options.

Another difficult scenario in home-based primary care is the patient with a chronic health condition and depression secondary to their medical condition. Chronic diabetes is a common problem, and patients become depressed because of the disability and prognosis. It is unfortunate that these patients are often unwilling to make the necessary lifestyle changes to improve their health and alleviate their depression. I have trouble using typical cognitive behavioral techniques because it seems that no matter how I try to stick with a collaborative approach, they perceive me as preaching to them about what they should do, just like every other health care professional. To avoid this trap, I empathize with their challenges and use motivational interviewing to increase health-promoting behaviors. It is a slow process to shift them into action, and I have to remind myself that changing lifelong habits takes time. I also keep in mind that maintaining the status quo is a victory when dealing with a progressively debilitating condition.

In summary, although it is difficult to follow an EBT protocol verbatim, there are many specific interventions within each EBT that can be used as designed. I think it is best to have the freedom to select bits and pieces from several EBTs and apply them as needed in each individual case.

CASE EXAMPLE

The patient is a 77-year-old, married Caucasian male veteran with chronic diabetes and associated neuropathy, including visual limitations. "Sam" is a retired truck driver and electrician with a high school education who was referred for the treatment of depression and anxiety. There were a total of 10 sessions, the last of which was primarily a check-in to monitor status and confirm treatment gains were being maintained. The following is a synopsis of the progress notes with elaborations on the techniques used.

Session 1

The first session is a psychological evaluation. Sam admits to being depressed, endorsing sadness, anhedonia, lack of energy, sleep disturbance (hypersomnia), and worthlessness. He scores a 6 on the Geriatric Depression Scale–15 (GDS-15; Yesavage et al., 1982–1983; see Appendix 4.5). Sam denies suicidal or homicidal thoughts, psychoticism, and substance problems. He feels somewhat helpless due to his visual limitations and hopeless because there is no cure for diabetes. He fears becoming injured secondary to the visual limitations and therefore must constantly remind himself to be cautious. He complains that he sleeps too much, with about 7 hours of sleep at night plus a 2-hour or longer nap each afternoon and sometimes also a 2-hour nap in the morning, and he states he would like to do all of his sleeping at night. Sam denies relationship problems and states that he and his wife get along well with each other. Brief evaluation of cognition indicates attention is intact; there are some deficits in working memory and recall, but recognition is intact. Overall, his pattern of cognitive deficits is consistent with the effects of depression, yet it is possible he is experiencing some mild cognitive impairment. Further testing would be necessary to discern this, but it is clear his memory is intact enough for psychotherapy, especially if I give him reminders and repeat important information. His visual limitations also prevent the use of written reminders, diagrams, and homework, which otherwise would have enhanced retention of treatment information. We agree to meet again in 2 weeks after he returns from vacation.

Session 2

Sam reports his mood has been "pretty good" and that they had a good vacation. He denies sadness and anhedonia, but he reports having nightmares and getting really angry several times while on vacation. He says the nightmares were not identical, but the content followed the general form of someone or something trying to kill him, and he awoke with a feeling of dread. I ask about his thoughts about death, and he says he gets claustrophobic whenever he envisions himself buried in a coffin, and he admits that is stupid because he knows he would be dead and it wouldn't matter. He also states he has very strong religious beliefs and has been a lifelong member of his church. Sam says he believes God has forgiven him, but although he has not done anything terribly wrong, he is not certain he will go to heaven when he dies. We discuss how this uncertainty would make the thought of death very uncomfortable, stressing the connection between thoughts and emotions. Sam then describes some of the incidents that triggered his anger while on vacation. In each instance, he got mad when someone disagreed with him or said something that he interpreted as being critical of him. Sam says this has been a long-standing problem for him, and it is his biggest problem. We did not have time remaining in this session for an intervention, so we agree to focus on this during our next session.

This session changed my conceptualization of Sam. In the first session, my impression was depression because he had not accepted his chronic illness and disability. However, by the end of the second session, a pattern of perfectionism, sensitivity to criticism, and general lack of self-acceptance emerged and appeared to be at the root of his problems, and this became my working hypothesis. I also noted I would need to tread lightly given his sensitivity to criticism and be cautious when challenging his viewpoints.

Session 3

Sam starts this session by engaging in life review, with a focus on his employment history, and admits he has always been very self-conscious, fearful of evaluation by others, and easily hurt by negative comments made by others. He says he knows it is wrong, but he has had trouble forgiving some who have hurt his feelings. He knows this is part of his anger problem.

To illustrate, Sam recalls an incident that occurred more than 30 years ago in his church. Sam describes his church as being a "small, close-knit congregation," and everyone is expected to take an active part in the worship service. This expectation of involvement is especially true for the men, who are expected to say prayers aloud each week as a regular part of the service. Sam says he heard one of the church elders at the end of the service say to someone, "You know, Sam can't even hardly speak right." Sam says it was wrong for anyone to say that sort of thing about another church member, and it was especially wrong for an elder, so he has still not forgiven him and is still angry. I explain the CT rationale of how emotions are connected to thoughts, and I ask Sam what else he is thinking and feeling. He admits he felt embarrassed and sad and that this incident made him even more fearful of public speaking. Sam's thoughts include "I cannot even pray well," "I'm not a good church member," and "If I speak in public again, I'll just embarrass myself." We discuss the connection between his thoughts and his emotions, and I cautiously emphasize that it was his thoughts rather than the elder's words that made him feel so bad. I then use the downward arrow technique as described in *Feeling Good* (Burns, 1980) and find that Sam thought he was worthless. I ask him what his expectation for himself was in regard to public prayer, and he says he should not be as good as the preacher but still pretty good. I ask if it were reasonable for all lay members of a congregation to be good public speakers and if public speaking was the only talent valued by a church. Sam agrees. He then explains how at that time he decided to contribute to the church through volunteer work on their electrical system instead of saying public prayers. Sam says he got really mad when after having worked all day Saturday on the church wiring, one of the church members chastised him for refusing to say a prayer during Sunday service:

> He told me I needed to start pulling my weight, and I told him I was doing other things than praying but I resented what he said and still feel bad about it even though it happened 30 years ago.

We review his thoughts, which were similar to the previous ones, except it is clear Sam expects himself to fulfill others' expectations and believed that if he did not, he was a failure. I agree with him that these other people were wrong to have said what they did, but it was his own beliefs and self-expectations causing the problem. We discuss how his need to satisfy others' expectations puts his emotional well-being in the hands of others. I encourage him, as homework, to monitor his feelings and note exactly what he feels and thinks such that we can review this information in the next session.

In this session, we used the CT rationale and verbally went through the three-column technique, and then we used the downward arrow technique to help identify the core negative beliefs. I did not do a thorough review of the evidence to dispute his negative thoughts because he responded quickly to rational disputation.

Session 4

Session 4 is essentially a repeat of Session 3, with no new content. Sam admits that his fear of evaluation and criticism has been a huge influence on his life and puts him at risk for overreacting with anger. We go back over the events he described in the previous session and review CT principles. I stress how we cannot control what other people say and think.

I am a little disappointed with the lack of new content but also realize there would likely be some repetition necessary for consolidation of the learning in the prior session. As I did at the end of the prior session, I encourage Sam to continue monitoring his emotions and to note exactly what he feels and thinks,. I also encourage Sam to not shy away from activities that subject him to evaluation and to use these activities as opportunities to practice monitoring his thoughts and emotions.

Session 5

Sam reports getting mad at a contractor who failed to live up to his promises. We explore his thoughts and identify "He is doing this to intentionally take advantage of me" and "I used to be able to do all this for myself, but now I have to rely on others." We focus on the former because his anger was far greater than his hopelessness and sadness. We review anger management principles with a focus on the mind-reading fallacy and how we can only see what people do, not why they are doing it. I ask Sam for alternative explanations for the contractor's behavior, and he offers the following: he could have encountered an unexpected delay, he could have had something critical come up, or he might be less responsible than I supposed he is, and this may be his normal work ethic. Sam reviews all of the possibilities and agrees he has no reason to suspect the contractor was deliberately taking advantage of him; his anger decreases accordingly. Sam says he still does not like being at the mercy of others, which leads us into an introduction of how to use acceptance.

Session 6

Sam reports that his mood has been angry since last session, and he is particularly upset by politics and all of the argument over changing the health care system. I review the general problem-solving model of doing whatever he can to solve a problem and then accepting the status quo if he is unable to make the change he wants. We discuss things he could do to influence politics. Sam says he called his congressman once and will not do it again, because it didn't help. Likewise, he is unwilling to get involved in a political organization at either the local or national level, and after discussion admits that national politics is beyond his control and influence. I suggest that he has the choice of continuing to be angry or using acceptance to cope with it. We review in more detail the principles of acceptance and how to apply them in anger management.

Session 7

Sam reports that he continues to be easily angered and cites an incident in which he lost his temper and said some harsh words to his wife. Sam says he was listening to TV and said something to his wife about being angry that they were devoting far more attention to a particular issue than was warranted and it was the same thing on all the channels. His wife said, "Well, nobody is making you watch the TV," and he said he got angry because he felt like she was demeaning him. I remind him that we cannot read anyone's mind and truly know their motives, and I ask him to consider what other reasons she might have had for making the comment. Sam admits she could have just been making a suggestion to him but also says she did not say what he wanted her to say. I ask what he was expecting, and he says he wanted her to simply agree with him that the coverage was excessive. We also discuss how it was possible she was tired of hearing him complain, and he says he can understand that. After reviewing the alternatives and considering how his wife was not one to say demeaning things to him, Sam agrees she probably meant her comment to be supportive or at worst was making an attempt to stop his complaining, and he felt much less angry. We also discuss how he sometimes allows himself to get angry over small issues and stress that his first step in coping with any upset is to ask himself whether it's a big enough issue to justify it.

Session 8

Sam reports that his mood has improved significantly and that he has had a good week. He says he talked with his wife, and they have improved their relationship. He says he got frustrated this week with a painter they hired but was able to use the principles we discussed to reduce his anger and deal effectively with him. In particular, he says he is getting better at not mind reading, not making mountains out of molehills, and acceptance. Sam says he is still having trouble with accepting things he does not like, but he admits it is necessary and useful.

Session 9

Sam says he had another good week. He says he was better able to control his anger and feels much better about himself. Sam says he no longer feels depressed, anxious, or angry. I suggest that our work together is finished and that we meet one more time in a month to monitor his status. Sam says he enjoys talking with me and is in no hurry to stop meeting, but we agree that we have accomplished the purpose and think a follow-up meeting is a good idea.

Session 10 (1 Month After Session 9)

Sam says he continues to do well and is having good control over his emotions. We review the techniques discussed in therapy. We discuss some possible challenges he might be facing in the future. He reports noticing his wife's worsening memory problems, and in light of her family history of Alzheimer's disease, he suspects she will eventually need care that he cannot provide because of his visual limitations. I ask how he is coping with this, and he explains how he has already talked with their children and feels confident they will both have the support they need in their final years. He denies significant anxiety and feels like they will cross that bridge when they get to it. I tell him that I am available if and when he needs to meet again, and he thanks me for all my help.

Final Comments

I feel like we fully addressed his anger problems and to a lesser extent his anxiety problems. I regret not more fully addressing his death anxiety, but on the occasions I brought up the topic it was not important to him. I think his need for approval from others is an issue that will continue to give him trouble occasionally if he does not continue to practice what he has learned. After all, we met for only 10 sessions, and he has held onto this belief for more than 70 years. I am optimistic, however, because his problem solving and his attitude about his future (which is uncertain but does not look very good) show excellent emotional coping.

APPENDIX 4.1: RESOURCES AND SUGGESTIONS
FOR FURTHER READING

Behavioral Therapy

Gallagher, D. E., & Thompson, L. W. (1981). *Depression in the elderly: A behavioral treatment manual.* Los Angeles: University of Southern California Press.

Lejuez, C. W., Hopko, D. R., & Hopko, S. D. (2001). A brief behavioral activation treatment for depression treatment manual. *Behavioral Modification, 25,* 255–286.

Lewinsohn, P., Biglan, A., & Zeiss, A. (1976). Behavioral treatment of depression. In P. Davidson (Ed.), *Behavioral management of anxiety, depression, and pain.* New York, NY: Brunner/Mazel.

Rider, K. L., Gallagher-Thompson, D., & Thompson, L. W. (2004). *California older person's pleasant events schedule: Manual.* Stanford University, Stanford, CA. Retrieved from http://oafc.stanford.edu/coppes.html

Teri, L. (1991). Behavioral assessment and treatment of depression in older adults. In P. A. Wisocki (Ed.), *Handbook of clinical behavior therapy with the elderly client* (pp. 225–243). New York, NY: Plenum Press.

Teri, L. (1994). Behavioral treatment of depression in patients with dementia. *Alzheimer Disease and Related Disorders, 8,* 66–73.

Cognitive Behavioral Therapy

Beck, A. T., Rush, A. J., Shaw, B. F., & Emery, G. (1979). *Cognitive therapy of depression.* New York, NY: Guilford Press.

Ellis, A. (1979). *Theoretical and empirical foundations of rational emotive therapy.* Monterey, CA: Brooks/Cole.

Emery, G. (1981). Cognitive therapy with the elderly. In G. Emery, S. Hollon, & R. Bedrosian (Eds.), *New directions in cognitive therapy* (pp. 84–98). New York, NY: Guilford Press.

Gallagher-Thompson, D., & Thompson, L. W. (2010). *Therapist guide: Treating late life depression: A cognitive-behavioral therapy approach.* New York, NY: Oxford University Press.

Thompson, L. W., Dick-Siskin, L., Coon, D. W., Powers, D. V., & Gallagher-Thompson, D. (2010). *Patient workbook: Treating late life depression: A cognitive-behavioral therapy approach.* New York, NY: Oxford University Press.

Yost, E. B., Beutler, L. E., Corbishley, M. A., & Allender, J. R. (1986). *Group cognitive therapy: A treatment approach for depressed older adults.* New York, NY: Pergamon Press.

Cognitive Bibliotherapy

Burns, D. D. (1980). *Feeling good*. New York, NY: Avon Books.

Problem-Solving Therapy

Nezu, A. M., & D'Zurilla, T. J. (2001). *Problem-solving therapies*. New York, NY: Guilford Press.

Reminscence Therapy

Birren, J. E., & Deutchman, D. E. (1991). *Guiding autobiography groups for older adults*. Baltimore, MD: Johns Hopkins University Press.

Kunz, J. A. & Soltys, F. G. (2007). *Transformational reminiscence: Life story work*. New York, NY: Springer.

Psychodynamic Psychotherapy

Evans, S., & Garner, J. (2004). *Talking over the years: A handbook of dynamic therapy with older adults*. New York, NY: Brunner/Routledge.

Morgan, A. C., & Goldstein, M. Z. (2003). Psychodynamic psychotherapy with older adults. *Psychiatric Services, 54*, 1592–1594.

APPENDIX 4.2: SAMPLE COGNITIVE BEHAVIORAL THERAPY SESSION OUTLINES

Session no.	Session outline
1–2	• Establish rapport • Elicit expectations about therapy • Explain therapy structure • Explain roles of therapist and client • Set goals for therapy • Explain rationale for cognitive therapy • Demonstrate cognitive therapy technique applied to a problem • Elicit reaction to session
3	• Effects of first session • Activity scheduling • Mastery and pleasure ratings • Problems since last session • Schedule of activities until next session • Agenda setting • Elicit reaction to session
4	• Prepare agenda • Effects of prior sessions • Review homework assignments • Explanation of unhelpful thoughts • Assign homework • Elicit reaction to session
5	• Prepare agenda • Effects of prior sessions • Review homework assignments • Further explanation of unhelpful thoughts • Assign homework • Elicit reaction to session
6	• Prepare agenda • Effects of prior sessions • Demonstrate identification and correction of unhelpful thoughts • Daily record of unhelpful thoughts • Assign homework • Elicit reaction to session
7–8	• Prepare agenda • Effects of prior sessions • Review homework assignments • Explain how to dealt with anger and anxiety • Explain relaxation • Assign homework • Elicit reaction to session

(continues)

Session no.	Session outline
9–12	• Increase responsibility for client for all activities in session • Prepare agenda • Effects of prior sessions • Review homework assignments • Explain assertiveness skills, overthinking, and problem solving • Assign homework • Elicit reaction to session
13–16	• Continue increased responsibility for client; move towards termination • Prepare agenda • Effects of prior sessions • Review homework assignments • Identification and testing of underlying assumptions • Assign homework • Anticipate problems and how to address them • Application of techniques as a life-long process—consolidate gains

APPENDIX 4.3: UNHELPFUL THOUGHTS WORKSHEET

	Responses
Step 1: Event	
Step 2: Unhelpful Thoughts	Rate how true you believe it is from 1 to 10:__
	Rate how true you believe it is **after Step 5 & 6:**__
Step 3: Unhelpful Thought (Circle type of unhelpful thought)	1) Name-Calling
	2) Should, Could, Would
	3) Tune Into Negative/Tune Out Positive
	4) Black & White Thinking
	5) Exaggerations
	6) What's the Use
	7) If Only
	8) Doomsday Thinking/Fortune telling
Step 4: Circle Emotions	Angry Sad Bothered Worried Scared Other_____
	Rate how strong your emotions are from 1 to 10:___
	Rate how you feel **after finishing Step 5 & 6:**___
Step 5: Way to Change Unhelpful Thoughts (Pick as many as needed)	1) Action
	2) Language
	3) As If (You Were A Friend)
	4) Consider Alternatives/In-Betweens
	5) Scale Technique
	6) Examine Consequences
	7) Credit Positives
	8) Helpful Thoughts
	9) Thought Stopping
Step 6: Helpful Thought	Rate how strongly you believe it from 1 to 10:__

From *Making the Golden Years Golden Again Workbook* (p. 30), by A. Shah, 2007, Tuscaloosa: University of Alabama. Copyright 2007 by A. Shah. Reprinted with permission.

APPENDIX 4.4: DAILY MOOD RATING FORM

DAILY MOOD RATING FORM

Dates: From _____ to _____

1. Please rate your mood for each day, i.e., how good or bad you felt, using the nine-point scale shown below. If you felt good, put a high number on the chart below. If you felt "so-so," mark a 5. And if you felt low or depressed mark a lower number.

☹ 1   2   3   4   5   6   7   8   9 ☺

very   "so-so"   very
depressed   happy

2. On the two lines next to your mood rating for each day, please briefly give two major reasons why you think you felt that way. Try to be as specific as possible.

Time of Day	Mood Score	Reasons why I felt this way:
Early Morning		
Noon		
Dinner		
Bedtime		
Average Daily Score:		

From *Treating Late-Life Depression: A Cognitive-Behavioral Therapy Approach, Workbook* (p. 184), by L. W. Thompson, L. Dick-Siskin, D. W. Coon, D. V. Powers, and D. Gallagher-Thompson, 2010, Oxford, England: Oxford University Press. Copyright 2010 by Oxford University Press. Reprinted with permission.

APPENDIX 4.5: MOOD SCREEN

Geriatric Depression Scale

Instructions: Answer yes or no for how you have felt over the past week on these questions.

1. Are you basically satisfied with your life?
2. Have you dropped many of your activities and interests?
3. Do you feel that your life is empty?
4. Do you often get bored?
5. Are you hopeful about the future?
6. Are you bothered by thoughts you can t get out of your head?
7. Are you in good spirits most of the time?
8. Are you afraid that something bad is going to happen to you?
9. Do you feel happy most of the time?
10. Do you often feel helpless?
11. Do you often get restless and fidgety?
12. Do you prefer to stay at home, rather than going out and doing new things?
13. Do you frequently worry about the future?
14. Do you feel you have more problems with memory than most?
15. Do you think it is wonderful to be alive now?
16. Do you often feel downhearted and blue?
17. Do you feel pretty worthless the way you are now?
18. Do you worry a lot about the past?
19. Do you find life very exciting?
20. Is it hard for you to get started on new projects?
21. Do you feel full of energy?
22. Do you feel that your situation is hopeless?
23. Do you think that most people are better off than you are?
24. Do you frequently get upset over little things?
25. Do you frequently feel like crying?
26. Do you have trouble concentrating?
27. Do you enjoy getting up in the morning?
28. Do you prefer to avoid social gatherings?
29. Is it easy for you to make decisions?
30. Is your mind as clear as it used to be?

Reprinted from "Development and Validation of a Geriatric Depression Screening Scale: Preliminary Report," by J. A. Yesavage, T. L. Brink, O. Lum, V. Huang, M. Adey, & V. O. Leirer, 1983, *Journal of Psychiatric Research, 17*, (p. 41). Scale in public domain.

APPENDIX 4.6: CALIFORNIA OLDER PERSON'S PLEASANT EVENTS SCHEDULE

CALIFORNIA OLDER PERSON'S PLEASANT EVENTS SCHEDULE

Dolores Gallagher-Thompson, Larry W. Thompson, Kenneth L. Rider

Name_____ Date_____

This is a list of 66 events that people tend to find pleasant. For each event, make 2 ratings:

How often did this event happen to you in the past month?

> 0 = Not at all
> 1 = 1-6 times
> 2 = 7 or more times

How pleasant, enjoyable, or rewarding was this event?
If the event did *not* occur, then please rate how pleasant you think it *would have been* if it *had* occurred.

> 0 = Was not or would not have been pleasant
> 1 = Was or would have been somewhat pleasant
> 2 = Was or would have been very pleasant

Here are two sample events with the answers properly filled in. Please remember to circle an answer for both HOW OFTEN and HOW PLEASANT for each event.

Please circle ONE number in EACH column for each item	HOW OFTEN in the past month? 0 = Not at all 1 = 1-6 times 2 = 7 or more times Circle ONE number	HOW PLEASANT was it or would it have been? 0 = Not pleasant 1 = Somewhat pleasant 2 = Very pleasant Circle ONE number
A. Winning the lottery	(0) 1 2	0 1 (2)
B. Writing a letter	0 (1) 2	0 (1) 2

Please circle ONE number in EACH column for each item	HOW OFTEN in the past month? 0 = Not at all 1 = 1-6 times 2 = 7 or more times Circle ONE number			HOW PLEASANT was it or would it have been? 0 = Not pleasant 1 = Somewhat pleasant 2 = Very pleasant Circle ONE number		
1. Looking at clouds	0	1	2	0	1	2
2. Being with friends	0	1	2	0	1	2
3. Having people show an interest in what I say	0	1	2	0	1	2
4. Thinking about pleasant memories	0	1	2	0	1	2
5. Shopping	0	1	2	0	1	2
6. Seeing beautiful scenery	0	1	2	0	1	2
7. Having a frank and open conversation	0	1	2	0	1	2
8. Doing a job well	0	1	2	0	1	2
9. Listening to sounds of nature	0	1	2	0	1	2
10. Having coffee, tea, etc., with friends	0	1	2	0	1	2
11. Thinking about myself	0	1	2	0	1	2
12. Being complimented or told I have done something well	0	1	2	0	1	2

Please circle ONE number in EACH column for each item	HOW OFTEN in the past month? 0 = Not at all 1 = 1-6 times 2 = 7 or more times Circle ONE number			HOW PLEASANT was it or would it have been? 0 = Not pleasant 1 = Somewhat pleasant 2 = Very pleasant Circle ONE number		
13. Doing volunteer work	0	1	2	0	1	2
14. Planning trips or vacations	0	1	2	0	1	2
15. Kissing, touching, showing affection	0	1	2	0	1	2
16. Being praised by people I admire	0	1	2	0	1	2
17. Meditating	0	1	2	0	1	2
18. Listening to music	0	1	2	0	1	2
19. Seeing good things happen to family or friends	0	1	2	0	1	2
20. Collecting recipes	0	1	2	0	1	2
21. Doing a project my own way	0	1	2	0	1	2
22. Seeing or smelling a flower or plant	0	1	2	0	1	2
23. Saying something clearly	0	1	2	0	1	2
24. Thinking about something good in the future	0	1	2	0	1	2
25. Looking at the stars or moon	0	1	2	0	1	2

Please circle ONE number in EACH column for each item	HOW OFTEN in the past month? 0 = Not at all 1 = 1-6 times 2 = 7 or more times Circle ONE number			HOW PLEASANT was it or would it have been? 0 = Not pleasant 1 = Somewhat pleasant 2 = Very pleasant Circle ONE number		
26. Being told I am needed	0	1	2	0	1	2
27. Working on a community project	0	1	2	0	1	2
28. Complimenting or praising someone	0	1	2	0	1	2
29. Watching a sunset	0	1	2	0	1	2
30. Thinking about people I like	0	1	2	0	1	2
31. Completing a difficult task	0	1	2	0	1	2
32. Amusing people	0	1	2	0	1	2
33. Baking because I feel creative	0	1	2	0	1	2
34. Reading literature	0	1	2	0	1	2
35. Being with someone I love	0	1	2	0	1	2
36. Having an original idea	0	1	2	0	1	2
37. Having peace and quiet	0	1	2	0	1	2
38. Listening to the birds sing	0	1	2	0	1	2
39. Making a new friend	0	1	2	0	1	2

Please circle ONE number in EACH column for each item	HOW OFTEN in the past month? 0 = Not at all 1 = 1-6 times 2 = 7 or more times Circle ONE number			HOW PLEASANT was it or would it have been? 0 = Not pleasant 1 = Somewhat pleasant 2 = Very pleasant Circle ONE number		
40. Being asked for help or advice	0	1	2	0	1	2
41. Bargain hunting	0	1	2	0	1	2
42. Reading magazines	0	1	2	0	1	2
43. Feeling a divine presence	0	1	2	0	1	2
44. Expressing my love to someone	0	1	2	0	1	2
45. Giving advice to others based on past experience	0	1	2	0	1	2
46. Solving a problem, puzzle, crossword	0	1	2	0	1	2
47. Arranging flowers	0	1	2	0	1	2
48. Helping someone	0	1	2	0	1	2
49. Getting out of the city (to the mountains, seashore, desert)	0	1	2	0	1	2
50. Having spare time	0	1	2	0	1	2
51. Being needed	0	1	2	0	1	2
52. Meeting someone new of the same sex	0	1	2	0	1	2

Please circle ONE number in EACH column for each item	HOW OFTEN in the past month? 0 = Not at all 1 = 1-6 times 2 = 7 or more times Circle ONE number			HOW PLEASANT was it or would it have been? 0 = Not pleasant 1 = Somewhat pleasant 2 = Very pleasant Circle ONE number		
53. Exploring new areas	0	1	2	0	1	2
54. Having a clean house	0	1	2	0	1	2
55. Doing creative crafts	0	1	2	0	1	2
56. Going to church	0	1	2	0	1	2
57. Being loved	0	1	2	0	1	2
58. Visiting a museum	0	1	2	0	1	2
59. Having a daily plan	0	1	2	0	1	2
60. Being with happy people	0	1	2	0	1	2
61. Listening to classical music	0	1	2	0	1	2
62. Shopping for a new outfit	0	1	2	0	1	2
63. Taking inventory of my life	0	1	2	0	1	2
64. Planning or organizing something	0	1	2	0	1	2
65. Smiling at people	0	1	2	0	1	2
66. Being near sand, grass, a stream	0	1	2	0	1	2

REFERENCES

Alexopoulos, G. S., Raue, P., & Arean, P. (2003). Problem-solving therapy versus supportive therapy in geriatric major depression with executive dysfunction. *The American Journal of Geriatric Psychiatry, 11*, 46–52.

Arean, P. A., Perri, M. G., Nezu, A. M., Schein, R. L., Christopher, F., & Joseph, T. X. (1993). Comparative effectiveness of social problem-solving therapy and reminiscence therapy as treatments for depression in older adults. *Journal of Consulting and Clinical Psychology, 61*, 1003–1010. doi:10.1037/0022-006X.61.6.1003

Beck, A. T., Rush, A. J., Shaw, B. F., & Emery, G. (1979). *Cognitive therapy of depression.* New York, NY: Guilford Press.

Birren, J. E., & Deutchman, D. E. (1991). *Guiding autobiography groups for older adults.* Baltimore, MD: Johns Hopkins University Press.

Bruce, M. L., Citters, V., & Bartels, S. J. (2005). Evidence-based mental health services for home and community. *Psychiatric Clinics of North America, 28*, 1039–1060. doi:10.1016/j.psc.2005.08.002

Burns, D. D. (1980). *Feeling good.* New York, NY: Avon Books.

Campbell, J. M. (1992). Treating depression in well older adults: Use of diaries in cognitive therapy. *Issues in Mental Health Nursing, 13*, 19–29. doi:10.3109/01612849209006882

Cole, M. G., & Yaffe, M. J. (1996). Pathway to psychiatric care of the elderly with depression. *International Journal of Geriatric Psychiatry, 11*, 157–161. doi:10.1002/(SICI)1099-1166(199602)11:2<157::AID-GPS304>3.0.CO;2-S

De Berry, S., Davis, S., & Reinhard, K. E. (1989). A comparison for reducing anxiety and depression in a geriatric population. *Journal of Geriatric Psychiatry, 22*, 231–247.

Dhooper, S. S., Green, S. M., Huff, M. B., & Austin-Murphy, J. (1989). Efficacy of a group approach to reducing depression in nursing home elderly residents. *Journal of Gerontological Social Work, 20*, 87–100.

Erickson, E. H. (1963). *Childhood and society* (2nd ed.). New York, NY: Norton.

Floyd, M., Scogin, F., McKendree-Smith, N. L., Floyd, D. L., & Rokke, P. D. (2004). Cognitive therapy for depression: A comparison of individual psychotherapy and bibliotherapy for depressed older adults. *Behavior Modification, 28*, 297–318. doi:10.1177/0145445503259284

Fry, P. S. (1984). Cognitive training and cognitive-behavioral variables in the treatment of depression in the elderly. *Clinical Gerontologist, 3*, 25–45. doi:10.1300/J018v03n01_04

Gallagher, D. E., & Thompson, L. W. (1982). Treatment of major depressive disorder in older adult outpatients with brief psychotherapies. *Psychotherapy: Theory, Research & Practice, 19*, 482–490. doi:10.1037/h0088461

Gallagher-Thompson, D., & Steffen, A. M. (1994). Comparative effects of cognitive-behavioral and brief psychodynamic psychotherapies for depressed family caregivers. *Journal of Consulting and Clinical Psychology*, 62, 543–549. doi:10.1037/0022-006X.62.3.543

Gallagher-Thompson, D., & Thompson, L.W. (2010). *Therapist guide: Treating late life depression: A cognitive-behavioral therapy approach.* New York, NY: Oxford University Press.

Gellis, Z.D., McGinty, J., Horowitz, A., Bruce, M.L., & Misener, E. (2007). Problem-solving therapy for late-life depression in home care: A randomized field trial. *The American Journal of Geriatric Psychiatry*, 15, 968–978. doi:10.1097/JGP.0b013e3180cc2bd7

Gellis, Z.D., McGinty, J., Tierney, L., Jordan, C., Burton, J., & Misener, E. (2008). Randomized controlled trial of problem-solving therapy for minor depression in home care. *Research on Social Work Practice*, 18, 596–606. doi:10.1177/1049731507309821

Goldwasser, A.N., Auerbach, S.M., & Harkins, S.W. (1987). Cognitive, affective, and behavioral effects of reminiscence group therapy on demented elderly. *The International Journal of Aging & Human Development*, 25, 209–222. doi:10.2190/8UX8-68VC-RDYF-VK4F

Haringsma, R., Engels, G.I., Cuijpers, P., & Spinhoven, P. (2006). Effectiveness of the coping with depression (CWD) course for older adults provided by the community-based mental health care system in the Netherlands: A randomized controlled field trial. *International Psychogeriatrics*, 18, 307–325. doi:10.1017/S104161020500253X

Horowitz, M., & Kaltreider, N. (1979). Brief therapy of the stress response syndrome. *The Psychiatric Clinics of North America*, 2, 365–377.

Hussian, R.A., & Lawrence, P.S. (1981). Social reinforcement of activity and problem-solving training in the treatment of depressed institutionalized elderly patients. *Cognitive Therapy and Research*, 5, 57–69. doi:10.1007/BF01172326

Hyer, L., Yeager, C.A., Hilton, N., & Sacks, A. (2009). Group, individual, and staff therapy: An efficient and effective cognitive behavioral therapy in long-term care. *American Journal of Alzheimer's Disease and Other Dementias*, 23, 528–539. doi:10.1177/1533317508323571

Jacobson, N.S., Dobson, K.S., Truax, P.A., Addis, M.E., Koerner, K., Gollan, J.K.,...Prince, S.E. (1996). A component analysis of cognitive-behavioral treatment for depression. *Journal of Consulting and Clinical Psychology*, 64, 295–304. doi:10.1037/0022-006X.64.2.295

Katon, W., & Ciechanowski, P. (2002). Impact of major depression on chronic medical illness. *Journal of Psychosomatic Research*, 53, 859–863. doi:10.1016/S0022-3999(02)00313-6

Klausner, E.J., Clarkin, J.F., Spielman, L., Pupo, C., Abrams, R., & Alexopoulos, A. (1998). Late-life depression and functional disability: The role of goal-focused group psychotherapy. *International Journal of Geriatric Psychiatry*, 13, 707–716.

Koenig, H.G., & Blazer, D.G. (1992). Epidemiology of geriatric affective disorders. *Clinics in Geriatric Medicine*, 8, 235–251.

Laidlaw, K., Davidson, K., Toner, H., Jackson, G., Clark, S., Law, J., ... Cross, S. (2008). A randomized controlled trial of cognitive behavior therapy vs. treatment as usual in the treatment of mild to moderate late life depression. *International Journal of Geriatric Psychiatry, 23,* 843–850. doi:10.1002/gps.1993

Laidlaw, K., Thompson, L.W., Dick-Siskin, L., & Gallagher-Thompson, D. (2003). *Cognitive behaviour therapy with older people.* New York, NY: Wiley. doi:10.1002/9780470713402

LaMascus, A.M., Bernard, M.A., Barry, P., Salerno, J., & Weiss, J. (2005). Bridging the workforce gap for our aging society: How to increase and improve knowledge and training. Report of an expert panel. *Journal of the American Geriatrics Society, 53,* 343–347. doi:10.1111/j.1532-5415.2005.53137.x

Landreville, P., & Bissonnette, L. (1997). Effects of cognitive bibliotherapy for depressed older adults with a disability. *Clinical Gerontologist, 17,* 35–55.

Landreville, P., & Bissonnette, L. (1998). Cognitive bibliotherapy for depression in older adults with a disability. *Clinical Gerontologist, 19,* 69–79.

Lewinsohn, P. (1974). A behavioral approach to depression. In R. Friedman & M. Katz (Eds.), *The psychology of depression: Contemporary theory and research* (pp. 157–176). New York, NY: Wiley.

Lewinsohn, P., Biglan, A., & Zeiss, A. (1976). Behavioral treatment of depression. In P. Davidson (Ed.), *Behavioral management of anxiety, depression, and pain* (pp. 91–146). New York, NY: Brunner/Mazel.

Lichtenberg, P.A., Kimbarow, M.L., Morris, P., & Vangel, S.J. (1996). Behavioral treatment of depression in predominately African-American medical patients. *Clinical Gerontologist, 17,* 15–33. doi:10.1300/J018v17n02_03

Meeks, S., Looney, S.W., Haitsma, K.V., & Teri, L. (2008). BE-ACTIV: A staff assisted behavioral intervention for depression in nursing homes. *The Gerontologist, 48,* 105–114. doi:10.1093/geront/48.1.105

Mossey, J.M., Knott, K.A., Higgins, M., & Talerico, K. (1996). Effectiveness of a psychosocial intervention, interpersonal counseling, for subdysthymic depression in medically ill elderly. *Journals of Gerontology: Series A: Biological & Medical Sciences, 51A,* M172–M178.

Mulsant, B.H., & Ganguli, M. (1999). Epidemiology and diagnosis of depression in late life. *The Journal of Clinical Psychiatry, 60(Suppl. 20),* 9–15.

Nezu, A.M., Nezu, C.M., & Perri, M.G. (1989). *Problem solving therapy for depression: Theory, research, and clinical guidelines.* Oxford, England: Wiley.

Pollock, B.G. (1999). Adverse reactions of antidepressants in elderly patients. *The Journal of Clinical Psychiatry, 60,* 4–8.

Rokke, P.D., Tomhave, J.A., & Jocic, Z. (1999). The role of client choice and target selection in self-management therapy for depression in older adults. *Psychology and Aging, 14,* 155–169. doi:10.1037/0882-7974.14.1.155

Rybarczyk, B., Gallagher-Thompson, D., Rodman, J., Zeiss, A., Gantz, F.E., & Yesavage, J. (1992). Applying cognitive-behavioral psychotherapy to the chronically ill elderly: Treatment issues and case illustration. *International Psychogeriatrics, 4,* 127–140. doi:10.1017/S1041610292000954

Scogin, F., Hamblin, D., & Beutler, L. (1987). Bibliotherapy for depressed older adults: A self-help alternative. *The Gerontologist, 27,* 383–387. doi:10.1093/geront/27.3.383

Scogin, F., Jamison, C., & Gochneaur, K. (1989). Comparative efficacy of cognitive and behavioral bibliotherapy for mildly and moderately depressed older adults. *Journal of Consulting and Clinical Psychology, 57,* 403–407. doi:10.1037/0022-006X.57.3.403

Scogin, F., Welsh, D., Hanson, A., Stump, J., & Coates, A. (2005). Evidence-based psychotherapies for depression in older adults. *Clinical Psychology: Science and Practice, 12,* 222–237. doi:10.1093/clipsy.bpi033

Serrano, J.P., Latorre, J.M., Gatz, M., & Montanes, J. (2004). Life review therapy using autobiographical retrieval practice for older adults with depressive symptomatology. *Psychology and Aging, 19,* 272–277. doi:10.1037/0882-7974.19.2.272

Shah, A. (2007). *Making the golden years golden again workbook.* Unpublished manuscript, Department of Psychology, University of Arizona, Tuscaloosa.

Sirey, J.A., Bruce, M.L., Alexopoulos, G.S., Perlick, D.A., Rave, P., Friedman, S.I., & Meyers, B.S. (2001). Perceived stigma as a predictor of treatment discontinuation in young and older outpatients with depression. *The American Journal of Psychiatry, 158,* 479–482. doi:10.1176/appi.ajp.158.3.479

Snarski, M., Scogin, F., DiNapoli, E., Presnell, A., McAlpine, J., & Marcinak, J. (2011). The effects of behavioral activation therapy with inpatient geriatric psychiatry patients. *Behavior Therapy, 42,* 100–108. doi:10.1016/j.beth.2010.05.001

Spek, V., Nyklicek, I., Smits, N., Cuijpers, P., Riper, H., Keyzer, J., & Pop, V. (2007). Internet-based cognitive behavioral therapy for subthreshold depression in people over 50 years old: A randomized controlled clinical trial. *Psychological Medicine, 37,* 1797–1806.

Steuer, J.L., Mintz, J., Hammen, C.L., Hill, M.A., Jarvik, L.F., McCarley, T., ...Rosin, R. (1984). Cognitive-behavioral and psychodynamic group psychotherapy in treatment of geriatric depression. *Journal of Consulting and Clinical Psychology, 52,* 180–189. doi:10.1037/0022-006X.52.2.180

Stinson, C.K., & Kirke, E. (2006). Structured reminiscence: An intervention to decrease depression and increase self-transcendence in older women. *Journal of Clinical Nursing, 15,* 208–218. doi:10.1111/j.1365-2702.2006.01292.x

Teri, L., Logsdon, R., Uomoto, J., & McCurry, S. (1997). Behavioral treatment of depression in dementia parents: A controlled clinical trial. *The Journals of Gerontology. Series B, Psychological Sciences and Social Sciences, 52B,* P159–P166. doi:10.1093/geronb/52B.4.P159

Thompson, L.W., Dick-Siskin, L., Coon, D.W., Powers, D.V., & Gallagher-Thompson, D. (2010). *Treating late life-depression: A cognitive-behavioral therapy approach, workbook.* New York, NY: Oxford University Press.

Thompson, L. W., Gallagher, D., & Breckenridge, J. S. (1987). Comparative effectiveness of psychotherapies for depressed elders. *Journal of Consulting and Clinical Psychology, 55*, 385–390. doi:10.1037/0022-006X.55.3.385

van Schaik, A., van Marwijk, H., Ader, H., van Dyck, R., de Haan, M., Penninx, B., ... Beekman, A. (2006). Interpersonal psychotherapy for elderly patients in primary care. *American Journal of Geriatric Psychiatry, 14*, 777–786.

Viney, L. L., Benjamin, Y. N., & Preston, C. A. (1989). An evaluation of personal construct therapy for the elderly. *British Journal of Medical Psychology, 62*, 35–41.

Wang, J. J. (2005). The effects of reminiscence on depressive symptoms and mood status of older institutionalized adults in Taiwan. *International Journal of Geriatric Psychiatry, 20*, 57–62. doi:10.1002/gps.1248

Wang, J. J. (2007). Group reminiscence therapy for cognitive and affective function of demented elderly in Taiwan. *International Journal of Geriatric Psychiatry, 22*, 1235–1240. doi:10.1002/gps.1821

Wang, P. S., Berglund, P., Olfson, M., Pincus, H. A., Wells, K. B., & Kessler, R. C. (2005). Failure and delay in initial treatment contact after first onset of mental disorders in the National Comorbidity Survey Replication. *Archives of General Psychiatry, 62*, 603–613. doi:10.1001/archpsyc.62.6.603

Watt, L. M., & Cappeliez, P. (2000). Integrative and instrumental reminiscence therapies for depression in older adults: Intervention strategies and treatment effectiveness. *Aging & Mental Health, 4*, 166–177. doi:10.1080/13607860050008691

Webster, J. D., Bohlmeijer, E. T., & Westerhof, G. J. (2010). Mapping the future of reminiscence: A conceptual guide for research and practice. *Research on Aging, 32*, 527–564. doi:10.1177/0164027510364122

Yesavage, J. A., Brink, T. L., Lum, O., Huang, V., Adey, M., & Leirer, V. O. (1982–1983). Development and validation of a geriatric depression screening scale: Preliminary report. *Journal of Psychiatric Research, 17*, 37–49. doi:10.1016/0022-3956(82)90033-4

5

EVIDENCE-BASED PSYCHOLOGICAL TREATMENTS FOR IMPROVING MEMORY FUNCTION AMONG OLDER ADULTS

GEORGE W. REBOK, JEANINE M. PARISI, ALDEN L. GROSS,
ADAM P. SPIRA, JEAN KO, QUINCY M. SAMUS, JANE S. SACZYNSKI,
STEVE KOH, AND RONALD E. HOLTZMAN

Memory loss is one of the most common complaints associated with aging (Balota, Dolan, & Duchek, 2000). Even among healthy older adults, memory impairments are a major concern and are often associated with physical health complaints, anxiety, and depression (Verhaeghen, Geraerts, & Marcoen, 2000). Difficulties with memory are especially bothersome because cognitive impairment often has a deleterious impact on one's personal, occupational, and social functioning, as well as overall quality of life (Bolla, Lindgren, Bonaccorsy, & Bleecker, 1991; Cutler & Grams, 1988; Fillenbaum, 1985; Fogel, Hyman, Rock, & Wolk-Klein, 2000; McCue, Rogers, & Goldstein, 1990; Ponds, van Boxtel, & Jolles, 2000). Although some loss in memory performance is a normal part of the aging process, in some cases, memory loss can be a sign of abnormal neurodegenerative processes (Albert, 2008).

Dementia, a neurodegenerative disorder characterized by memory loss and impairment in least one other cognitive domain (American Psychiatric Association, 2000), is becoming more common as our population ages and as the average life expectancy grows longer (Wan et al., 2005). Starting from 65 years of age, it has been estimated that the prevalence of dementia in the population doubles with each 5-year increase in age. Estimates also suggest that at least 7% of individuals who live to be older than 65 years will eventually suffer from

Alzheimer's disease, the most common form of dementia (Evans et al., 1989; McDowell, 2001), and an even greater number of individuals will experience memory decline severe enough to impede their daily activities.

Although the risk of developing dementia or pathological memory impairment increases with age, this is not considered a normal or inevitable consequence of aging. Over the last few decades, the scientific and medical communities have changed their view of memory loss in older individuals. Recent scientific findings suggest that it may be possible to help individuals maintain their memory function well into advanced age. As such, memory training programs with healthy, community-dwelling older individuals have proliferated in recent years. The immediate goal of these programs is most often to enhance performance on various memory tasks. More remote, long-term goals strive for maintaining or even improving functional independence and quality of life (Hertzog, Kramer, Wilson, & Lindenberger, 2008; Jobe et al., 2001; G. G. McDougall et al., 2010). A number of studies have supported the effectiveness of memory training programs for older adults (e.g., Ball et al., 2002; Best, Hamlett, & Davis, 1992; Calero & Navaro, 2007; Caprio-Prevette & Fry, 1996; Cavallini, Pagnin, & Vecchi, 2003; Kliegl, Smith, & Baltes, 1989; Lachman, Weaver, Bandura, Elliott, & Lewkowicz, 1992; O'Hara et al., 2007; Rasmusson, Rebok, Bylsma, & Brandt, 1999; Rebok & Balcerak, 1989; Scogin, Storandt, & Lott, 1985; Verhaeghen, Marcoen, & Goossens, 1992; Willis et al., 2006; Woolverton, Scogin, Shackelford, Black, & Duke, 2001), suggesting that many of the cognitive difficulties experienced by older people can be lessened or even reversed.

Promising findings also have emerged from studies of cognitively impaired populations, implying that individuals with neurodegenerative disorders may still have the ability to learn and retain information and skills despite their memory difficulties (e.g., Bäckman, 1992; Belleville, 2008; Bourgeois et al., 2003; Camp, Foss, O'Hanlon, & Stevens, 1996; Camp, Foss, Stevens, & O'Hanlon, 1996; Camp & Stevens, 1990; Cipriani, Bianchetti, & Trabucchi, 2006; De Vreese, Neri, Fioravanti, Belloi, & Zanetti, 2001; Floyd & Scogin, 1997; Gatz et al., 1998; Grandmaison & Simard, 2003; Little, Volans, Hemsley, & Levy, 1986; Sitzer, Twamley, & Jeste, 2006; Storandt, 1991). Table 5.1 outlines many of the memory strategies and programs that have been empirically tested in both cognitively healthy and impaired populations.

Consistent with these behavioral findings, animal and neuroimaging studies have provided additional evidence that training-induced neural plasticity continues into old age (Bor & Owen, 2007; Briones, Klintsova, & Greenough, 2004; Mahncke, Bronstone, & Merzenich, 2006). Thus, there is great hope for the continual optimization of memory performance in later life (Baltes & Baltes, 1990; Schaie, 2005) and the potential for memory training to influence everyday behavior (Willis et al., 2006).

TABLE 5.1
Memory Training Strategies

Memory strategies	Populations in which strategies have been tested			EBT-eligible studies that taught this strategy
	Normal	MCI	Dementia	
Internal mnemonic strategies				
Elementary strategies				
Association	X	X	X	2, 5, 7, 8, 9, 10, 13, 18, 19, 26, 29, 32, 39
Categorization/cluster/chunking	X	X	X	2, 5, 7, 8, 9, 10, 22, 23, 34, 35, 36, 37, 41
Visual imagery	X	X	X	1, 2, 4, 5, 7, 8, 9, 11, 18, 22, 23, 24, 26, 31, 32, 35, 36, 37, 39, 42
Rehearsal	X	X	X	13, 19, 24, 25
Attention/concentration	X	X		6, 8, 9, 10, 15, 19, 26, 27, 28, 30, 38, 39
More complicated strategies				
Method of loci	X	X	X	2, 5, 7, 8, 9, 10, 22, 24, 34, 35, 36, 37, 39, 41
Face–name/name learning/name recall	X	X	X	1, 2, 4, 5, 8, 9, 10, 13, 16, 23, 29, 31, 33, 35, 36, 37, 38, 40, 42, 43, 44
Number mnemonics	X	X		8, 9, 17, 25
Story mnemonics	X	X		14, 24
External memory aids	X	X	X	1, 5, 10, 14, 22, 33, 35, 36, 37, 41
Program techniques				
Spaced retrieval			X	12, 16, 28
Self-guided training	X			1, 17, 18, 22, 30, 35, 36, 37, 41
Procedural			X	20, 21, 28, 40, 44, 45
Cognitive control	X	X	X	4, 10, 31, 32, 34
Relaxation therapy	X	X	X	3, 4, 31, 32, 34, 39, 43

Note. EBT = evidence-based treatment; MCI = mild cognitive impairment. EBT-eligible studies follow (with corresponding number from the table listed in brackets before each listed study): [1] Andrewes et al., 1996; [2] Ball et al., 2002; [3] Beck, 1988; [4] Beck et al., 2002; [5] Best et al., 1992; [6] Buschkuel et al., 2008; [7] Cahn-Weiner et al., 2003; [8] Calero & Navarro, 2007; [9] Calero-Garcia & Navarro-Gonzalez, 2007; [10] Caprio-Prevette et al., 1996; [11] Carretti et al., 2007; [12] Cherry et al., 1999; [13] Clare et al., 2003; [14] Craik et al., 2007; [15] Dahlin et al., 2008; [16] Davis et al., 2001; [17] Derwinger et al., 2005; [18] Dunlosky et al., 2007; [19] Fabre et al., 2002; [20] Farina et al., 2002; [21] Farina et al., 2006; [22] Flynn & Storandt, 1990; [23] Hill et al., 1990; [24] Hill et al., 1991; [25] Hill et al., 1997; [26] Lachman et al., 1992; [27] Li et al., 2008; [28] Loewenstein et al., 2004; [29] Lustig & Flegal, 2008; [30] Mahncke et al., 2006; [31] McDougall et al., 2009; [32] Mohs et al., 1998; [33] Nolan et al., 2001; [34] Rapp et al., 2002; [35] Scogin & Prohaska, 1992; [36] Scogin et al., 1985; [37] Scogin et al., 1998; [38] Smith et al., 2009; [39] Stigsdotter & Bäckman, 1989; [40] Woods et al., 2006; [41] Woolverton et al., 2001; [42] Yesavage, 1983; [43] Yesavage & Rose, 1984; [44] Zanetti et al., 1997; [45] Zanetti et al., 2001.

Although it is clear that memory is critical to everyday function and maintaining independence (McCue et al., 1990; Royall et al., 2007), it remains unclear how best to maintain or improve it with behavioral interventions. We conducted a review of memory training research with older adults to determine which, if any, memory training procedures have sufficient empirical support to warrant classification as evidence based according to established criteria (Weisz & Hawley, 2001). To develop evidence-based recommendations, we conducted a comprehensive review of research studies published between January 1967 and December 2008 that focused on memory training interventions for older persons with varying levels of cognitive impairment, ranging from cognitively healthy older adults to individuals with a clinical diagnosis of dementia. To identify relevant studies, we searched computerized databases (i.e., PsycINFO, PsycLiT, PubMed), using combinations of the following key words: *memory, mnemonic, cognitive, cognition, intervention, training, rehabilitation, stimulation, learning, improvement, enhancement, older adult, aging, elderly, dementia, impairment,* and *Alzheimer's disease*. To increase the breadth of our search, we also searched published reviews and meta-analyses (De Vreese et al., 2001; Floyd & Scogin, 1997; Grandmaison & Simard, 2003; G. J. McDougall, 2000; Sitzer et al., 2006; Storandt, 1991; Verhaeghen et al., 1992) and performed hand searches of journals (e.g., *Applied Cognitive Psychology, Educational Gerontology, Cognitive Technology*), as well as reference lists from journal articles and book chapters. Further, we contacted authors of cognitive training studies for recently published or in-press articles.

In the following sections, we discuss our findings, provide recommendations for the use of particular memory interventions for older adults with varying levels of cognitive ability, and present a case example, highlighting the clinical implications of translating these findings into practice.

The Evidence

George W. Rebok, Jeanine M. Parisi, Alden L. Gross, Adam P. Spira, Jean Ko, Quincy M. Samus, Jane S. Saczynski, Steve Koh, and Ronald E. Holtzman

We initially identified 402 memory training studies published between 1967 and 2008. Two independent reviewers reviewed each study to assess the intervention, study design, population, cognitive outcomes, and evidence for treatment effectiveness. In keeping with established criteria for evaluating evidence-based treatments (EBTs; Weisz & Hawley, 2001), several key requirements had to be met for studies to be considered for review. Studies had to report original data on older adults, all of whom were at least 60 years of age at the time of training. Studies had to use a nonpharmacologic approach targeted at memory and be published in English. Specific to our review, we excluded (a) theoretical or review articles or book chapters without original memory training treatment data, (b) studies that combined memory training and pharmacotherapy or memory training and exercise therapy, (c) studies in which the active condition only involved practice of memory tasks but no actual training program, and (d) articles that were follow-up studies of prior interventions.

On the basis of these criteria, 46 of the 402 identified studies provided adequate information to determine whether the applied techniques could be considered an evidence-based practice. Further, these 46 studies provided 50 separate treatment–control comparisons (three using mild cognitive impairment [MCI] populations, 13 using dementia populations, and 35 using healthy older adult populations) and information for 15 different memory training approaches to be considered as evidence based. A majority of eligible studies, to be classified as evidence based, using the same population and evaluating the same treatment program must show the treatment group to be better than the control or comparison condition, as defined by both statistically significant effects on memory outcomes and effect sizes (ESs) of at least 0.20 (Weisz & Hawley, 2001). In this chapter, average pretest to posttest ESs were calculated to quantitatively compare strategies across studies. For each outcome memory measure provided by a study, the mean difference between the posttraining and pretraining scores for an appropriate no-contact or active control group was subtracted from the analogous difference for the memory trained group. This difference in differences was then divided by a pooled standard deviation to place all ESs on the same scale. These ESs represent standardized differences in memory change after training between trained and control groups. Table 5.2 presents our findings regarding the evidence-based effectiveness for each strategy investigated.

Memory interventions often provided training and practice with elementary strategies, such as associating or categorizing items to be remembered, as well as more complicated techniques, such as the method of loci and number mnemonics. Reviewed programs involved training programs that ranged in total duration from 30 minutes to 45 hours (average duration was 1 hour per session) and were distributed across anywhere from one to 45 sessions (average length of training was 10 sessions). Most interventions were conducted in a group format and adhered to a training protocol, with the exception of some training programs conducted with patients with dementia, for which individually tailored treatments were implemented.

TABLE 5.2
Evidence-Based Strategies

Key strategies	Populations			Total no. receiving treatment	Proportion of supportive studies[a]	Average treatment			M effect size among EBT studies
	Normal	MCI	Dementia			Duration per session (in min)	No. of sessions	EBT?	
Internal mnemonic strategies									
Elementary strategies									
At least 3 of 4: method of loci, association, categorization, visual imagery	X	X		955	9/14	60–90	8–14	Yes	0.506
Association	X	X		943	9/15	60–90	4–14	Yes	0.446
Categorization/cluster/chunking	X	X		949	9/15	60–90	4–10	Yes	0.566
Visual imagery	X	X		1,524	13/24	60–120	9–14	Yes	0.457
Rehearsal	X			298	3/3	120	2–9	Yes	0.892
Attention/concentration	X	X		277	7/13	60–90	8–14	Yes	0.388
More complicated strategies									
Method of loci	X	X		955	9/15	60–90	8–14	Yes	0.463
Face–name/name learning/Name recall	X	X		1213	11/20	60–90	6–14	Yes	0.424
Number mnemonics	X	X		184	3/6	60	3–14	No	0.425
Story mnemonics	X			295	1/2	180	14	No	0.408
External memory aids	X			298	4/10	60–120	4–24	No	0.478
Training program techniques									
Spaced retrieval			X	54	1/3	45–100	3–24	No	0.176
Self-guided training: Overall	X			234	5/12	60–120	4–40	No	0.422
Self-guided training: Subset[b]	X			87	1/4	90–120	2–9	Yes	0.775
Procedural			X	74	2/6	45–60	14–30	No	0.077
Cognitive control	X			287	1/5	90–120	4–10	No	0.158
Relaxation therapy	X			260	2/6	90	6–9	No	0.242

Notes. MCI = mild cognitive impairment; EBT = evidence-based treatment.

[a]The proportion of supportive studies column provides the number of EBT-eligible studies supportive of the technique over the total number of studies that used that technique. Because most studies trained on more than one technique, this column adds up to more than the total number of eligible studies we found. Similarly, participants may be double counted in the same size estimate. For example, ACTIVE's 620 memory training participants are included under method of loci, association, categorization, and visual imagery.
[b]This represents a subset of studies applying self-guided memory training that involved a more focused number of sessions and session durations. See the text for details.

In this review, we distinguish strategies by their difficulty, although we recognize that some elementary strategies may not be easier than some more complex ones. Most studies in our review were conducted in generally healthy samples of older adults or with older adults with MCI, and the two populations did not seem to differ in their responsiveness to treatments or types of strategies taught. Because the effectiveness of each of these strategies varies among individuals, one should use strategies with which they are personally comfortable but that are still effective (Saczynski & Rebok, 2004).

ELEMENTARY STRATEGIES: HEALTHY AND MCI POPULATIONS

In the general population and also for those with MCI, we found that programs that trained individuals on elementary strategies, including (a) association (M ES = 0.45), (b) categorization (M ES = 0.57), (c) visual imagery (M ES = 0.46), (d) attention (M ES = 0.39), and (e) rehearsal (M ES = 0.89), training were supported by a sufficient number of positive studies to be considered evidence based. These elementary strategies were not supported as evidence-based practices for individuals with dementia. We now provide a detailed description of each of these strategies.

Association entails making connections between items or pieces of information, and might be made with respect to time (e.g., remembering to take morning medications with breakfast), environment (e.g., retracing steps through the house to locate lost keys), or specific characteristics of a person (e.g., "Claire, with the big hair"). It is a broad concept, and one can argue that nearly all of learning relies on association to some degree (West, 1985). *Categorization* involves grouping (also referred to as *chunking* or *clustering*) items by shared attributes. For example, one might group items on a grocery list by color or food group to facilitate remembering (Gobet et al., 2001). *Visual imagery*, on the other hand, entails mentally picturing items to be remembered in logical or illogical contexts (Poon, Walsh-Sweeney, & Fozard, 1980; Rankin, Karol, & Tuten, 1984; Rasmusson et al., 1999; Sharps & Price-Sharps, 1996). Older adults tend to remember bizarre images more easily because of well-preserved distinctive processing abilities; this phenomenon is called the *bizarreness effect* (McDaniel, Einstein, & Jacoby, 2008). For example, when trying to learn three words (*elephant, tea, nest*) for later recall, an individual may visualize an *elephant* hosting a *tea* party in a bird's *nest*. *Attentional* or concentration training teaches participants to focus on and attend to important details of stimuli while learning to filter out irrelevant information (Lachman et al., 1992). Attentional training exercises might include scanning photographs for familiar faces, or scanning blocks of randomly positioned letters on a page (Gordon & Berger, 2003). Finally, *rehearsal* emphasizes the importance of repetition and practice to facilitate learning and improve recall (Gordon & Berger, 2003; Heun, Burkart, & Benkert, 1997). An example would be repeating a phone number to oneself after looking it up, to facilitate later recall.

COMPLEX STRATEGIES: HEALTHY AND MCI POPULATIONS

More complicated strategies for improving memory performance are often derived from a combination of simpler ones. In our review, two complex strategies were supported by a sufficient number of positive studies to be considered evidence based: the method of loci (M ES = 0.46) and face–name mnemonics (M ES = 0.42). The *method of loci* is a mnemonic link system based on places, such as locations on the body or sites along one's route to work. Each location is paired with a to-be-remembered item, and it is this structured sequence of images that provides memory cues to enable recall (e.g., Ball et al., 2002; Cavallini et al., 2003; Hill, Allen, & McWhorter, 1991; Kliegl et al., 1989; Rebok & Balcerak, 1989; Verhaeghen & Marcoen, 1996; Yesavage & Rose, 1984). In practice, an individual chooses an area with which they are familiar (e.g., their home). Next, the individual selects a series of different places or loci around this area (e.g., driveway, front door, stairway). The individual then goes through the series of selected loci and mentally pictures an item that they want to remember at each locus. To recall this information, an individual would simply retrace his or her steps around the home (in this case) and remember the item associated with the loci. For instance, if trying to remember a grocery list, one can imagine eggs frying on the driveway, tomato vines growing on the red front door, and milk flowing down the stairway.

Face–name recognition involves learning to couple faces with names by integrating mnemonic devices, phonemic aids, and visual imagery. There are many variants of this technique. Typical face–name association training programs involve priming a person with a set of unfamiliar faces with common names and then presenting an individual face with multiple names to choose from, or vice versa. For example, a clinician or caregiver may have an individual first select a distinctive feature of a face that is to be remembered (e.g., nose), then select a word or phrase that sounds like the name (e.g., *fairy* for *Mary*). The last step involves creating an interactive image linking the distinctive feature with the keyword (e.g., a tiny fairy dancing on the tip of a nose). This procedure is repeated over several trials, using different faces to enable the individual to practice their association and imagery skills (e.g., Verhaeghen & Marcoen, 1996; Woolverton et al., 2001; Yesavage & Rose, 1984). Once again, bizarre, exaggerated, or silly associations are often more memorable than others (McDaniel et al., 2008; West, 1985). Another strategy for remembering names and faces includes paying attention to the name when it is first presented and then rehearsing the name while looking at the face. One might try saying the name out loud or if at a social gathering, introducing the person to someone else (West, 1985). Similarly, *name learning* and *name recall* are meant to help an individual remember names. These techniques often include combinations of strategies such as simple repetition, categorization, association, or imagery (Andrewes, Kinsella, & Murphy, 1996). For more details on strategies for remembering names and associating them with faces, please refer to West (1985).

Two frequently used strategies—*number* and *story mnemonics*—are also worth mentioning; although these techniques produced high mean ESs (see Table 5.2), neither met our criteria to be considered evidence based. Number mnemonics are used to remember strings of numbers such as dates, phone numbers, and addresses. Training for this type of strategy involves first associating numbers with characters or phonemes to create a codebook of sorts to translate numbers to letters. For example, one may associate letters with their corresponding number on a telephone dial or keypad, link letters to their numeric alphabetical order, or use some other idiosyncratic method that works for an individual. From this codebook of number–letter associations, words or phrases are generated to remember the pattern of letters formed by the numbers. These words or phrases are encoded into memory using some memory strategy like clustering, association, or repetition. Finally, the word can be decomposed back into the original numbers (Derwinger, Stigsdotter-Neely, MacDonald, & Bäckman, 2005; Hill, Campbell, Foxley, & Lindsay, 1997). For instance, the phone number 474-8386 may be converted to the phrase IS-IT-FUN, using a telephone's keypad as the codebook, and this phrase should be easier to later recall than the number sequence.

Story or sentence mnemonics involves creating a story or sentence using to-be-remembered items to enable later recall (e.g., Hill et al., 1991). For instance, a person (Amy) may need to plan out a day that involves practicing for an important presentation, preparing for a meeting with Marissa, and shopping for a shirt and birthday cake. So, Amy may form the sentence, "I will *talk Marissa* out of eating that *cake* so she'll fit into her lucky *presentation shirt*." The items might also be organized in whatever fashion is most conducive to later recall, such as in alphabetical or temporal order. This strategy is facilitated by distilling a thought or item into one word or phrase to represent the to-be-remembered information (Small, 2002).

Although both number and story mnemonics produced high mean ESs (see Table 5.2), the studies reviewed were equally divided in terms of evidence-based eligibility. According to EBT criteria, the majority of applicable studies must support the treatment (Weisz & Hawley, 2001); therefore, the evidence for these techniques should be considered inconclusive at this time. Similarly, relaxation therapy, cognitive control, and use of external memory aids also yielded relatively high mean ESs; however, in each case fewer than half of the reviewed studies met the criteria to be considered evidence based (Weisz & Hawley, 2001).

SELF-GUIDED TRAINING TECHNIQUES: HEALTHY AND MCI POPULATIONS

Most research on memory training programs to date entails small group sessions with a trainer, though self-guided training has been used among older adults to train the mnemonic strategies described previously. Most of these programs involve take-home manuals (Dunlosky et al., 2007; Scogin et al., 1985), but computerized training is growing in popularity (Li et al., 2008; Mahncke et al., 2006; Morrell et al., 2006). In our review, self-guided training did not meet criteria to be defined as evidence based when considering the full range of available studies (see Table 5.2; Self-Guided Training: Overall). However, it is worth noting that when studies were analyzed according to similarity of number and length of sessions, a subset (five of 12) of self-guided training studies were supported by evidence-based criteria (see Table 5.2; Self-Guided Training: Subset). Considering that the subset of studies is probably more reflective of this program technique, self-guided training may be considered conditionally evidence based.

TRAINING PROGRAMS: COGNITIVELY DISABLED POPULATIONS

Training interventions also have been designed for older adults with cognitive deficits, including those with dementia and Alzheimer's disease. The ultimate goals of these interventions are generally to restore or improve particular functions, maintain quality of life, and prevent further functional and cognitive decline (Acevedo & Loewenstein, 2007). Memory training approaches for more impaired populations use skills that are relatively well-preserved or that place low demands on disrupted cognitive processes (Clare, 2006; Kasl-Godley & Gatz, 2000). For instance, some evidence has been reported for programs that focus on cognitive stimulation (e.g., discussions, supervised leisure activities, list memorization, reality orientation) and cognitive rehabilitation interventions. The latter are individually tailored programs centered on specific instrumental activities of daily living, such as getting to appointments on time, medication adherence, or remembering names (Acevedo & Loewenstein, 2007; Clare & Woods, 2004; Woods et al., 2006).

Interventions that have been applied with some success among impaired older adults include spaced retrieval training (e.g., Camp, Foss, Stevens et al., 1996; Camp & Stevens, 1990; Cherry, Simmons, & Camp, 1999; Davis, Massman, & Doody, 2001; Logan & Balota, 2008; McKitrick, Camp, & Black, 1992; Ozgis, Rendell, & Henry, 2009), procedural memory learning (Zanetti et al., 1997, 2001), and training in the use of external aids (Hanley & Lusty, 1984; McPherson et al., 2001; Nolan, Mathews, & Harrison, 2001; Woods et al., 2006). *Spaced retrieval* takes advantage of implicit memory, which is fairly well-preserved in the early stages of dementia (Heindel, Salmon, Shults, Walicke, & Butters, 1989). This procedure uses a schedule of practice in which information is repeatedly presented to an individual. Between-trial delays are increased incrementally according to a learner's performance (e.g., Camp, 1989; Camp, Foss, Hanlon, et al., 1996; Camp & Stevens, 1990). For example, a clinician or caregiver might tell a patient with dementia to remember the address, "13425 Hickory Way," and ask her to repeat this information. This is repeated with increasing amounts of time between the stimulus presentation and recall. The gaps in time are interspersed with distracting conversation to prevent rote repetition of the information. If after a sufficient delay the address is recalled correctly, it is judged to have been encoded in the patient's long-term memory.

Procedural memory, or *reality orientation therapy*, enables one to learn or improve performance of a motor task through repeated practice (Saint-Cyr et al., 1988; Ullman, 2001). A typical training program might entail assigning older adults to basic instrumental activities of daily living tasks, such as washing hands, brushing teeth, or counting money (Zanetti et al., 1997). Moreover, research has suggested that the use of external aids (e.g., calendars, reminder notes) in combination with internal memory strategies may be particularly effective for impaired persons (Bourgeois et al., 2003; Bourgeois & Mason, 1996; Fleming, Shum, Strong, & Lightbody, 2005; West, 1985).

Although such evidence is promising, evidence-based criteria have not yet been used to evaluate the body of research around cognitive stimulation, rehabilitation, external memory aids, or procedural memory programs in individuals with cognitive impairments or dementia. At the present time, too few studies conducted with this population met our criteria for inclusion to draw conclusions about strategies or techniques that can be EBT supported. This lack of evidence may be reflective of the fact that we excluded many within-group studies of Alzheimer's disease patients due to inadequate control groups. Both of the studies among dementia populations that were EBT supportive used procedural memory training (Loewenstein, Acevedo, Czaja, S. J., & Duara, 2004; Woods et al., 2006), but they did not constitute a majority of studies that used such a technique.

Adapting Evidence-Based Treatments for the Real World

George W. Rebok

As we described earlier, only recently have significant cognitive impairment and decline been viewed as abnormal and potentially modifiable phenomena. Thus, relatively few mental health practitioners have provided older adults with cognitive training, beyond recommending that patients complete crossword or Sudoku puzzles. As the population of older adults grows and the public becomes more aware of the malleability of cognition in late life, clinicians will likely experience more requests for memory training programs that are evidence based.

My name is Dr. George W. Rebok, and I am a licensed psychologist and professor of mental health and psychiatry and behavioral sciences at Johns Hopkins University. I am not a practicing clinician, but I have clinical experience with older adults and over 30 years of experience administering memory training interventions to older adults through research trials. I describe myself as a life-span developmental researcher, but my research is focused on cognitive outcomes in older adults and interventions to prevent late-life cognitive loss and functional decline.

In adapting memory training for older people, there are several generalizable insights based on my clinical experience that I would like to share with you. First, older people bring varying backgrounds and skills to bear on their learning of memory techniques, including the use of self-generated and idiosyncratic strategies. If you uncritically apply EBTs for all memory problems, you may overlook these personally generated techniques. You may find that a hybrid approach works best for many older patients whereby you integrate EBTs with self-designed techniques that may be effective, more familiar, and that have been used over long periods of time. On the other hand, you also need to be aware of strategies that older adults may be using that are ineffective and that interfere with EBT strategies. I would feel free to deviate from the evidence-based protocol when it makes clinical sense to do, for example, when the evidence-based technique does not seem to be producing the intended results.

You also may discover that some older people are resistant to certain memory training approaches, in particular, those like method of loci that incorporate complicated mnemonics and strange, interactive visual imagery and associations and that may strike them as impractical. In these cases, it is unwise to pressure the person to adapt a particular technique; instead, you should consider offering alternative techniques that may involve many of the same underlying memory principles (e.g., association, visual imagery) but that are less cognitively effortful or threatening. This is especially important when you are working with a depressed or anxious patient who may not want to tackle something that is so mentally taxing. Usually, you can get an older patient to at least try a given technique, and once they find that it is effective and can be practically useful they are more likely to continue to want to use it. Frequently, I find that some older adult patients question the relevance of memory training to their everyday lives and view mnemonic techniques as gimmicks or tricks that may work in the clinic but that do not apply in the real world. To address these concerns, I am careful never to refer to memory training techniques as "tricks," and I spend a lot of time encouraging patients to think of everyday life situations to which these techniques apply. I also ask them to practice the techniques at home and then come back to the clinic and tell me how they fared. Some patients readily agree to do this, whereas others are more reluctant. A phone call reminder or external aid to remind them to practice at home may boost compliance rates. It also helps if you can spend the beginning of the next training session reviewing their attempts to implement the technique and providing feedback and suggestions for further practice.

I try to create realistic expectations at the beginning of training about how much one can reasonably expect to improve after memory training and how much practice will be required without undermining the person's motivation. Often patients have seen advertisements or infomercials about memory improvement products that make exaggerated claims about effectiveness. For example, some products promise instantaneous improvement, with little effort, and even go so far as to say that the user will never forget anything again. I would let your client know that there is little evidence to support such claims. Further, let him or her know that memory training takes time, that the course of training is not always marked by steady improvements, and that improving your memory, like any other learned ability, requires considerable practice. At the same time, it is important to provide continual encouragement and feedback that will motivate the client to continue with the training program, even if progress is slow.

Memory training can be conducted in many settings, including memory clinics, the offices of a private practice, nursing homes, rehabilitation centers, community colleges, and senior centers. Next, I outline the process of implementing memory training strategies and programs and share my experience administering memory training. I emphasize the conduct of memory training in clinical settings, such as private practice or nursing home settings, rather than in more educational settings, such as community colleges and senior centers.

PRETREATMENT ASSESSMENT

Before beginning memory training, it is important to screen for variables that might contribute to memory impairment or prevent memory improvement. These include your patients' medical conditions and medications, their current cognitive status, and any symptoms that might indicate the presence of a mental disorder. I find that older adults who are already experiencing advanced mental or functional decline are less amenable to memory instruction than better functioning older adults, even if the latter present with memory complaints. Results of our evidence-based review support this notion. In addition, for those who might need help completing a memory training program, it is important that you help patients identify someone like a husband or wife who can serve as a "coach" to assist with home practice of the skills. I discuss each of these considerations in greater detail below.

Numerous medical conditions—many treatable—negatively affect memory. For example, chronic obstructive pulmonary disease (COPD) and sleep disorders are linked to lower cognitive performance. Cardiovascular disease can even lead to vascular dementia through significant vascular changes in the brain. It is also important to consider that older adults with medical problems can be taking several medications that, on their own or through interactions with other drugs, are linked to cognitive problems. For example, sedative-hypnotic medications—particularly benzodiazepines—are associated with cognitive impairment. Consideration of these issues, and consultation with a patient's physicians when concerns about medications or illnesses arise, can help ensure your patients are in a position to benefit from memory training.

Your patient's baseline (i.e., current) cognitive status has significant implications for your decision to implement a memory training program. Memory interventions have been evaluated in older adults with normal cognition, as well as those with mild cognitive impairment and dementia. In my experience, those with normal cognition and MCI appear to derive similar benefits from programs that meet criteria for evidence-based interventions, whereas older adults with dementia often do not benefit. This means that valid cognitive assessment and diagnosis are needed to guide your decision making in regard to the value of implementing memory training versus an alternative intervention to optimize functioning. Cognitive assessment is particularly important when treating older adults in memory clinics, rehabilitation centers, or long-term-care facilities, where a substantial proportion of patients or clients demonstrate cognitive impairment. If you do not have adequate training in neuropsychological assessment, refer the patient to a clinician who is qualified to provide these services (Rebok, Parisi, Gross, & Spira, 2010). In my experience, it is also useful to collect information about a patient's memory beliefs at baseline; this can be done by using a number of standardized tools like the Memory Functioning Questionnaire (Gilewski, Zelinski, & Schaie, 1990), the Metamemory in Adulthood Questionnaire (Dixon, Hultsch, & Hertzog, 1988), and the Memory Toolbox (Troyer, 2001). These data will be essential for you to evaluate training-related changes in these areas.

In addition to a patient's baseline cognitive status, pretreatment assessment should include screening for depression, anxiety, and substance abuse. These and other conditions are predictors of memory training success (for a review, see Hill, Bäckman, & Stigsdotter-Neely, 2000). Symptoms of depression and anxiety are associated with cognitive impairment in older adults. If a mood or anxiety disturbance is contributing to cognitive impairment, failure to treat the root disturbance might prevent your patient from adhering to or benefiting from a memory training program (Hill et al., 2000). For patients with severe symptoms of depression or anxiety, you should first treat these problems to reduce patients' distress before beginning memory training. Although our review identifies strategies and programs as evidence based, few randomized trials included in our review focused exclusively on older adults with depression or anxiety, so it is not possible to determine if these strategies would be evidence based among such individuals. For patients with milder symptoms of depression and anxiety, you should treat these symptoms and initiate memory training simultaneously while monitoring the extent to which adherence to and progress with the training protocol are affected by patients' symptoms.

In a related area, active substance abuse (including abuse of alcohol and/or prescription and illicit drugs) and dependence affect cognition among older adults. Before beginning memory training, it is important to screen for these problems and carefully consider how they might affect the results of a memory intervention.

Caregivers can play an important role in the treatment of individuals with cognitive impairment. You should determine the extent to which someone with relatively intact cognition is available to assist an individual with mild impairment who presents for memory training, with home practice of skills learned in your sessions. Although older adults with cognitive deficits often present in clinical settings with a family member, in my experience this individual may or may not self-identify as a caregiver and will not necessarily live with the patient. Because the term *caregiver* might seem inappropriate to individuals with mild impairment and their family members, you might use the term *coach* to describe this role. A coach is helpful to a patient with MCI who has some executive dysfunction that can obstruct routine, structured practice, or with patients whose memory problems interfere with the ability to choose particular strategies. Even an older adult with intact cognitive function can also benefit from having a coach motivate them with consistent practice of strategies. You should work closely with coaches to clearly outline their role in the treatment plan and troubleshoot potential problems (e.g., scheduling time for in-home practice, strategies for increasing patients' cooperation with training exercises).

OTHER CLINICAL CONSIDERATIONS

You should consider several other issues in your clinical practice. In the majority of the studies we reviewed, a trained facilitator led group-based memory training program sessions. In practice, however, interventions might need to be conducted without the support of research staff or clinical supervision. Although some programs are designed to be self-directed, simply providing your patients with an instruction manual without regular support lowers the chances that they will follow the program to completion. This is especially true if the manual is lengthy, complicated, or given to a patient with MCI. In such situations, you should work closely with patients and their coaches to elaborate on instructions provided in the manual, soliciting questions regarding the program material and regularly encouraging and checking up on patients' out-of-session practice of memory strategies.

A second important consideration is the amount of training time needed for an individual to learn and benefit from a memory technique. The importance of practicing strategies cannot be overstated (Bjorklund & Coyle, 1995; Hertzog et al., 2008; Light, 1991), but it is not always the case that more is better. In my experience, excessively long training programs lead to fatigue. This notion is underscored by our findings regarding self-guided training methods among cognitively normal older adults and procedural memory training among those with dementia: Two studies using procedural memory training that were ineffective in changing memory outcomes by our standards lasted 2 and 4 times longer than a procedural memory training program that met evidence-based criteria (Farina et al., 2002, 2006). With regard to the actual number of sessions, I have found that as few as two or three sessions can produce noticeable gains, but you may want to vary the training dose depending on patient characteristics and scope of the training. If you are training on one specific technique or memory outcome with someone who is not suffering from pronounced memory loss, then two or three sessions might suffice. However, interventions with multiple components focusing on different aspects of memory (e.g., memory for names, faces, appointments, text, telephone numbers) may require more time but may produce broader and more durable memory improvements.

Third, as a memory trainer I do my best to be aware of a patient's preferences, lifestyles, and circumstances to find out what works for different individuals. I once worked with an active older adult who was a former math teacher; we found that she enjoyed learning and using number mnemonics to aid her memory. Patients with computers in the home have access to potentially helpful online resources for memory improvement that others do not have. Attending to past interests, using remaining skills and abilities, and tailoring programs to an individual's current lifestyle and level of mental functioning may increase the likelihood that a given strategy or set thereof may be appropriately applied in the context of daily life.

A fourth important clinical consideration is that you will undoubtedly encounter individuals who, regardless of the strength of the evidence for the efficacy of the technique implemented, do not appear to benefit from memory training or who are unsatisfied with results. Several explanations account for this. The technique might have been a poor fit with a patient's particular cognitive strengths. Someone with poor visuospatial abilities might have more difficulty with the method of loci than someone with stronger abilities in this area. Alternatively, the patient may not have learned the strategy correctly or practiced it sufficiently to benefit from memory training, you may not have communicated the method effectively, or a longer course of training may be needed. Another explanation is that you might have failed to detect a preexisting cognitive deficit that is interfering with the individual's ability to benefit from training (Hill et al., 2000).

In the event of a poor treatment outcome—defined by either patient satisfaction with gains or objective measures of memory improvement—a frank yet sensitive conversation about the results is warranted. During this conversation, you can discuss with the patient their beliefs about the treatment outcome, which can help determine the best course of remediation (e.g., troubleshoot obstacles to patient practice, pursue further neuropsychological testing, implement an alternative memory strategy that better fits patient strengths). Keep in mind that patients will have a range of memory outcomes following these interventions and that the ESs we report here are based on group averages across trials in which participants' performances also varied. I would remind patients of this to put unexpected negative results in perspective.

In the following section, I present a case example to illustrate how clinicians might practically integrate evidence-based memory training methods into their practice. This case provides an example of memory training with an older adult woman with memory complaints and anxious mood who was cognitively normal for her age and educational level (adapted from Rebok et al., 2010).

CASE EXAMPLE

Mrs. G is a 67-year-old White woman with 18 years of education whose husband died several years ago after a 5-year bout with lung cancer. At a recent checkup appointment with her primary care physician, Mrs. G reported anxiety and memory problems over the prior 3 months. Mrs. G's physician contacted me and informed me that Mrs. G was in very good health; her only medical problems were mild arthritis in her knees and well-controlled COPD. Mrs. G agreed to meet with me, and in our initial session she explained that she had experienced the same cognitive symptoms after her husband passed away but that they had resolved in the year following his death. I administered a depression and anxiety screening measure and referred Mrs. G to a neuropsychologist colleague for a cognitive evaluation. Consistent with her complaints, results indicated that Mrs. G had noteworthy deficits in verbal episodic memory that were probably due to mild anxiety. I explained to Mrs. G that her deficits might be explained by her mood disturbance, and we completed 10 weeks of cognitive behavioral therapy aimed at alleviating her anxiety symptoms.

Mrs. G's somatic symptoms decreased substantially with treatment and eventually went into full remission, although she still complained of forgetfulness. Further neuropsychological testing indicated that Mrs. G's memory was within the normal range for an individual of her age and level of education. On the basis of Mrs. G's complaints and her desire to do something to improve her memory, I suggested we begin a memory training program. Mrs. G was open to this suggestion, and after I explained more and Mrs. G consented, she completed a comprehensive baseline memory assessment. This included standardized tests of visual, verbal, and procedural memory, as well as an assessment of Mrs. G's beliefs about how malleable her memory is. Mrs. G also agreed to keep a daily memory diary, in which she recorded instances of memory successes and memory lapses over 1 week. Memory diaries were not used in any training studies we reviewed, but in my clinical judgment they are helpful. Although Mrs. G often failed to record memory successes, to her surprise, completing this diary exercise revealed that she had relatively few memory lapses that tended to occur in particular contexts. Specifically, Mrs. G had difficulty recalling the names of new acquaintances, and she found this awkward and embarrassing when she subsequently encountered them.

On the basis of Mrs. G's normal neuropsychological test results, her pattern of self-reported memory lapses, and the existing evidence base, I decided that a multicomponent intervention involving both face–name and name-learning interventions would be the most appropriate, and I obtained Mrs. G's informed consent to begin this treatment. Prior to implementing the intervention, I conducted a pretreatment assessment by presenting Mrs. G with 15 pictures of individuals I cut out of magazines, telling her their (made-up) names and instructing her to remember them. Ten minutes later after some other tasks, I showed Mrs. G the same photos and asked her to recall these individuals' names. I recorded the number that Mrs. G named correctly, to serve as a measure of baseline performance. Fifteen faces is a lot to remember, but I wanted to be sure Mrs. G would not recall all the faces and names because I hoped to see improvement later on.

I explained that learning to remember names is similar to other skills and that it requires consistent practice. In addition to encouraging Mrs. G to practice face–name and name-learning methods in her everyday life, I provided her with in-home practice materials, which I prepared by cutting 50 different faces out of magazines, pasting them to the back of index cards, and writing names for each individual on the back of the cards. I also knew that Mrs. G had a computer at home, so asked her to find some free online face–name tests by conducting an online search for face–name games. We agreed Mrs. G would learn the names of 10 individuals each week on her own and that I would quiz her during our weekly session. Mrs. G consistently completed these in-home exercises, and we plotted her progress on a chart during each of our weekly sessions. Over the next 5 weeks, Mrs. G showed steady improvement on her quiz scores and improvement from baseline.

After eight sessions, to assess changes in subjective memory, I asked Mrs. G to complete the memory diary once again over the course of 1 week. Consistent with her objective improvement on the objective name-learning exercises, Mrs. G recorded fewer name-related memory failures and more successes. She noted that these gains enhanced her confidence and her desire to socialize. Given the resolution of her mood symptoms and her memory improvement, I suggested that we stop meeting weekly but that we check in once every 6 months to evaluate her mood and complete a booster session to review name-learning and face–name strategies as needed.

RESOURCES

Several resources are commercially available to help a clinician select memory exercises and develop a training curriculum, including books, games, and websites (see Appendix 5.1). It should be noted, however, that there are numerous additional resources that have been designed to "train the brain" and provide various examples of the techniques and mnemonic strategies (e.g., association, visualization, method of loci) that we have outlined in this chapter. There is also a long-standing interest in commercially available programs for cognitive enrichment, such as Memory Master, The Memory Works, MegaMemory, Happy Neuron, Nintendo Brain Age, or Big Brain Academy (e.g., Burden, 1988). They are readily available at relatively low costs and can be pretty challenging. These programs often incorporate tips on memory training, memory training strategies, and various exercises to strengthen neural connections. However, to our knowledge only one randomized trial has been conducted in an epidemiologic context to test the effectiveness of any of these programs (Rasmusson et al., 1999); therefore, it is difficult to objectively determine the effectiveness of these programs. They are, however, potentially useful off-the-shelf resources for the clinician interested in helping to enhance a patient's memory.

CONCLUDING REMARKS

As older persons live longer, putting them at risk for neurodegenerative diseases such as dementia, we will inevitably observe an increase in the prevalence of cognitive impairment and dementia. Interest in identifying evidence-based interventions has been driven by a growing desire to maintain or even reverse age-related cognitive decline. To date, the majority of evidence for the optimization of cognition in adulthood has been garnered through findings from select intervention studies, which may produce misleading evidence in support of or against an intervention's efficacy. Using a uniform set of criteria to evaluate the entire body of research on a specific intervention, however, provides more compelling evidence of its effectiveness or ineffectiveness. This is not to argue that the evidence garnered from research should replace clinical experience and expertise. EBTs should integrate high-quality, reliable research with proven, expert clinical practices to provide advice on how best to treat memory concerns and decline in specific populations.

Our review identified eight different memory training techniques (association, categorization, visual imagery, rehearsal, attention–concentration, method of loci, face–name, a subset of self-guided training; see Table 5.2) beneficial for improving memory in cognitively intact or mildly cognitively impaired older adults. Although the findings are promising, several limitations need to be addressed. First, we only included published studies of memory interventions. We do not include results from unpublished programs that may have been conducted in hospitals or continuing care facilities (e.g., DeMont & Wood, 2008). Second, although memory was the primary outcome in all studies, particular memory measures varied widely across studies. Further, we only considered performance memory tasks as our outcome measure, neglecting effects on other cognitive, social, or psychological factors. Therefore, we are unable to determine whether an application of a specific technique would generalize to other cognitive domains (e.g., executive functioning, processing speed, language), measures of everyday functioning, or across levels of neuropsychiatric syndromes (e.g., depression, anxiety). Third, we did not consider approaches that combined memory training with forms of pharmacotherapy (Yesavage et al., 2007), exercise (Colcombe & Kramer, 2003), or nutrition (González-Gross, Marcos, & Pietrzik, 2001). Such combinations of approaches may be better or less effective than any single training program for promoting memory performance among older adults, a topic that merits future investigation (Rebok, Carlson, & Langbaum, 2007; Studenski et al., 2006). We did, however, examine programs that incorporated self-guided practice, cognitive control, or relaxation therapy; none of these programs met our criteria to be considered evidence based (see Table 5.2; under Training Program Techniques). Fourth, this review does not consider long-term benefits for either memory or functional ability that may result from memory training. Several studies have provided some evidence of long-term effects of memory training on both memory and functional outcomes; however, relatively few studies have provided follow-up information beyond 1 year (see Ball et al., 2002; Farina et al., 2006; Willis et al., 2006). Last, we excluded studies if any participant in the sample was under 60 years of age, and consequently, many studies that could have added value to our review were not included (Bagwell & West, 2008; Belleville et al., 2006; Bherer et al., 2006; Boman, Lindstedt, Hemmingsson, & Bartfai, 2004; Erickson et al., 2007; Fiszdon et al., 2005; Fleming et al., 2005; Frankel et al., 2006; Hawley & Cherry, 2004; Hildebrandt et al., 2006; Hohaus, 2007; Jaeggi et al., 2008; Jennings, Webster, Kleykamp, & Dagenbach, 2005; Johnson et al., 2005; Londos et al., 2008; Melton & Bourgeois, 2005; Olesen, Westerberg, & Klingberg, 2004; Sveistrup et al., 2004; Turkstra & Bourgeois, 2005; R. L. West, Bagwell, & Dark-Freudeman, 2008; Westerberg et al., 2007; Yamamoto-Mitani, Matsuoka, & Fujii, 2007).

Given the relatively small number of studies that met criteria to be considered evidence based, continued investigations of memory programs and interventions are warranted to evaluate the effectiveness and generalizability of these interventions across different sites, programs, and individuals. Continued memory training research is particularly important among populations with MCI and dementia.

APPENDIX 5.1: RESOURCES AND SUGGESTIONS FOR FURTHER READING

Websites

Memory Works offers (for sale) a variety of science-based memory training CD-ROM programs. Educational materials, discussion about memory and memory impairments, and other resources are available at no cost: http://www.memoryzine.com/memoryworks.html

Lumosity provides exercises to improve memory and attention, detailed feedback, and improvement tracking: http://www.lumosity.com

Brainist.com includes Memory, Math, Mnemonics, Strategy Games, Trivia, Riddles, and Logic Puzzles. Also, includes educational articles explaining the benefits of each game on the brain: http://www.brainist.com

SharpBrains contains a variety of Brain Teasers and Games, as well as presents some educational information about memory and the brain: http://www.sharpbrains.com/teasers

Fit Brains includes games designed to target each of the five major brain categories: Memory, Concentration & Attention, Language Skills, Visual & Spatial, and Executive Functions (Logic & Reasoning): http://www.fitbrains.com

HAPPYneuron brings you Brain Fitness through entertaining games designed to challenge the brain. The comprehensive program stimulates your attention, language, memory, visual-spatial and executive function skills: http://www.happy-neuron.com

Posit Science offers (for sale) a variety of auditory and visual brain training software programs. These programs were designed to help an individual think faster, focus better, and remember more: http://www.positscience.com

Books

Arden, J. B. (2002). *Improving your memory for dummies.* New York, NY: Wiley.

Provides information on memory, how the brain works, and establishing memory power, as well as on other lifestyle tips for a healthy memory (nutrition, stress reduction, sleep). Chapters are dedicated to mnemonics strategies, including strategies for remembering a list, remembering people, and remembering dates (appointments, birthdays).

Bendheim, P. E. (2009). *The brain training revolution: A proven workout for healthy brain aging.* Naperville, IL: Sourcebooks.

Discusses what to expect as your brain grows older and provides information about how to boost your brain's performance in midlife and beyond. Includes a bonus DVD with interactive mental exercises.

Gediman, C., & Crinella, F. M. (2005). *Brainfit: 10 minutes a day for a sharper mind and memory.* Nashville, TN: Rutledge Hill.

Discusses ways to maintain your brain and includes mental agility challenges, exercises, and a memory preassessment.

Gediman, C. L., & Crinella, F. M. (2008). *Supercharge your memory! More than 100 exercises to energize your mind.* Nashville, TN: Rutledge Hill.

Includes various mental agility exercises designed to challenge and energize the mind.

Green, C. R. (2001). *Total memory workout: 8 easy steps to maximum memory fitness.* New York, NY: Bantam Books.

Discusses how to maximize memory potential and includes several techniques to keep memory sharp. Exercises are designed to facilitate list learning, story recall, and remembering faces.

Higbee, K. L (2001). *Your memory: How it works and how to improve it.* New York, NY: Marlowe & Company.

Provides an understanding of memory processes and tips for how to improve them. Chapters cover the basic principles for remembering; including several mnemonics strategies and techniques (e.g., link and story mnemonics, peg mnemonics, loci method, visualization, organization, remembering names and faces).

Katz, L., & Rubin, M. (1998). *Keep your brain alive: 83 neurobic exercises.* New York, NY: Workman.

Includes exercises for your memory. Exercises are designed to benefit memory across several contexts (e.g., commuting, work, market, leisure).

Lorayne, H. (1985). *Page-a-minute memory book.* New York, NY: Random House.

Offers practice with mnemonic techniques (e.g., substitute word system, link system, peg system).

Lorayne, H. (2007). *Ageless memory: Simple secrets for keeping your brain young: Foolproof methods for people over 50.* New York, NY: Black Dog & Leventhal.

Discusses how memory training works and provides exercises for several memory techniques and strategies (e.g., association, link system, remembering words and meanings, names, faces, numbers, shopping lists, errands, and appointments).

Mark, V. H., & Mark, J. P. (1999). *Reversing memory loss: Proven methods for regaining, strengthening, and preserving your memory.* New York, NY: Houghton Mifflin.

Provides information on memory and memory impairments, as well as on other lifestyle tips for a healthy memory (e.g., nutrition, depression, alcoholism, stress reduction, sleep).

Mason, D. J., Kohn, M. L., & Clark, K. A. (2001). *The memory workbook: Breakthrough techniques to exercise your brain and improve your memory.* Oakland, CA: New Harbinger.

Highlights several aspects of memory (e.g., visual and verbal memory), as well as covers major structures of the brain and their function. Provides exercises to aid in memory recall.

Noir, M., & Croisile, B. (2006). *Get your brain in the fast lane: Turbocharge your memory with more than 100 brain building exercises*. New York, NY: McGraw-Hill.

Provides exercises at various difficulty levels (e.g., easy, medium, and difficult) and solutions.

Noir, M., & Croisile, B. (2009). *Protein shakes for the brain: 91 games and exercises to work your minds muscle to the max*. China: McGraw-Hill.

Discusses the benefits of exercising the brain. Provides exercises at various difficulty levels (e.g., easy, medium, and difficult) and solutions.

O' Brien, D. (2005). *How to develop a brilliant memory week by week*. London, England: Duncan Baird.

Discusses a variety of mnemonic techniques (e.g., acronyms, link method, journal method, concentration, number-rhyme system, alphabet system, remembering names and faces, directions, spellings, jokes, and telephone numbers and important dates). Includes self-tests for all lessons.

Small, G. (2003). *The memory bible: An innovative strategy for keeping your brain young*. New York, NY: Hyperion Books.

Covers a wide variety of topics, such as the effects of lifestyle, medications, diet, and stress on memory Includes memory training skills and memory assessments.

Small, G., & Vorgan, G. (2004). *The memory prescription: Dr. Gary Small's 14-Day plan to keep your brain and body young*. New York, NY: Hyperion Books.

Covers a wide variety of topics, such as the effects of physical fitness, diet, and stress on memory. Chapters include mental and physical fitness assessments, a 14-day memory prescription, and a 2-week check-up-gauge success.

REFERENCES

Acevedo, A., & Loewenstein, D. A. (2007). Nonpharmacological cognitive interventions in aging and dementia. *Journal of Geriatric Psychiatry and Neurology*, 20, 239–249. doi:10.1177/0891988707308808

Albert, M. (2008). The neuropsychology of the development of Alzheimer's disease. In F. I. M. Craik & T. A. Salthouse (Eds.), *The handbook of Aging and cognition* (4th ed., pp. 97–132). London, England: Academic Press.

American Psychiatric Association. (2000). *Diagnostic and statistical manual of mental disorders* (4th ed., text revision). Washington, DC: Author.

Andrewes, D. G., Kinsella, G., & Murphy, M. (1996). Using a memory handbook to improve everyday memory in community-dwelling older adults with memory complaints. *Experimental Aging Research*, 22, 305–322. doi:10.1080/03610739608254013

Bäckman, L. (1992). Memory training and memory improvement in Alzheimer's disease: Rules and exceptions. *Acta Neurologica Scandinavica*, 85, 84–89.

Bagwell, D. K., & West, R. L. (2008). Assessing compliance: Active versus inactive trainees in a memory intervention. *Clinical Interventions in Aging, 3,*

Ball, K., Berch, D. B., Helmers, K. F., Jobe, J. B., Leveck, M. D., Marsiske, M., ... Willis, S. L. (2002). Effects of cognitive training interventions with older adults: A randomized controlled trial. *Journal of the American Medical Association*, 288, 2271–2281. doi:10.1001/jama.288.18.2271

Balota, D. A., Dolan, P. O., & Duchek, J. M. (2000). Memory changes in healthy older adults. In E. Tulving & F. I. M. Craik (Eds.), *Handbook of memory* (pp. 395–410). New York, NY: Oxford University Press.

Baltes, P. B., & Baltes, M. M. (1990). Selective optimization with compensation. In P. B. Baltes & M. M. Baltes (Eds.), *Successful aging: Perspectives from the behavioral sciences* (pp. 1–34). New York, NY: Cambridge University Press. doi:10.1017/CBO9780511665684.003

Beck, C., Heacock, P., Mercer, S., Thatcher, R., & Sparkman, C. (1988). The impact of cognitive skills remediation training on persons with Alzheimer's disease or mixed dementia. *Journal of Geriatric Psychiatry*, 21, 73–88.

Becker, H., McDougall, G. J., Douglas, N. E., & Arheart, K. L. (2008). Comparing the efficiency of eight-session versus four-session memory intervention for older adults. *Archives of Psychiatric Nursing*, 22, 87–94. doi:10.1016/j.apnu.2007.05.003

Belleville, S. (2008). Cognitive training for persons with mild cognitive impairment. *International Psychogeriatrics*, 20, 57–66. doi:10.1017/S104161020700631X

Belleville, S., Gilbert, B., Fontaine, F., Gagnon, L., Ménard, E., & Gauthier, S. (2006). Improvement of episodic memory in persons with mild cognitive impairment and healthy older adults: Evidence from a cognitive intervention program. *Dementia and Geriatric Cognitive Disorders*, 22, 486–499. doi:10.1159/000096316

Best, D.L., Hamlett, K.W., & Davis, S.W. (1992). Memory complaints and memory performance in the elderly: The effects of memory-skills training and expectancy change. *Applied Cognitive Psychology*, 6, 405–416. doi:10.1002/acp.2350060505

Bherer, L., Kramer, A.F., Peterson, M.S., Colcombe, S., Erickson, K., & Becic, E. (2006). Testing the limits of cognitive plasticity in older adults: Application to attentional control. *Acta Psychologica*, 123, 261–278. doi:10.1016/j.actpsy.2006.01.005

Bjorklund, D.F., & Coyle, T.R. (1995). Utilization deficiencies in the development of memory strategies. In F.E. Weinert & W. Scheider (Eds.), *Memory performance and competencies: Issues in growth and development* (pp. 161–180). Mahwah, NJ: Lawrence Erlbaum Associates.

Bolla, K.I., Lindgren, K.N., Bonaccorsy, C., & Bleecker, M.L. (1991). Memory complaints in older adults. Fact or fiction? *Archives of Neurology*, 48, 61–64. doi:10.1001/archneur.1991.00530130069022

Boman, I.L., Lindstedt, M., Hemmingsson, H., & Bartfai, A. (2004). Cognitive training in home environment. *Brain Injury*, 18, 985–995. doi:10.1080/02699050410001672396

Bor, D., & Owen, A.M. (2007). Cognitive training: Neural correlates of expert skills. *Current Biology*, 17, 95–97. doi:10.1016/j.cub.2007.01.019

Bourgeois, M.S., Camp, C.J., Rose, M., White, B., Malone, M., Carr, J., & Rovine, M. (2003). A comparison of training strategies to enhance use of external aids by persons with dementia. *Journal of Communication Disorders*, 36, 361–378. doi:10.1016/S0021-9924(03)00051-0

Bourgeois, M., & Mason, L.A. (1996). Memory wallet intervention in an adult day-care setting. *Behavioral Interventions*, 11, 3–18. doi:10.1002/(SICI)1099-078X(199601)11:1<3::AID-BRT150>3.0.CO;2-0

Briones, T.L., Klintsova, A.Y., & Greenough, W.T. (2004). Stability of synaptic plasticity in the adult rat visual cortex induced by complex environment exposure. *Brain Research*, 1018, 130–135. doi:10.1016/j.brainres.2004.06.001

Burden, B. (1988). *The memory master method*. Dallas, TX: Billy Burden School of Memory & Attitude.

Cahn-Weiner, D.A., Ready, R.E., & Malloy, P. (2003). Neuropsychological predictors of everyday memory and everyday functioning in patients with mild Alzheimer's disease. *Journal of Geriatric Psychiatry and Neurology*, 16, 84–89. doi:10.1177/0891988703016002004

Calero, M.D., & Navarro, E. (2007). Cognitive plasticity as a modulating variable on the effects of memory training in elderly persons. *Archives of Clinical Neuropsychology*, 22, 63–72. doi:10.1016/j.acn.2006.06.020

Calero-García, M.D., & Navarro-Gonzalez, E. (2007). Effectiveness of a memory training programme in the maintenance of status in elderly people with and without cognitive decline. *Psychology in Spain*, 11, 106–112.

Camp, C. J. (1989). Facilitation of new learning in Alzheimer's disease. In G. Gilmore, P. Whitehouse, & M. Wykle (Eds.), *Memory and aging: Theory, research, and practice* (pp. 212–225). New York: Springer.

Camp, C. J., Foss, J. W., O'Hanlon, A. M., & Stevens, A. B. (1999). Memory interventions for persons with dementia. *Applied Cognitive Psychology, 10*, 193–210. doi:10.1002/(SICI)1099-0720(199606)10:3<193::AID-ACP374>3.0.CO;2-4

Camp, C. J., Foss, J. W., Stevens, A. B., & O'Hanlon, A. M. (1996). Improving prospective memory task performance in Alzheimer's Disease. In M. Brandimonte, G. Einstein, & M. McDaniel (Eds.), *Prospective memory: Theory and applications* (pp. 351–367). Mahwah, NJ: Lawrence Erlbaum Associates.

Camp, C. J., & Stevens, A. B. (1990). Spaced-retrieval: A memory intervention for dementia of the Alzheimer's type (DAT). *Clinical Gerontologist: The Journal of Aging and Mental Health, 10*, 58–60.

Caprio-Prevette, M. D., & Fry, P. S. (1996). Memory enhancement program for community-based older adults: Development and evaluation. *Experimental Aging Research, 22*, 281–303. doi:10.1080/03610739608254012

Carretti, B., Borella, E., & De Beni, R. (2007). Does strategic memory training improve the working memory performance of younger and older adults? *Experimental Psychology, 54*, 311–320. doi:10.1027/1618-3169.54.4.311

Cavallini, E., Pagnin, A., & Vecchi, T. (2003). Age and everyday memory: The beneficial effect of memory training. *Archives of Gerontology and Geriatrics, 37*, 241–257. doi:10.1016/S0167-4943(03)00063-3

Cherry, K. E., Simmons, S. S., & Camp, C. J. (1999). Spaced retrieval enhances memory in older adults with probable Alzheimer's disease. *Journal of Clinical Geropsychology, 5*, 159–175. doi:10.1023/A:1022983131186

Cipriani, G., Bianchetti, A., & Trabucchi, M. (2006). Outcomes of a computer-based cognitive rehabilitation program on Alzheimer's disease patients compared with those on patients affected by mild cognitive impairment. *Archives of Gerontology and Geriatrics, 43*, 327–335. doi:10.1016/j.archger.2005.12.003

Clare, L. (2006). Multi-technique program approaches. In D. Attix & K. Welsh-Bohmer (Eds.), *Geriatric neuropsychology: Assessment and intervention* (pp. 293–314). New York, NY: Guilford Press.

Clare, L., Wilson, B. A., Carter, G., & Hodges, J. R. (2003). Cognitive rehabilitation as a component of early intervention in Alzheimer's disease: A single case study. *Aging & Mental Health, 7*, 15–21. doi:10.1080/1360786021000045854

Clare, L., & Woods, R. T. (2004). Cognitive training and cognitive rehabilitation for people with early-stage Alzheimer disease: A review. *Neuropsychological Rehabilitation, 14*, 385–401. doi:10.1080/09602010443000074

Colcombe, S., & Kramer, A. F. (2003). Fitness effects on the cognitive function of older adults: A meta-analytic study. *Psychological Science, 14*, 125–130. doi:10.1111/1467-9280.t01-1-01430

Craik, F. I. M., Winocur, G., Palmer, H., Binns, M. A., Edwards, M., Bridges, K., ...Stuss, D. T. (2007). Cognitive rehabilitation in the elderly: Effects on memory. *Journal of the International Neuropsychological Society, 13,* 132–142. doi:10.1017/S1355617707070166

Cutler, S.J., & Grams, A.E. (1988). Correlates of self-reported everyday memory problems. *Journal of Gerontology, 43,* S82–S90.

Dahlin, E., Nyberg, L., Bäckman, L., & Neely, A.S. (2008). Plasticity of executive functioning in young and older adults: Immediate training gains, transfer, and long-term maintenance. *Psychology and Aging, 23,* 720–730. doi:10.1037/a0014296

Davis, R.N., Massman, P.J., & Doody, R.S. (2001). Cognitive intervention in Alzheimer disease: A randomized placebo-controlled study. *Alzheimer Disease and Associated Disorders, 15,* 1–9. doi:10.1097/00002093-200101000-00001

De Vreese, L., Neri, M., Fioravanti, M., Belloi, L., & Zanetti, O. (2001). Memory rehabilitation in Alzheimer's Disease: A review of progress. *International Journal of Geriatric Psychiatry, 16,* 794–809. doi:10.1002/gps.428

DeMont, M., & Wood, M.R. (2008, November). *The relation between memory strategy use, stress, and memory ability.* Poster presented at the annual meeting of the Gerontological Society of America, Washington, DC.

Derwinger, A., Stigsdotter-Neely, A., MacDonald, S., & Bäckman, L. (2005). Forgetting numbers in old age: Strategy and learning speed matter. *Gerontology, 51,* 277–284. doi:10.1159/000085124

Dixon, R.A., Hultsch, D.F, & Hertzog, C. (1988). The metamemory in adulthood (MIA) questionnaire. *Psychopharmacology Bulletin, 24,* 671–688.

Dunlosky, J., Cavallini, E., Roth, H., McGuire, C.L., Vecchi, T., & Hertzog, C. (2007). Do self-monitoring interventions improve older adult learning? *The Journal of Gerontology: Psychological Sciences and Social Sciences, 62,* 70–76. doi:10.1093/geronb/62.special_issue_1.70

Erickson, K.I., Colcombe, S.J., Wadhwa, R., Bherer, L., Peterson, M.S., Scalf, P.E., ...Kramer, A.F. (2007). Training-induced plasticity in older adults: Effects of training on hemispheric asymmetry. *Neurobiology of Aging, 28,* 272–283. doi:10.1016/j.neurobiolaging.2005.12.012

Evans, D.A., Funkenstein, H.H., Albert, M.S., Scherr, P.A., Cook, N.R., Chown, M.J.,...Taylor, J.O. (1989). Prevalence of Alzheimer's disease in a community population of older persons. Higher than previously reported. *Journal of the American Medical Association, 262,* 2551–2556. doi:10.1001/jama.1989.03430180093036

Fabre, C., Chamari, K., Mucci, P., Massé-Biron, J., & Préfaut, C. (2002). Improvement of cognitive function by mental and/or individualized aerobic training in healthy elderly subjects. *International Journal of Sports Medicine, 23,* 415–421. doi:10.1055/s-2002-33735

Farina, E., Fioravanti, R., Chiavari, L., Imbornone, E., Alberoni, M., Pomati, S., ...Mariani, C. (2002). Comparing two programs of cognitive training in Alzheimer's disease: A pilot study. *Acta Neurologica Scandinavica, 105,* 365–371. doi:10.1034/j.1600-0404.2002.01086.x

Farina, E., Mantovani, F., Fioravanti, R., Pignatti, R., Chiavari, L., Imbornone, E., ...Nemni, R. (2006). Evaluating two group programmes of cognitive training in mild-to-moderate AD: Is there any difference between a 'global' stimulation and a 'cognitive-specific' one? *Aging & Mental Health, 10*, 211–218. doi:10.1080/13607860500409492

Fillenbaum, G. G. (1985). Screening the elderly: A brief instrumental activities of daily living measure. *Journal of the American Geriatrics Society, 33*, 698–706.

Fiszdon, J. M., Whelahan, H., Bryson, G. J., Wexler, B. E., & Bell, M. D. (2005). Cognitive training of verbal memory using a dichotic listening paradigm: Impact on symptoms and cognition. *Acta Neurologica Scandinavica, 112*, 187–193. doi:10.1111/j.1600-0447.2005.00565.x

Fleming, J. M., Shum, D., Strong, J., & Lightbody, S. (2005). Prospective memory rehabilitation for adults with traumatic brain injury: A compensatory training programme. *Brain Injury, 19*, 1–10. doi:10.1080/02699050410001720059

Floyd, M., & Scogin, F. (1997). Effects of memory training on the subjective memory functioning and mental health of older adults: A meta-analysis. *Psychology and Aging, 12*, 150–161. doi:10.1037/0882-7974.12.1.150

Flynn, T. M., & Storandt, M. (1990). Supplemental group discussions in memory training. *Psychology and Aging, 5*, 178–181. doi:10.1037/0882-7974.5.2.178

Fogel, J. F., Hyman, R. B., Rock, B., & Wolk-Klein, G. (2000). Predictors of hospital length of stay and nursing home placement in an elderly medical population. *Journal of the American Medical Directors Association, 1*, 202–210.

Frankel, J. E., Marwitz, J. H., Cifu, D. X., Kreutzer, J. S., Englander, J., & Rosenthal, M. (2006). A follow-up study of older adults with traumatic brain injury: Taking into account decreasing length of stay. *Archives of Physical Medicine and Rehabilitation, 87*, 57–62. doi:10.1016/j.apmr.2005.07.309

Gatz, M., Fiske, A., Fox, L. S., Kaskie, B., Kasl-Godley, J. E., McCallum, T. J., ...Wetherell, J. L. (1998). Empirically validated psychological treatments for older adults. *Journal of Mental Health and Aging, 4*, 9–45.

Gilewski, M. J., Zelinski, E. M., & Schaie, K. W. (1990). The Memory Functioning Questionnaire for assessment of memory complaints in adulthood and old age. *Psychology and Aging, 1*, 150–158.

Gobet, F., Lane, P. C. R., Croker, S., Cheng, P. C. H., Jones, G., Oliver, I., & Pine, J. M. (2001). Chunking mechanisms in human learning. *Trends in Cognitive Sciences, 5*, 236–243. doi:10.1016/S1364-6613(00)01662-4

González-Gross, M., Marcos, A., & Pietrzik, K. (2001). Nutrition and cognitive impairment in the elderly. *The British Journal of Nutrition, 86*, 313–321. doi:10.1079/BJN2001388

Gordon, B., & Berger, L. (2003). *Intelligent memory*. New York: Penguin Books.

Grandmaison, E., & Simard, M. (2003). A critical review of memory stimulation programs in Alzheimer's disease. *The Journal of Neuropsychiatry and Clinical Neurosciences, 15*, 130–144. doi:10.1176/appi.neuropsych.15.2.130

Hanley, I. G., & Lusty, K. (1984). Memory aids in reality orientation: A single-case study. *Behaviour Research and Therapy, 22*, 709–712. doi:10.1016/0005-7967(84)90134-7

Hawley, K. S., & Cherry, K. E. (2004). Spaced-retrieval effects on name-face recognition in older adults with probable Alzheimer's disease. *Behavior Modification, 28*, 276–296. doi:10.1177/0145445503259283

Heindel, W. C., Salmon, D. P., Shults, C. W., Walicke, P. A., & Butters, N. (1989). Neuropsychological evidence for multiple implicit systems: A comparison of Alzheimer's, Huntington's, and Parkinson's disease patients. *The Journal of Neuroscience, 9*, 582–587.

Hertzog, C., Kramer, A. F., Wilson, R. S., & Lindenberger, U. (2008). Enrichment effects on adult cognitive development: Can the functional capacity of older adults be preserved and enhanced? *Psychological Science in the Public Interest, 9*, 1–65.

Heun, R., Burkart, M., & Benkert, O. (1997). Improvement of picture recall by repetition in patients with dementia of Alzheimer type. *International Journal of Geriatric Psychiatry, 12*, 85–92. doi:10.1002/(SICI)1099-1166(199701)12:1<85::AID-GPS470>3.0.CO;2-U

Hildebrandt, H., Bussmann-Mork, B., & Schwendemann, G. (2006). Group therapy for memory impaired patients: A partial remediation is possible. *Journal of Neurology, 253*, 512–519. doi:10.1007/s00415-006-0013-6

Hill, R. D., Allen, C., & McWhorter, P. (1991). Stories as a mnemonic aid for older learners. *Psychology and Aging, 6*, 484–486. doi:10.1037/0882-7974.6.3.484

Hill, R. D., Bäckman, L., & Stigsdotter-Neely, A. (2000). *Cognitive rehabilitation in old age.* New York: Oxford University Press.

Hill, R. D., Campbell, B. W., Foxley, D., & Lindsay, S. (1997). Effectiveness of the number-consonant mnemonic for retention of numeric material in community-dwelling older adults. *Experimental Aging Research, 23*, 275–286. doi:10.1080/03610739708254284

Hill, R. D., Storandt, M., & Simeone, C. (1990). The effects of memory skills training and incentives on free recall in older learners. *Journal of Gerontology, 45*, 227–232.

Hohaus, L. (2007). Remembering to age successfully: Evaluation of a successful aging approach to memory enhancement. *International Psychogeriatrics, 19*, 137–150. doi:10.1017/S1041610206003760

Jaeggi, S. M., Buschkuehl, M., Jonides, J., & Perrig, W. J. (2008). Improving fluid intelligence with training on working memory. *Proceedings of the National Academy of Sciences of the United States of America, 105*, 6829–6833. doi:10.1073/pnas.0801268105

Jennings, J. M., Webster, L. M., Kleykamp, B. A., & Dagenbach, D. (2005). Recollection training and transfer effects in older adults: Successful use of a repetition-lag procedure. *Aging, Neuropsychology, & Cognition, 12*, 278–298.

Jobe, J. B., Smith, D. M., Ball, K., Tennstedt, S. L., Marsiske, M., Willis, S. L., …Kleinman, K. (2001). ACTIVE: A cognitive intervention trial to promote independence in older adults. *Controlled Clinical Trials, 22*, 453–479. doi:10.1016/S0197-2456(01)00139-8

Johnson, A.M., Pollard, C.C., Vernon, P.A., Tomes, J.L., & Jog, M.S. (2005). Memory perception and strategy use in Parkinson's disease. *Parkinsonism & Related Disorders, 11*, 111–115. doi:10.1016/j.parkreldis.2004.06.005

Kasl-Godley, J., & Gatz, M. (2000). Psychosocial interventions for individuals with dementia: An integration of theory, therapy, and a clinical understanding of dementia. *Clinical Psychology Review, 20*, 755–782. doi:10.1016/S0272-7358(99)00062-8

Kliegl, R., Smith, J., & Baltes, P.B. (1989). Testing the limits and the study of adult age differences in cognitive plasticity of a mnemonic skill. *Developmental Psychology, 25*, 247–256. doi:10.1037/0012-1649.25.2.247

Lachman, M.E., Weaver, S.L., Bandura, M., Elliott, E., & Lewkowicz, C.J. (1992). Improving memory and control beliefs. *Journal of Gerontology, 47*, 293–299.

Li, S.C., Schmiedek, F., Huxhold, O., Röcke, C., Smith, J., & Lindenberger, U. (2008). Working memory plasticity in old age: Practice gain, transfer, and maintenance. *Psychology and Aging, 23*, 731–742. doi:10.1037/a0014343

Light, L. (1991). Memory and aging: Four hypotheses in search of data. *Annual Review of Psychology, 42*, 333–376. doi:10.1146/annurev.ps.42.020191.002001

Little, A.G., Volans, P.J., Hemsley, D.R., & Levy, R. (1986). The retention of new information in senile dementia. *The British Journal of Clinical Psychology, 25*, 71–72. doi:10.1111/j.2044-8260.1986.tb00673.x

Loewenstein, D.A., Acevedo, A., Czaja, S.J., & Duara, R. (2004). Cognitive rehabilitation of mildly impaired Alzheimer Disease patients on cholinesterase inhibitors. *American Journal of Geriatric Psychiatry, 12*, 395–402.

Logan, J.M., & Balota, D.A. (2008). Expanded vs. equal interval spaced retrieval practice: Exploring different schedules of spacing and retention interval in younger and older adults. Aging. *Neuropsychology and Cognition, 15*, 257–280. doi:10.1080/13825580701322171

Londos, E., Boschian, K., Lindén, A., Persson, C., Minthon, L., & Lexell, J. (2008). Effects of a goal-oriented rehabilitation program in Mild Cognitive Impairment: A pilot study. *American Journal of Alzheimer's Disease and Other Dementias, 23*, 177–183. doi:10.1177/1533317507312622

Lustig, C., & Flegal, K.E. (2008). Targeting latent function: Encouraging effective encoding for successful memory training and transfer. *Psychology and Aging, 23*, 754–764. doi:10.1037/a0014295

Mahncke, H.W., Bronstone, A., & Merzenich, M.M. (2006). Memory enhancement in healthy older adults using a brain plasticity-based training program: A randomized, controlled study. *Proceedings of the National Academy of Sciences, 103*, 12523–12528. doi:10.1073/pnas.0605194103

McCue, M., Rogers, J.C., & Goldstein, G. (1990). Relationships between neuropsychological and functional assessment in elderly neuropsychiatric patients. *Rehabilitation Psychology, 35*, 91–99. doi:10.1037/h0079052

McDaniel, M.A., Einstein, G.O., & Jacoby, L.J. (2008). New considerations in aging and memory. In F.I.M. Craik & T.A. Salthouse (Eds.), *The handbook of aging and cognition* (4th ed., pp. 251–310). London, England: Academic Press.

McDougall, G. G., Becker, H., Pituch, K., Vaughan, P., Acee, T., & Delville, C. (2010). The SeniorWISE study: Improving everyday memory in older adults. *Archives of Psychiatric Nursing, 24*, 291–306.

McDougall, G. J. (2000). Memory improvement in assisted living elders. *Issues in Mental Health Nursing, 21*, 217–233. doi:10.1080/016128400248202

McDowell, I. (2001). Alzheimer's disease: Insights from epidemiology. *Aging, 13*, 143–162.

McKitrick, L. A., Camp, C. J., & Black, F. W. (1992). Prospective memory intervention in Alzheimer's disease. *Journal of Gerontology, 47*, 337–343.

McPherson, A., Furniss, F. G., Sdogati, C., Cesaroni, F., Tartaglini, B., & Lindes, A. (2001). Effects of individualized memory aids on the conversation of persons with severe dementia: A pilot study. *Aging & Mental Health, 5*, 289–294. doi:10.1080/13607860120064970

Melton, A. K., & Bourgeois, M. S. (2005). Training compensatory memory strategies via the telephone for persons with TBI. *Aphasiology, 19*, 353–364. doi:10.1080/02687030444000804

Mohs, R. C., Ashman, T. A., Jantzen, K., Albert, M., Brandt, J., Gordon, B., ... Stern, Y. (1998). A study of the efficacy of a comprehensive memory enhancement program in healthy elderly persons. *Psychiatry Research, 77*, 183–195. doi:10.1016/S0165-1781(98)00003-1

Morrell, R. W., Rager, R., Harley, J. P., Herrmann, D. J., Rebok, G. W., & Parente, R. (2006). Developing an online intervention for memory improvement: The sharper memory project. *Cognitive Technology, 11*, 34–46.

Nolan, B. A., Mathews, R. M., & Harrison, M. (2001). Using external memory aids to increase room finding by older adults with dementia. *American Journal of Alzheimer's Disease and Other Dementias, 16*, 251–254. doi:10.1177/153331750101600413

O'Hara, R., Brooks, J. O., Friedman, L., Schröder, C. M., Morgan, K. S., & Kraemer, H. C. (2006). Long-term effects of mnemonic training in community-dwelling older adults. *Journal of Psychiatric Research, 41*, 585–590. doi:10.1016/j.jpsychires.2006.04.010

Olesen, P. J., Westerberg, H., & Klingberg, T. (2004). Increased prefrontal and parietal activity after training of working memory. *Nature Neuroscience, 7*, 75–79. doi:10.1038/nn1165

Ozgis, S., Rendell, P. G., & Henry, J. D. (2008). Spaced retrieval significantly improves prospective memory performance of cognitively impaired older adults. *Gerontology, 55*, 229–232. doi:10.1159/000163446

Ponds, R. W. H. M., van Boxtel, M. P. J., & Jolles, J. (2000). Age-related changes in subjective cognitive functioning. *Educational Gerontology, 26*, 67–81. doi:10.1080/036012700267402

Poon, L. W., Walsh-Sweeney, L., & Fozard, J. L. (1980). Memory skill training for the elderly: Salient issues on the use of imagery mnemonics. In L. W. Poon, J. L. Fozard, L. S. Cermak, D. Arenberg, & L. W. Thompson (Eds.), *New directions* in memory and aging: Proceedings of the George A. Talland Memorial Conference (pp. 461–484). Hillsdale, NJ: Erlbaum.

Rankin, J. L., Karol, R., & Tuten, C. (1984). Strategy use, recall, and recall organization in young, middle-aged, and elderly adults. *Experimental Aging Research, 10,* 193–196. doi:10.1080/03610738408258463

Rapp, S., Brenes, G., & Marsh, A. P. (2002). Memory enhancement training for older adults with mild cognitive impairment: A preliminary study. *Aging & Mental Health, 6,* 5–11. doi:10.1080/13607860120101077

Rasmusson, D. X., Rebok, G. W., Bylsma, F. W., & Brandt, J. (1999). Effects of three types of memory training in normal elderly. *Aging, Neuropsychology, and Cognition, 6,* 56–66. doi:10.1076/anec.6.1.56.790

Rebok, G. W., & Balcerak, L. J. (1989). Memory self-efficacy and performance differences in young and old adults: Effect of mnemonic training. *Developmental Psychology, 25,* 714–721. doi:10.1037/0012-1649.25.5.714

Rebok, G. W., Carlson, M. C., & Langbaum, J. B. S. (2007). Training and maintaining memory abilities in healthy older adults: Traditional and novel approaches. *The Journals of Gerontology. Series B, Psychological Sciences and Social Sciences, 1(Spec No),* 53–61. doi:10.1093/geronb/62.special_issue_1.53

Rebok, G. W., Parisi, J. M., Gross, A. L., & Spira, A. P. (2010). Assessment of cognitive training. In P. A. Lichtenberg (Ed.), *Handbook of assessment in clinical gerontology* (2nd ed., pp. 211–228). New York, NY: Elsevier. doi:10.1016/B978-0-12-374961-1.10008-9

Royall, D. R., Lauterbach, E. C., Kaufer, D., Malloy, P., Coburn, K. L., Black, K. J., & Committee on Research of the American Neuropsychiatric Association. (2007). The cognitive correlates of functional status: A review from the Committee on Research of the American Neuropsychiatric Association. *The Journal of Neuropsychiatry and Clinical Neurosciences, 19,* 249–265. doi:10.1176/appi.neuropsych.19.3.249

Saczynski, J. S., & Rebok, G. W. (2004). Strategies for memory improvement in older adults. *Topics in Advanced Practice Nursing eJournal, 4.* Retrieved from http://www.medscape.com/viewarticle/465740

Saint-Cyr, J. A., Taylor, A. E., & Lang, A. E. (1988). Procedural learning and neostriatal dysfunction in man. *Brain: A Journal of Neurology, 111,* 941–960. doi:10.1093/brain/111.4.941

Schaie, K. W. (2005). *Developmental influences on adult intelligence: The Seattle Longitudinal Study.* New York, NY: Oxford University Press. doi:10.1093/acprof:oso/9780195156737.001.0001

Scogin, F., & Prohaska, M. (1992). The efficacy of self-taught memory training for community-dwelling older adults. *Educational Gerontology, 18,* 751–766. doi:10.1080/0360127920180801

Scogin, F., Prohaska, M., & Weeks, E. (1998). The comparative efficacy of self-taught and group memory training for older adults. *Journal of Clinical Geropsychology, 4,* 301–314.

Scogin, F., Storandt, M., & Lott, L. (1985). Memory-skills training, memory complaints, and depression in older adults. *Journal of Gerontology, 40*, 562–568.

Sharps, M. J., & Price-Sharps, J. L. (1996). Visual memory support: An effective mnemonic device for older adults. *The Gerontologist, 36*, 706–708. doi:10.1093/geront/36.5.706

Sitzer, D. I., Twamley, E. W., & Jeste, D. V. (2006). Cognitive training in Alzheimer's Disease: A meta-analysis of the literature. *Acta Psychiatrica Scandinavica, 114*, 75–90. doi:10.1111/j.1600-0447.2006.00789.x

Small, G. (2002). *The Memory Bible*. New York: Hyperion.

Smith, G. E., Housen, P., Yaffe, K., Ruff, R., Kennison, R. F., Mahncke, H. W., & Zelinski, E. M. (2009). A cognitive training program based on principles of brain plasticity: Results from the Improvement in memory with plasticity-based adaptive cognitive training (IMPACT) study. *Journal of Geriatric Psychiatry, 57*, 594–603.

Stigsdotter, A., & Bäckman, L. (1989). Multifactorial memory training with older adults. *Gerontology, 35*, 260–267. doi:10.1159/000213035

Storandt, M. (1991). Memory-skills training for older adults. *Nebraska Symposium on Motivation, 39*, 39–62.

Studenski, S., Carlson, M. C., Fillit, H., Greenough, W. T., Kramer, A., & Rebok, G. W. (2006). From bedside to bench: Does mental and physical activity promote cognitive vitality in late life? *Science of Aging Knowledge Environment, 2006*, 21. doi:10.1126/sageke.2006.10.pe21

Sveistrup, H., Thornton, M., Bryanton, C., McComas, J., Marshall, S., Finestone, H., . . . Bisson, E. (2004). Outcomes of intervention programs using flatscreen virtual reality. *Annual International Conference of the IEEE Engineering in Medicine and Biology Society, 7*, 4856–4858.

Troyer, A. K. (2001). Improving memory knowledge, satisfaction, and functioning via an education and intervention program for older adults. *Aging, Neuropsychology, and Cognition, 8*, 256–268.

Turkstra, L. S., & Bourgeois, M. (2005). Intervention for a modern day HM: Errorless learning of practical goals. *Journal of Medical Speech-Language Pathology, 13*, 205–212.

Ullman, M. T. (2001). The declarative/procedural model of lexicon and grammar. *Journal of Psycholinguistic Research, 30*, 37–69. doi:10.1023/A:1005204207369

Verhaeghen, P., Geraerts, N., & Marcoen, A. (2000). Memory complaints, coping, and well-being in old age: A systemic approach. *The Gerontologist, 40*, 540–548. doi:10.1093/geront/40.5.540

Verhaeghen, P., & Marcoen, A. (1996). On the mechanisms of plasticity in young and older adults after instruction in the method of loci: Evidence for an amplification model. *Psychology and Aging, 11*, 164–178. doi:10.1037/0882-7974.11.1.164

Verhaeghen, P., Marcoen, A., & Goossens, L. (1992). Improving memory performance in the aged through mnemonic training: A meta-analytic study. *Psychology and Aging, 7*, 242–251. doi:10.1037/0882-7974.7.2.242

Wan, H., Sengupta, M., Velkoff, V. A., & DeBarros, K. A. (2005). U.S. Census Bureau, current population reports, 65+ in the United States: 2005. Washington, DC: U.S. Government Printing Office.

Weisz, J. R., & Hawley, K. M. (2001). *Procedural and coding manual for identification of evidence-based treatments*. Los Angeles: University of California.

West, R. (1985). *Memory fitness over 40*. Gainesville, FL: Triad Publishing.

West, R. L., Bagwell, D. K., & Dark-Freudeman, A. (2008). Self-efficacy and memory aging: The impact of a memory intervention based on self-efficacy. *Aging, Neuropsychology, and Cognition, 15*, 302–329.

Westerberg, H., Jacobaeus, H., Hirvikoski, T., Clevberger, P., Ostensson, M. L., Bartfai, A., & Klingberg, T. (2007). Computerized working memory training after stroke: A pilot study. *Brain Injury, 21*, 21–29. doi:10.1080/02699050601148726

Willis, S. L., Tennstedt, S. L., Marsiske, M., Ball, K., Elias, J., Koepke, K. M., . . . Wright, E. (2006). Long-term effects of cognitive training on everyday functional outcomes in older adults. *Journal of the American Medical Association, 296*, 2805–2814. doi:10.1001/jama.296.23.2805

Woods, B., Thorgrimsen, L., Spector, A., Royan, L., & Orrell, M. (2006). Improved quality of life and cognitive stimulation therapy in dementia. *Aging & Mental Health, 10*, 219–226. doi:10.1080/13607860500431652

Woolverton, M., Scogin, F., Shackelford, J., Black, S., & Duke, L. (2001). Problem-targeted memory training for older adults. *Aging, Neuropsychology, and Cognition, 8*, 241–255. doi:10.1076/anec.8.4.241.5637

Yamamoto-Mitani, N., Matsuoka, K., & Fujii, M. (2007). Home-based rehabilitation program for older adults with cognitive impairment: Preliminary results. *Psychogeriatrics, 7*, 14–20. doi:10.1111/j.1479-8301.2007.00193.x

Yesavage, J. A. (1983). Imagery pretraining and memory training. *Gerontology, 29*, 271–275. doi:10.1159/000213126

Yesavage, J. A., Hoblyn, J., Friedman, L., Mumenthaler, M., Schnieder, B., & O'Hara, R. (2007). Should one use medications in combination with cognitive training? If so, which ones? *Journal of Gerontology: Psychological Sciences and Social Sciences, 62*, 11–18. doi:10.1093/geronb/62.special_issue_1.11

Yesavage, J. A., & Rose, T. L. (1984). The effects of a face-name mnemonic in young, middle-aged, and elderly adults. *Experimental Aging Research, 10*, 55–57. doi:10.1080/03610738408258543

Zanetti, O., Binetti, G., Magni, E., Rozzini, L., Bianchetti, A., & Trabucchi, M. (1997). Procedural memory stimulation in Alzheimer's disease: Impact of a training programme. *Acta Neurologica Scandinavica, 95*, 152–157. doi:10.1111/j.1600-0404.1997.tb00087.x

Zanetti, O., Zanieri, G., DiGiovanni, G., De Vreese, L. P., Pezzini, A., Metitieri, T., & Trabucchi, M. (2001). Effectiveness of procedural memory stimulation in mild Alzheimer's disease patients: A controlled study. *Neuropsychological Rehabilitation, 11*, 263–272. doi:10.1080/09602010042000088

6

EVIDENCE-BASED TREATMENTS FOR BEHAVIORAL DISTURBANCES IN LONG-TERM CARE

KIM J. CURYTO, KELLY M. TREVINO, SUZANN OGLAND-HAND, AND PETER LICHTENBERG

Currently, 4.5 million persons in the United States have Alzheimer's disease, with an estimated increase to 11 million to 16 million persons by the year 2050 (Hebert, Scherr, Bienias, Bennett, & Evans, 2003). A hallmark issue when caring for persons with dementia is addressing challenging or disruptive behavior. Approximately 66% of community-dwelling older adults with dementia and 77% of older adults in nursing homes with dementia demonstrate disruptive behaviors (Bartels et al., 2003; Chan, Kasper, Black, & Rabins, 2003). Untreated, these behaviors can lead to decreased quality of life, increased family and staff caregiver burden, staff burnout and turnover, use of restraints, and institutionalization or psychiatric hospitalization. As a result, disruptive behavior can also increase the cost of care (Brotons & Pickett-Cooper, 1996; Burgio, Jones, Butler, & Engler, 1988; Conely & Campbell, 1991; Daniel, 2000).

Disruptive behaviors in dementia have been categorized into three types (Beck et al., 1998; Cohen-Mansfield & Deutsch, 1996): (a) *verbal agitation*—repetitive sentences or questions, calling out, constant unwarranted requests, complaining, and negativism; (b) *physically nonaggressive behavior*—repetitious mannerisms, inappropriate robing–disrobing, eating or handling things inappropriately, pacing, aimless wandering, trying to get to a different place, general restlessness, hiding, and hoarding; and (c) *verbal and physical aggression* (combined because they have similar correlates)—cursing, verbal threats, screaming, making strange noises, making verbal and physical sexual advances, hurting oneself or others, throwing, tearing, scratching, grabbing, pushing, spitting, hitting, kicking, and biting. Many well-used measures assess most or all of these disruptive behaviors.

Research indicates that pharmacological therapies for these behaviors are not particularly effective and have significant and potentially fatal side effects (Streim, 2004). Consistent with these findings, a consensus statement from the American Association for Geriatric Psychiatry reports the need for effective combinations of behavioral and pharmacological interventions. Unfortunately, although systems are in place to diagnose, treat, reimburse, and evaluate the pharmacological management of disruptive behaviors, similar systems do not exist for nonpharmacological interventions (Cohen-Mansfield & Mintzer, 2005).

Fortunately, extensive research on nonpharmacological interventions for disruptive behavior has been conducted. Three theoretical frameworks can be used to organize this research: the learning behavior model (LBM), the person–environment fit model, and the need-driven behavior model. The next section of this chapter discusses each model and its supporting evidence. In practice, these models overlap and often lead to similar interventions, as they all focus on how the environment can be changed (to change antecedents–consequences, to adjust to abilities and disabilities, or to meet needs respectively).

The Evidence

Kim J. Curyto, Kelly M. Trevino, and Peter Lichtenberg

NONPHARMACOLOGICAL INTERVENTIONS FOR DISRUPTIVE BEHAVIOR

Researchers have identified numerous interventions that successfully decrease disruptive behavior and increase positive behavior across settings (for reviews, see Cohen-Mansfield, 2001; McCabe, Davison, & George, 2007; Opie, Rosewarne, & O'Connor, 1999). However, although the literature on disruptive behavior and related treatment options is extensive, research that meets criteria for evidence-based treatments (EBTs) for disruptive behavior is relatively small. The focus of this chapter is on EBT for disruptive behavior in long-term care (LTC). LTC includes care for frail older adults who require assistance with activities of daily living provided in nursing homes, assisted living facilities, and in the family home.

This review of the literature expands on the review by Logsdon, McCurry, and Teri (2007) by applying their established search strategy to research conducted between 2006 and 2009. The methods used to identify EBTs are described in detail in the introductory chapter of this book. As a summary, to be labeled as an EBT, interventions need at least two supporting peer-reviewed, published studies using the same or a similar treatment approach. The research methodology must include a randomized phase design (i.e., ABA), and/or random assignment to treatment conditions that demonstrates that the treatment effect would not have occurred in another condition. In addition, the results must demonstrate significant reductions in behavioral symptoms. Finally, interventions must be based in psychological theory and be delivered or supervised by mental health professionals.

In the original review (Logsdon et al., 2007), seven studies were identified as EBTs for disruptive behavior in LTC. These studies provided evidence for training of staff and informal caregivers in behavioral management and pleasant events scheduling. In the 3 years since that publication, several noteworthy articles on behavioral approaches have been published. These added eight new studies that meet EBT criteria, as well as offered a new approach for behavior management, simulated presence therapy. In addition, our review uncovered six studies that outlined two interventions that show promise but do not meet full criteria for EBT: activity programming and personalized interdisciplinary care planning. Thus, we will be reviewing 21 studies.

An overview of the EBT approaches and their research support follows. The EBTs are grouped under the three models of behavior intervention described above. Tables 6.1, 6.2, and 6.3 include details on sample size, interventions implemented, study design, measures used, and outcomes. Although the research reports on many outcomes (cognition, physical functioning, caregiver functioning), only outcomes related to behavior and mood are included in this review.

LEARNING BEHAVIOR MODEL INTERVENTIONS

The LBM focuses on the learned relationship between behaviors and their antecedents and consequences. The antecedents provide stimulus control for the behaviors, whereas consequences reinforce or punish behaviors (Cohen-Mansfield, 2001). Behavioral change is achieved by manipulating the antecedents and consequences to promote adaptive behaviors and reduce disruptive behaviors. Interventions for behavior associated with dementia using the LBM have been conducted in both residential and home care settings (see Table 6.1).

TABLE 6.1
Description of Evidence-Based Interventions Based on the Learning Behavior Model (LBM)

LBM	Sample	Intervention	Design	Behavior measures	Outcomes
Residential Proctor et al., 1999; nursing home	$N = 105$; age of treatment, $M = 83.4$, $SD = 5.5$; control, $M = 82.7$, $SD = 9.1$	1. Seven 60-min staff training seminars 2. Weekly visits by psychiatric nurse to assist in care planning; length = 6 months	Matched randomized unit control Control group = usual care	CRBRS	1. Behavior frequency ↑ in both conditions 2. No significant group differences in behavior 3. Greater ↓ in depression in intervention group
Teri, Huda, et al., 2005; assisted living	$N = 120$; total sample age, $M = 85.8$, $SD = 7.0$	Train staff on the ABC model and increasing pleasant events using 2 half-day group sess. and 4 individual sess.; length = 2 months	Randomized control group Control group = usual training (needs of older adults, memory impairment)	RMBPC; ABID; NPI	1. Greater ↓ in behavior in the treatment group 2. Greater ↓ in depression and anxiety in treatment group
Lichtenberg et al., 2005; nursing home	$N = 20$; age of treatment, $M = 84.8$, $SD = 4.9$; control, $M = 85.0$, $SD = 5.1$	1. 5-hr didactic staff training, weekly onsite supervision, monthly conference calls, treatment observed 4 weeks into treatment 2. 20–30 min pleasant event 3/week Length = 3 months	Randomized unit control Control unit = usual care	BEHAVE-AD	1. Behavior frequency ↓ in both units 2. Behavior severity ↓ in treatment condition and ↑ in control condition 3. No change in depression
Davison et al., 2007; nursing home	$N = 113$; total sample age, $M = 85$, $SD = 9$	1. Eight 60–90 min staff training sess. 2. Five 30-min peer support groups Length = 8 weeks	Randomized unit Conditions 1. Training + peer support 2. Training only 3. Usual care	CMAI	1. No change in behavior

Study/Setting	Sample	Intervention	Design	Measure	Results
Visser et al., 2008; nursing home	N = 76; age of training only, M = 87.15, SD = 4.37; training + peer support, M = 87.64, SD = 7.67; control, M = 83.13, SD = 6.99	1. Same as Davison et al. (2006) except peer support groups conducted 4 times; length = 8 weeks	Randomized facility control Conditions 1. Training + peer support 2. Training only 3. Wait-list control	CMAI	1. No change in behavior 2. No change in mood
Home care Teri et al., 1997	N = 72; age of BT-PE, M = 72.8, SD = 8.2; BT-PS, M = 78.5, SD = 7.9; typical care, M = 79.5, SD = 6.9; wait list, M = 76.8, SD = 8.2	1. BT-PE: Caregivers taught to increase activities and changing behavioral and mood contingencies; nine 60-min sess. 2. BT-PS: Caregivers taught to problem-solve; provided education, advice, support; nine 60-min sess.; length = 9 weeks	Randomized control group Control conditions: 1. Typical care 2. Wait list	HDRS	1. 17% of participants with psychomotor agitation or retardation at baseline did not exhibit symptoms after treatment 2. Greater ↓ in depression in treatment groups
Teri et al., 2003	N = 153; age of treatment, M = 78, SD = 6; control, M = 78, SD = 8	1. Twelve 60-min caregiver training sess. focused on behavior management and increasing activities 2. 30 min/day moderate exercise; length = 11 weeks of training and 3 follow-up sess. (1/month) group	Randomized control Control group = usual care	RMBPC	1. More participants in control group institutionalized due to behavior than in treatment group (11 vs. 4) 2. Greater ↓ in depression in treatment group

(continues)

TABLE 6.1

Description of Evidence-Based Interventions Based on the Learning Behavior Model (LBM)   *(Continued)*

LBM	Sample	Intervention	Design	Behavior measures	Outcomes
Teri, McCurry, et al., 2005	$N = 95$; age of treatment, $M = 81.4$, $SD = 6.2$; control, $M = 78.5$, $SD = 8.7$	1. Train community consultants in two training sess. using reading materials, pilot case, ongoing supervision through audiotape 2. Eight weekly 60-min caregiver training sess. by consultants focused on behavior management, communication, activities, and caregiver support 3. Four monthly follow-up calls Length = 8 weeks and 4 monthly follow-up calls	Randomized control group Control condition = usual care	Caregiver ratings of behavior frequency, severity, disturbance; NPI; RMBPC	1. Greater ↓ in frequency and severity of behavior in treatment group

Note. sess. = session; CRBRS = Crichton Royal Behavioural Rating Scale (Sixsmith, Stilwell, & Copeland, 2004); RMBPC = Revised Memory and Behavior Problem Checklist (Teri et al., 1992); ABID = Agitated Behavior in Dementia Scale (Logsdon et al., 1999); NPI = Neuro-Psychiatric Inventory (Cummings et al., 1994); BEHAVE-AD = Behavioral Pathology in Alzheimer's Disease Rating Scale (Reisberg et al., 1987); CMAI = Cohen-Mansfield Agitation Inventory (Cohen-Mansfield, Marx, & Rosenthal, 1989); BT-PE = Behavior Treatment–Pleasant Events; BT-PS = Behavior Treatment–Problem Solving; HDRS = Hamilton Depression Rating Scale (Hamilton, 1960, 1967).

TABLE 6.2

Description of Evidence-Based Interventions Based on the Progressively Lowered Stress Threshold (PLST) Model

PLST	Sample	Intervention	Design	Behavior measures	Outcomes
Residential Woods & Ashley, 1995 (feasibility); nursing home	$N = 27$; total sample age range = 76–94	Simulated presence therapy: (a) 15-min audiotape about positive past events, most cherished memories; (b) only family side of conversation is taped; (c) used when problem behavior is displayed; length = 1 month	Postassessment	Staff report using behavior logs	1. 81.5% of participants' disruptive behaviors improved during intervention
Woods & Ashley, 1995 (pilot); nursing home	$N = 9$; total sample age $M = 82$, range = 71–97	Simulated presence therapy: (a) 15-min audiotape as stated above; (b) used 2 ×/day when behaviors typically occur; length = 2 months	Pre–post quasi-experimental	Staff behavior log; DBRS; rating scales for severity of disruptive behavior and affect	1. Behavior improved during 91% of intervention observations and ↓ pre- to posttest 2. All exhibited positive responses for some episodes of behavior
Camberg et al., 1999; nursing home	$N = 54$; total sample age $M = 82.7$, $SD = 7.5$	Simulated presence therapy: (a) 15-min audiotape as above; (b) used at least twice a day when behaviors occur; (c) staff did not use consistently as directed; length = 17 days over 4 weeks	Facilities randomly rotated between treatment and control phases with 10-day washout period Control conditions: 1. placebo tape of newspaper reading 2. usual care	AARS–interest and plea-sure; CMAI–SF; MOSES; SOAPD; Staff obser-vation logs	1. Greater ↓ in number and frequency of behaviors in treatment phase (67% of time) 2. Greater ↑ in level of interest in treatment phase

(continues)

TABLE 6.2

Description of Evidence-Based Interventions Based on the Progressively Lowered Stress Threshold (PLST) Model   (Continued)

PLST	Sample	Intervention	Design	Behavior measures	Outcomes
Garland et al., 2007; nursing home	$N = 30$; total sample age $M = 79$, range $= 66–93$	1. Simulated family presence: once a day, 3 days a week 2. 15-min of music preferred in earlier life: once a day, 3 days a week; length = 3 weeks	Groups randomly rotated between three phases with 2-day washout period; observations conduced at 15-min intervals (ABA) Control conditions: 1. usual care 2. placebo activity reading from horti-culture text	Direct observation by trained researchers	1. Greater ↓ in frequency of physically agitated behavior in both treatment phases, which continued 15 min after 2. Greater ↓ in verbally agitated behavior in simulated presence phase only, continued 15 min after
Rovner et al., 1996; nursing home	$N = 81$; total sample age $M = 82$, $SD = 8$	1. Activity programming: 10 a.m.–3 p.m., structure, stimulation, and reinforce social skills 2. After 2 weeks, medication prescribed for remaining depression or delusions–hallucinations 3. Educational rounds 1 hr/week with psychiatrist; length = 2 weeks	Randomized control group Control condition = usual care	CMAI; observation of engagement; PDRS (staff rated); use of restraints and anti-psychotics	1. Greater number in the control group met criteria for a behavior disorder at 6 months 2. Those in control group twice as likely to be restrained or receive antipsychotics at 6 months 3. Intervention group 10 times more likely to participate in activities

Study	Sample	Intervention	Design	Measure	Outcomes
Volicer et al., 2006; state vets nursing home "The Club"	N = 28; sample age M = 77.3, range: 62–91	Continuous activity programming: flexible around current resident schedules, adjusted to ability; available all day; length = 3 months	Pre–post quasi-experimental	MDS	1. ↓ in use of psychotropic meds 2. ↓ in social isolation
Volicer et al., 2006; VA nursing home "Vets Club"	N = 28; sample age M = 77.3, range: 62–91	Continuous activity programming: morning only; length = 7 months	Repeated measures (monthly)	MDS; informal staff report	1. ↓ in use of antianxiety and hypnotic meds 2. ↓ in wandering, pacing, agitation 3. ↑ time participating in activities
Volicer et al., 2006; VA nursing home TAC	N = 22; sample age M = 77.3, range = 62–91	Continuous activity programming: available all day; length = 3–4 months	Within-subjects comparison of TAC vs. Club days	Chart review; behavioral logs	1. ↓ in use of as-needed psychoactive meds compared with Vets Club 2. Less days of observed agitation in TAC than Vets Club 3. ↓ sleep disturbance after TAC participation vs. Vets Club
Putnam et al., 2007; nursing home	N = 13; total sample age M = 83	Small group between 2:30 and 4:30 p.m.—calmer environment, resident-driven activity based on mood and behavior; length = 3 months	Prepost quasi-experimental Home care	CMAI	1. ↓ in CMAI total, and screaming and complaining behaviors specifically
Gerdner et al., 2002	N = 237; total sample age M = 64.8, SD = 13.8	Individualized care plan including structured routine and environmental modifications created with family; length = 2 weeks	Randomized comparison group Control condition = 1. routine info 2. referral for case management, community services, support groups	MBPC	1. Greater ↓ in frequency of disruptive behaviors with nonspousal caregiver report only

(continues)

TABLE 6.2
Description of Evidence-Based Interventions Based on the Progressively Lowered Stress Threshold
(PLST) Model   *(Continued)*

PLST	Sample	Intervention	Design	Behavior measures	Outcomes
Huang et al., 2003	N = 48; total sample age M = 75.8, SD = 6.4	1. 2–3-hr sess. of caregiver training focused on modifying causative environmental stimuli 2. Follow-up telephone consults every 2 weeks Length = 2 weeks and 2 weeks follow-up	Randomized control group Control condition = written educational materials	CMAI-Chinese version	1. ↓ in behaviors in treatment condition
Gitlin et al., 2008	N = 30; total sample age M = 79, SD = 9.4	1. Six 90-min home visits 2. Two 15-min phone contacts 3. Develop pleasant events schedule, plan activities matched to ability 4. Caregiver relaxation training length = 4 months	Randomized blind wait-list control	ABID (16-item); RMBPC (2-item); developed 5-item engagement index	1. Greater ↓ in number of and frequency of disruptive behaviors in treatment group 2. Greater ↓ in caregiver reported behavior. 3. Greater ↑ in engagement

Note. sess. = session; DBRS = Disruptive Behavior Rating Scale (Mungas, Weiler, Franzi, & Henry, 1989); AARS = Apparent Affect Rating Scale (Lawton, Van Haitsma, & Klapper, 1996); CMAI-SF = Cohen-Mansfield Agitation Inventory–Short Form (Cohen-Mansfield, 1991); MOSES = Multidimensional Observation Scale for Elderly Subjects (Helmes, Csapo, & Short, 1987); SOAPD = Scale for the Observation of Agitation in Persons with Dementia (Camberg et al, 1999); CMAI = Cohen-Mansfield Agitation Inventory; PDRS = Psychogeriatric Dependency Rating Scale (Evans, 1984); MOSES = Multidimensional Observation Scale for Elderly Subjects (Helmes, Csapo, & Short, 1987); SOAPD = Scale for the Observation of Agitation in Persons with Dementia (Camberg et al, 1999); MBPC = Memory and Behavior Problem Checklist (Zarit, Todd, & Zarit, 1986); ABID = Agitated Behavior in Dementia Scale (Logsdon et al., 1999); RMBPC = Revised Memory and Behavior Problem Checklist (Teri et al., 1992); MDS = Minimum Data Set (Morris et al., 1990); VA = Veterans Affairs.

TABLE 6.3

Description of Evidence-Based Interventions Based on the Need-Driven Behavior (NDB) Model

NDB	Sample	Intervention	Design	Behavior measures	Outcomes
Residential Cohen-Mansfield et al., 2007; nursing home	N = 167; sample age M = 86, SD = 7.6	Individualized interventions based on NDB through TREA and implemented during 4-hr peak agitation; length = 10 days	Randomized facility control (2 facilities refused random assignment); control condition = usual care	ABMI AARS	1. Greater ↓ in overall nonaggressive agitation in treatment group 2. Greater ↑ in pleasure and interest in treatment group
Curyto et al., 2007; assisted living	N = 24; sample age M = 74.4, SD = 9.4	Individualized interventions based on NDB model through TREA and implemented through a structured plan at individually based times through an interdisciplinary team; length = 2 weeks	Prospective prepost-follow-up (ABC)	ABMI; DBS; APS	1. ↓ total disruptive behavior 2. ↑ activity participation
Opie et al.., 2002; nursing home	N = 99; M = 83.9	Individualized interventions implemented through a structured plan; length = 4 weeks	Prospective prepost with randomized delay	BAGS; daily observation counts	1. ↓ frequency and severity of disruptive behavior

Note. TREA = treatment routes for exploration of agitation (Cohen-Mansfield, 2000); ABMI = Agitated Behavior Mapping Instrument (Cohen-Mansfield, Werner, & Marx, 1989); AARS = Apparent Affect Rating Scale (Lawton, Van Haitsma, & Klapper, 1996); APS = Activity Participation Scale (Lawton et al., 1998); BAGS = behavior assessment graphical system (Prodger, Hurley, Clarke, & Bauer, 1991); DBS = Disruptive Behavior Scale (Beck et al., 1998).

Residential Settings

Five studies investigated interventions for disruptive behavior in dementia in residential settings (Davison et al., 2007; Lichtenberg, Kemp-Havican, MacNeill, & Schafer Johnson, 2005; Proctor et al., 1999; Teri, Huda, Gibbons, Young, & van Leynseele, 2005; Visser et al., 2008). Caregiver training was the core component of all interventions. Topics covered across studies and training sessions included basic information on dementia and psychiatric diagnoses, therapeutic approaches to care, Antecedent–Behavior–Consequences (ABCs) of behavior management, methods for increasing pleasant events, and communication between individuals with dementia and their family member. Training duration and frequency varied across studies, ranging from two half-day workshops plus four individual 60-minute sessions, to seven 60-minute sessions, to eight 60- to 90-minute sessions. In addition, one study provided an intervention that included 5 hours of didactic training, weekly onsite supervision, monthly conference calls with the project leader, and observation of the behavioral treatment 4 weeks into implementation.

Additional components of the interventions varied across studies. One included individualized behavior management planning in which a nurse practitioner visited the home weekly and assisted with development of behavioral interventions (Proctor et al., 1999). In another, nursing staff identified pleasurable activities for each resident and implemented these activities individually (Lichtenberg, Kemp-Havican, MacNeill, & Schafer Johnson, 2005). Finally, two studies included a peer-support program for staff that was held for 30 to 60 minutes after the education sessions (Davison et al., 2006; Visser et al., 2008). Control conditions across studies consisted of either usual care or wait list.

Two of the five studies revealed significant improvement in decreasing either the frequency or severity of behaviors (Lichtenberg, Kemp-Havican, MacNeill, & Schafer Johnson, 2005; Teri, Huda, et al., 2005). Although disruptive behaviors were not significantly improved in three of the five studies, improvements were found in mood problems (depression, anxiety) and caregiver outcomes (e.g., self-efficacy in dementia care, nursing performance, knowledge and skills in dementia care).

Home Care Settings

Three studies examined interventions using the LBM in home settings (Teri et al., 2003; Teri, Logsdon, Uomoto, & McCurry, 1997; Teri, McCurry, Logsdon, & Gibbons, 2005). All three studies demonstrated reductions in behavior frequency, severity, or both. Two studies were based on the Seattle

Protocol, which trains caregivers in interventions for improving behavior and depression.

In one study, training in behavior therapy consisted of strategies for increasing pleasant events and problem-solving techniques for altering contingencies of depression and behavioral problems (Teri et al., 1997). The intervention was provided in nine 60-minute sessions, with control participants receiving usual care or placed on a wait list. Those in the treatment condition demonstrated a reduction in behavioral symptoms of depression (i.e., psychomotor agitation or retardation): 17% of participants who demonstrated these behaviors at baseline did not exhibit behaviors after treatment.

In the second study, caregiver training in behavior management was combined with a home-based exercise program (Teri et al., 2003). The intervention was provided in twelve 60-minute sessions with three follow-up 60-minute sessions over 3 months. The exercise program consisted of at least 30 minutes per day of moderate intensity exercise. Results indicated that 11 control participants were institutionalized because of behavioral problems compared with four participants in the treatment condition. It is interesting to note that caregiver-reported disruptive behavior was not significantly different between treatment and control groups.

In the third study, community health care providers who had master's degrees in counseling, psychology, or social work served as consultants to caregiver–patient dyads (Teri, McCurry, et al., 2005). The consultants provided instruction in modification of the antecedents and consequences of disruptive behavior, communication strategies, and strategies to increase pleasant events. They also provided caregiver support. Consultants visited the home for eight weekly sessions and provided four monthly telephone calls to ensure maintenance of the intervention. Participants in the control conditions received routine medical care. Results indicated that the frequency and severity of disruptive behaviors and caregiver reactivity to behavior decreased over the course of the intervention in the treatment condition. In addition, at the 6-month follow-up, caregivers in the treatment condition reported fewer memory-related behavior problems than in the control condition.

PERSON–ENVIRONMENT FIT MODEL INTERVENTIONS

The person–environment fit model, or progressively lowered stress threshold model, is based on the premise that the dementia process results in a greater reliance on the environment and a lower threshold at which stimuli affect behavior (Lawton & Nahemow, 1973). A poor fit between the abilities of the person and the demands of the environment can impair functioning and contribute to disruptive behavior. Treatment focuses on matching the environmental demands to the person's abilities to obtain optimal levels of stimulation and to decrease excess disability. As with LBM interventions, interventions based on the person–environment fit model have been conducted in residential and home care settings (see Table 6.2).

Residential Settings

Interventions based on this model have used simulated presence therapy and activity programming to address disruptive behavior. Simulated presence therapy relies on preserved memories to create a low-stress environment that is familiar, comforting, and provides individually appropriate levels of stimulation. In this intervention, a family member audiotapes a conversation (typically 15 minutes in length) about positive past events and cherished memories in the life of the individual with dementia. The tape only includes the family member's portion of the conversation to allow the individual time to respond and interact. The tape is played during episodes of disruptive behavior or when behaviors tend to occur. Headphones are used to exclude ambient noise and allow freedom of movement.

Three studies evaluated the impact of simulated presence therapy on disruptive behavior (Camberg et al., 1999; Garland, Beer, Eppingstall, & O'Connor, 2007; Woods & Ashley, 1995). A feasibility and pilot study showed improvements in behavior with the use of simulated presence therapy (Woods & Ashley, 1995). In the feasibility study, 81.5% of participants showed decreased disruptive behavior based on nursing staff report. A pilot study included in the same article (Woods & Ashley, 1995) demonstrated a decrease in disruptive behaviors in 91% of observations with use of simulated presence therapy and significant improvement from pre- to postintervention. In addition, all participants responded positively to the intervention for at least some episodes of disruptive behavior. In a similar study, 67% of behavior logs indicated reductions in staff-observed agitation, which was significantly better than the usual care and placebo conditions (Camberg et al., 1999). A final study indicated that simulated presence therapy reduced the occurrence of physical and verbal agitation compared with the placebo and usual care conditions. However, simulated presence therapy did not differ from individualized music therapy (Garland et al., 2007).

Activity programming is another type of intervention based on the person–environment fit model and is designed to reduce disruptive behaviors by creating an environment that is calm, engaging, and avoids overstimulation. These interventions accommodate for the difficulties of those with dementia in processing large amounts of information and initiating meaningful activities

(Putman & Wang, 2007; Rovner, Steele, Shmuely, & Folstein, 1996; Volicer, Simard, Pupa, Medrek, & Riordan, 2006). Activity programming represents a promising area of intervention for disruptive behavior. We located one randomized controlled trial; thus, this intervention does not yet meet the criteria for EBT. The study provided a modular-based intervention titled, "the Activities, Guidelines for Psychotropic Medications, and Education program" (AGE program; Rovner, Steele, Shmuely, & Folstein, 1996), which designs activities based on individuals' mental and physical abilities. Compared with a usual care control group, participants in the program were 10 times more likely to participate in activities. In addition, participants in the control group were significantly more likely to meet criteria for a behavior disorder and twice as likely to be restrained or receive antipsychotic medications as participants in the intervention group.

Further, two additional activity interventions were evaluated by using prospective pre- and postevaluations over 3 months, again not meeting criteria as an EBT because the design does not prove that a change would not have happened if an intervention was not implemented. Because they demonstrate activity interventions as a promising area of intervention, they are included here. One study evaluated three continuous activity programs guided by the principles that residents are never alone in the activities room, they need times of stimulation and rest, and activities are provided by staff in all disciplines (Volicer et al., 2006). In addition, activities were adjusted to participants' abilities and schedules and included periods of stimulation and rest. In the first program, "The Club" in a state nursing home, staff were provided with education on dementia, communication, and behaviors, and activities were available during all three shifts and were provided by staff from various disciplines. Pre–post data were collected over 3 months. The results indicated a significant reduction in the use of psychotropic medication, improved nutritional status, and decreased social isolation. The second program, "The Vet's Club," provided continuous activities during the morning. Results from data, collected monthly for 7 months, indicated a reduction in use of antianxiety–hypnotic medications, a reduction in physical agitation, and increased time participating in activities. The third program, the therapeutic activity center (TAC), provided continuous activity programming from 9 a.m. to 3 p.m. in a large-group format. A within-subjects design was used to compare days spent in all-day programming (TAC) to days in half-day programming (The Vet's Club). During all-day activities (TAC), residents required less psychoactive medication and exhibited less agitation and sleep disturbance than when during half-day activities.

In a final study, participants were placed in small groups during peak times of unit activity during the afternoon. They were involved in activities that were individualized to eliminate environmental and psychosocial factors involved in disruptive behaviors. Results indicated that activity scheduling was associated with a significant decrease in frequency of disruptive behavior (Putman & Wang, 2007).

Home Care Settings

Interventions based on the person–environment fit model in home settings provide caregivers with training on environmental modifications and creation of a daily schedule that support the individual's cognitive limitations. Other facets of these interventions include training on incorporation of pleasant activities into a structured daily routine, caregiver communication skills, and caregiver behavior management skills. Three studies have demonstrated the effectiveness of these interventions (Gerdner et al., 2002; Gitlin et al., 2008; Huang, Shyu, Chen, Chen, & Lin, 2003). In one study, nonspousal family caregivers in the intervention group reported significantly fewer behavior problems compared with nonspousal family caregivers in the usual care control group. However, a treatment effect did not emerge for spousal caregivers (Gerdner et al., 2002). In a second study, results indicated that caregivers in the treatment condition reported decreases in overall behavioral problems, physically nonaggressive behaviors, and verbally aggressive and nonaggressive behaviors over time, whereas these same behaviors increased or remained the same in the control condition (Huang et al., 2003). Finally, an evaluation of the tailored activity program that coupled environmental modifications with activity scheduling revealed a significant decrease in frequency of disruptive behavior in the intervention group. In addition, after 4 months, significantly fewer caregivers in the intervention group reported agitation compared with the control group (Gitlin et al., 2008).

NEED-DRIVEN BEHAVIOR MODEL

The need-driven behavior model states that the dementia process interferes with individuals' abilities to meet their basic needs. Disruptive behaviors are the individual's response to the unmet need (Algase et al., 1996). Treatment focuses on adjusting the physical and social environment and building on the abilities, personality, and preferences of the individual to meet the unmet needs and eliminate the behavior (Kolanowski, Richards, & Sullivan, 2002). This model also emphasizes the importance of personal history and the need to tailor interventions to individuals' unique characteristics, preferences, and abilities.

Although a number of personal characteristics and environmental conditions are associated with all disruptive behaviors, specific conditions have been linked to certain clusters of behavior (see Beck et al., 1998; Cohen-Mansfield & Deutsch, 1996). These associations help to identify the unmet needs that underlie the behavior and are the foundation for the treatment routes for exploration of agitation intervention (TREA; Cohen-Mansfield, 2000), a general strategy for identifying a treatment approach for disruptive behaviors. A decision tree guides the caregiver through behavioral correlates for each subtype of behavior to identify the unmet need most likely contributing to the behavior, separately for verbal agitation (see Figure 6.1), physical nonaggressive behavior (see Figure 6.2), and aggressive behavior (see Figure 6.3). Interventions to meet the need are chosen on the basis of the individual's background, specific needs, and abilities. Interventions based on the unmet needs model show promise but do not yet fully meet criteria for evidence-based interventions (see Table 6.3).

Three studies exhibit evidence for the use of interventions based on this model. Two studies used a randomized controlled design but with significantly different methodologies. The first study used decision trees to identify individualized interventions implemented by research assistants (Cohen-Mansfield, Libin, & Marx, 2007). The second used an interdisciplinary team to identify and implement individualized interventions for behaviors based on identified needs and structured behavior management plans (Opie, Doyle, & O'Connor, 2002). The third study used a prospective within-subjects design to evaluate interventions based on the decision-tree strategy and structured behavior management plans implemented by an interdisciplinary team (Curyto, Ogland-Hand, & Vriesman, 2008).

The first study evaluated the use of the TREA treatment strategy (Cohen-Mansfield, 2000) to develop interventions for agitated behavior in nursing home residents with dementia (Cohen-Mansfield et al., 2007). Using the TREA decision trees and demographic and medical information,

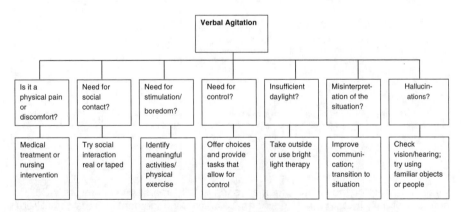

Figure 6.1. Approaches to management of verbal agitation. From "Nonpharmacological Management of Behavioral Problems in Persons With Dementia: The TREA Model," by J. Cohen-Mansfield, 2000, *Alzheimer's Care Quarterly, 1,* p. 26. Copyright 2000 by Jiska Cohen-Mansfield. Reprinted with permission.

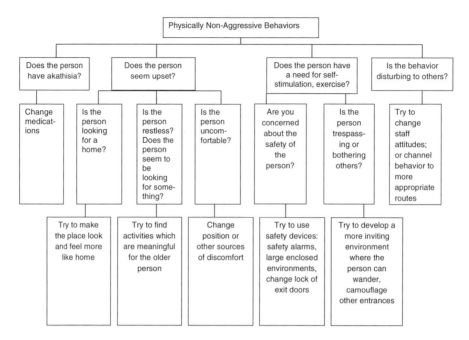

Figure 6.2. Approaches to management of physically nonaggressive behaviors. From "Nonpharmacological Management of Behavioral Problems in Persons With Dementia: The TREA Model," by J. Cohen-Mansfield, 2000, *Alzheimer's Care Quarterly, 1,* p. 28. Copyright 2000 by Jiska Cohen-Mansfield. Reprinted with permission.

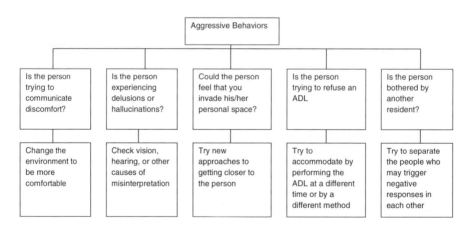

Figure 6.3. Approaches to management of physically aggressive behaviors. ADL = activities of daily living. From "Nonpharmacological Management of Behavioral Problems in Persons With Dementia: The TREA Model," by J. Cohen-Mansfield, 2000, *Alzheimer's Care Quarterly, 1,* p. 29. Copyright 2000 by Jiska Cohen-Mansfield. Reprinted with permission.

interventions were created to fit the individual's identity, preferences, and abilities. Implementation of these interventions by a paid research assistant decreased overall agitation and increased pleasure and interest from baseline in comparison to a control condition.

The second study evaluated the impact of an interdisciplinary process for development and implementation of individualized interventions for disruptive behavior (Opie et al., 2002). Detailed information about the individual's background, personality, interests, social networks, and medical and psychiatric history was obtained through semistructured interviews with the person with dementia and family members. A consultant team of four members trained in psychiatry, psychology, and nursing used assessments of personal history and behavior to develop individualized strategies for specific behaviors. The team created structured, written behavior management plans listing the goal, rationale, description, timing, and responsible staff. These plans focused on meeting unmet needs by adjusting the environment based on abilities and personal history. However, the TREA decision trees were not used. Results indicated significant reductions in restlessness, verbal disruption, inappropriate behaviors, and total disruptive behaviors across the course of the intervention. At a 1-month follow-up, staff reported that the frequency and severity of target behaviors had decreased.

The third study evaluated the implementation of the unmet needs model and TREA treatment strategy through an interdisciplinary team (Curyto, Ogland-Hand, et al., 2008). Outcomes were evaluated before, during, and after intervention implementation. Participants were residents in a behavioral treatment program for individuals with dementia. The interdisciplinary team used the TREA decision trees to develop, implement, and assess individualized interventions for disruptive behavior. Over 6 months, staff reported significant reductions in the frequency of total disruptive behavior and physical and verbal aggression. Verbal agitation and physically nonaggressive behavior declined but did not reach significance. In addition, activity participation increased significantly.

Adapting EBT to the Real World

Kim J. Curyto, Kelly M. Trevino, and Suzann Ogland-Hand

Although more research is needed to document evidence for the interventions discussed above, a number of interventions meet the criteria for EBT. Some studies refer to manuals that can be requested or purchased from the author (Huang et al., 2003; Teri, McCurry, et al., 2005). However, applying EBTs in different settings within the LTC system is rarely as simple as following a manual exactly. All EBTs for disruptive behavior focus on changing the environment, which is a complex, multifaceted, situation-specific construct. Adapting EBTs to the specific context and setting as well as the individual's unique history and ability is a great challenge. In the paragraphs that follow, we discuss our thoughts and experience with implementation of evidence-based practice around disruptive behaviors in LTC settings.

Kim Curyto is currently a full-time clinician in the Veterans Affairs system in a 90-bed skilled nursing facility, called the community living center. She also spends a small but significant portion of her time in applied research activities, evaluating the effectiveness of implementing EBTs in this setting or adapting evidence-based practice demonstrated with other populations and in other settings to the veterans in the community living center. The residents are predominantly older adults and have a mixture of mental disorders (e.g., dementia, depression, anxiety disorders, psychotic disorders) and health problems (e.g., chronic pain, chronic illness, disability). Her approach is primarily behavioral and focused on functional analysis and behavioral activation, but it also includes social learning theory. She has established her role as a psychologist in the Veterans Affairs community living center as an integral part of the treatment team, which is fairly uncommon in community nursing home settings. Prior to taking on her current role, she worked as a consultant to community nursing homes and assisted living facilities. She also worked as the clinical director of a specialized assisted living program for individuals with dementia and disruptive behaviors. We refer to all of these roles in the following section to illustrate a range of challenges when implementing EBTs for disruptive behavior.

Kelly Trevino is also a full-time clinical psychologist in a Veterans Affairs system 120-bed LTC and medical rehabilitation facility. The residents of the facility are predominately older adults and are medical and psychiatrically complex. Disruptive behavior is relatively common and typically secondary to dementia. We use an interdisciplinary approach to behavior management in which all disciplines collaborate to develop and implement interventions based on the models described above.

Suzann Ogland-Hand is a full-time clinical psychologist in a nonprofit free-standing behavioral health service organization, and she currently provides outpatient psychotherapy and consultation to patients in home and congregate care settings. Some of her outpatient practice involves working with patients with dementia with disruptive behaviors, and/or co-morbid mood disorders such as depression or anxiety. There, she works with "treatment team segments" (see Ogland-Hand & Zeiss, 2000) in her clinic and community to attempt to administer interventions based on the models described above. Prior to her current role, she worked as a consultant to community congregate care settings, a geropsychiatric inpatient unit, and a specialized assisted living program for individuals with dementia and disruptive behaviors.

Like most clinical psychologists, we believe in following the science of EBTs to guide our work as clinicians. However, we have experienced difficulty following treatment manuals exactly. We have spent time considering what revisions can be made to implement the treatment protocol with minimal reduction of the impact of the intervention on the desired outcome. In the next sections, we describe some of the barriers we have encountered to implementing EBTs for disruptive behaviors in LTC and discuss ways we have adjusted to be able to implement EBTs in a way that is feasible and successful.

SELECTION CONSIDERATIONS

The selection of a treatment for disruptive behaviors will depend on the potential outcomes desired (narrowly defined, or broadly defined as impacting improvement in quality of life). Many EBTs include methods to assess additional outcomes, such as mood, positive and negative affect, cognition, physical function, and engagement, as well as caregiver burden, distress and self-efficacy. In many ways, it is important to consider whether the goals of the intervention are only to impact disruptive behavior or to have broader impact on other areas such as the ones listed. This is especially true in clinical work, in which multiple issues and comorbid conditions are common.

In this review, only psychological interventions were included. However, other studies demonstrate successful treatment strategies by other disciplines (e.g., nursing interventions that address participation in activities of daily living, care to decrease disruptive behavior) that require consideration in combination with psychological EBTs. Selecting the EBT protocol or which aspects of each EBT to implement will also depend on factors such as resources available, level of organizational support, and the level of flexibility of the environment and services provided.

ORGANIZATIONAL SUPPORT

As clinicians, we have become very aware of the impact that administrative and facility support has on the implementation of EBTs for disruptive behavior. For example, caregiver training requires financial resources for purchase of manuals and materials and caregiver time (Camp & Nasser, 2003).

Implementing EBTs requires the readiness of the organization to implement a new way of addressing disruptive behavior. There is a great deal of information on assessing readiness for change and implementation of evidence-based practice (Levkoff, Chen, Fisher, & McIntyre, 2006). This includes the active support of all executive decision makers and health care providers, and a collaborative and open relationship among them. A few of the EBT protocols include inservices for leadership within the LTC facility, such as the STAR (staff in assisted living residences) manual designed around the LBM (Teri, Huda, et al., 2005).

Kim Curyto and Suzann Ogland-Hand experienced firsthand the importance of ongoing leadership engagement and continued information sharing. In one facility, initial support was obtained for a specialized assisted living facility designed around implementation of EBTs. As a result of this support, all staff were consistently trained in EBTs, and the facility's budget reflected the training and ongoing support needed. However, with turnover in a number of facility administrators, this support gradually faded, and the treatment program reduced in size and eventually closed.

CAREGIVER TRAINING

Convincing LTC administrators to invest in training caregivers in an EBT for disruptive behavior is often difficult. However, successful implementation of EBTs requires that all team members monitor the targeted behavior symptoms and consistently implement the treatment plan. Caregivers in home care and institutional LTC settings vary in the level of formal or informal training in dementia, dementia care, and management of disruptive behavior they receive (Logsdon et al., 2007). Caregivers with limited knowledge of dementia and dementia care will likely have greater difficulty in implementing EBTs for disruptive behavior. Therapeutic nihilism, or the belief that the progressive nature of dementia precludes effective behavioral treatment, can interfere with caregiver's willingness to implement treatment. Caregiver training can address caregiver attitudes and expectations and provide accurate information about what can be achieved (Rewilak, 2007). A review of the effectiveness of caregiver training programs for behavioral problems with dementia found that training not only increases knowledge and skills and reduces frequency of behavioral problems but also improves caregiver satisfaction and turnover rates (McCabe, Davison, & George, 2007).

In our experience, when evidence-based training is provided, caregivers are better able to work with mental health professionals to reduce disruptive behavior. In addition, trained caregivers are more active and motivated to address disruptive behaviors, have more accurate expectations of the outcomes, and view themselves as valuable to the process of reducing disruptive behavior. However, implementation of caregiver training based on a manual is often not feasible in clinical settings. We have found that the time caregivers are able to spend in training is much less than the amount of time devoted to training in EBT protocols. Being flexible and willing to adjust to the time and resources available is important in teaching caregivers the skills taught in EBT protocols.

For example, Kim Curyto has adjusted the implementation of training caregivers in EBTs by using the ABC approach and TREA decision trees to seven 30-minute sessions, provided over multiple times during shift report (7:30–8 a.m., 1:30–2:00 p.m., 3:30–4:00 p.m.) and multiple days. This schedule has allowed her to train more staff than if she held to the original protocols. For caregivers and other staff who are unable to attend formal training, she incorporates key points of training into informal case discussions. She also illustrates key training points when working with caregivers in the moment on how to assess and approach a person who is demonstrating disruptive behaviors.

TEAMWORK

We have found that an integral part of creating active support for a new approach to addressing disruptive behaviors from health care providers is to develop the interdisciplinary team, based on the principle "we help support what we create" from organization psychology. When everyone is involved in creating the structured plan to address challenging behavior, then each team member is motivated to do what he or she can to help implement the behavior plan and to achieve the best outcome.

Research indicates improved efficiency and outcomes when treatment for complex and chronic conditions is coordinated within an interdisciplinary team (Zeiss & Steffen, 1996). The most successful teams are interdisciplinary (not multidisciplinary), where all disciplines are actively involved to provide a breadth of resources and work together to create shared team goals and treatment plans rather than separate treatment plans and goals for each discipline (Zeiss & Steffen, 1996). The team collaboratively identifies the behaviors to change, obtains an accurate and comprehensive understanding of the disruptive behaviors, and determines the best approach to treatment given the goals of the team. No single discipline is held accountable. Rather, the whole team accepts the responsibility of the outcome of treatment.

However, turf battles often occur when developing and implementing individualized behavioral intervention plans. Different caregivers, disciplines, and shifts may often disagree about the goals and content of a successful treatment plan. For example, a resident named "Mrs. Smith" is a lifelong walker. She enjoys walking and uses it to relieve stress. She now has advanced dementia and demonstrates unsteady gait. She falls frequently but forgets to request assistance with transfers and ambulation. When a caregiver redirects her or reminds her that she is not safe to walk, she becomes anxious and repeatedly calls out and asks questions. Nursing staff are focused on the need for safety for Mrs. Smith, and they insist that she needs to have supervision at all times while walking. However, the family is focused on Mrs. Smith's desire to be able to get up when she chooses and the extreme level of distress during times she is required to stay sitting. They are focused on the need for autonomy and want to allow her to be able to walk when she desires. This example illustrates the competing goals of safety and autonomy. This conflict of goals and values can also occur across shifts. In another example, evening caregivers may prefer that a resident rest in the afternoon to eliminate fatigue as a trigger for agitation during evening care. However, day caregivers may believe that the resident should be engaged and out of bed during the day.

In our experience, when these conflicts are not openly discussed and addressed, tension within the team develops and becomes a barrier to successfully intervening with disruptive behaviors. Meeting consistently as a team can help to obtain an accurate, complete picture of the disruptive behaviors caregivers are facing. Regular meetings with all caregivers, shifts, and disciplines can be a time to discuss different perspectives and opinions and to identify the goals of care based on different values and goals represented by team members. These types of interdisciplinary team meetings are critical for successful implementation of a treatment plan over time. Learning skills for successful participation in interdisciplinary treatment team meetings, as well as regular attention to the process of communication with the interdisciplinary team, are two additional variables essential for success (see Zeiss & Steffen, 1996; and Ogland-Hand & Zeiss, 2000, for more information on interdisciplinary team function in LTC).

COMMUNICATION AND DOCUMENTATION OF BEHAVIOR

A vital component of effective treatment of disruptive behavior is consistent treatment implementation, particularly for behavior interventions that focus on changing the environment (Davis & Burgio, 1999). Creating this consistency can be difficult, particularly in institutional settings where there are many caregivers and members of the treatment team that span disciplines and shifts. A documented structured behavioral plan makes it clear to all caregivers what behaviors are targeted, what the goals of the intervention plan are, what interventions are to be implemented, and by whom. To create a successful person-centered behavior plan, it is important for caregivers to consistently document frequency and severity of disruptive behaviors over 24 hours to create a better understanding of what is occurring across time. This information can be used to identify patterns of behaviors that can guide interventions and review, evaluate, and revise the behavior plan regularly. Evaluating the effectiveness of a behavior plan requires continued documentation of the occurrence of the behavior over time. Consistent documentation improves understanding of the behavior and informs development and refinement of the behavior plan.

The EBTs described above all include standardized, validated measures for assessing disruptive behavior, typically by caregiver report. These measures assess the frequency of a comprehensive list of disruptive behaviors within a specific time frame and involve caregivers' subjective, retrospective report. They rely on caregivers' ability to accurately observe, describe, and sometimes remember disruptive behaviors. These measures may also assess the level of severity or disruptiveness of the behaviors. However, they do not indicate the clinical importance of behavior symptoms or which disruptive behaviors are most problematic or distressing. Rather, they are designed to document change in behavioral symptoms to demonstrate outcomes of behavior interventions.

One of the most common measures is the Cohen-Mansfield Agitation Inventory (CMAI; Cohen-Mansfield, Marx, Rosenthal, 1989), a list of 29 agitated behaviors rated by caregivers on a 7-point scale for frequency over a 2-week period (see Appendices 6.1 and 6.2). These behaviors are broken down into the behavioral subtypes, described above. The Revised Memory and Behavior Problem Checklist (Teri et al., 1992) assesses the frequency of a list of 24 problematic behaviors on the basis of caregiver report (see Appendix 6.3). In addition, it assesses the caregiver's reaction to these behaviors so that interventions can target those most upsetting to caregivers. It includes three factors: mood, disruption, and memory-related problems. The Behavioral Pathology in Alzheimer's Disease Rating Scale (BEHAVE-AD; Reisberg et al., 1987) assesses a range of behavior symptoms on the basis of caregiver report, including delusions, hallucinations, activity disturbances, aggressiveness, sleep–wake disturbances, affective disturbances, anxieties, and phobias (ranges from 0 to 75; see Appendix 6.4). In addition to a total score, there is also a global rating of the magnitude of trouble the behavior is to the caregiver or the level of danger to the patient. Finally, the Minimum Data Set (MDS; Morris et al., 1990) assesses behavior problems routinely in nursing home settings on the basis of staff-initiated quarterly assessments of the presence of specific behavioral problems.

Other measures involve direct observation by a trained observer, such as the Agitated Behavior Mapping Instrument (Cohen-Mansfield, Werner,

& Marx, 1989), the Apparent Affect Rating Scale (Lawton, Van Haitsma, & Klapper, 1996), and the Scale for the Observation of Agitation in Persons With Dementia (Camberg et al., 1999). These observational measures involve significant amounts of training and require a sampling strategy to accurately capture the disruptive behaviors as they occur and also document when they do not occur. However, they have the advantage of reflecting behavioral symptom frequency, duration, and intensity as they occur and documenting the context in which they occur (see Curyto, Van Haitsma, & Vriesman, 2008, for a review).

Using comprehensive measures of disruptive behavior in clinical work can be challenging. Person-centered, nonpharmacological interventions for disruptive behaviors in clinical settings often focus on one or two key disruptive behaviors that are assessed as the most challenging or disruptive. The above measures assess all possible disruptive behaviors and may not capture significant change in the targeted behaviors of the intervention. We have found it useful clinically to use a comprehensive behavioral assessment measure initially and at key points in the intervention process to ensure that the targeted behavior symptoms are decreasing and not being replaced with other behaviors. For example, we administer a comprehensive measure such as the CMAI on intake and annually, and also when a change in behavior has been noticed. It is also useful to track a person's response to treatment frequently (e.g., weekly) by asking caregivers to rate the targeted behavioral items only.

These measures do not replace the need for a systematic method of documenting the context in which a specific behavior occurred, the implementation of the interventions, and the impact of the interventions on the behavior. Traditional behavior logs typically ask caregivers to describe details of the behavior, when it occurred, where it occurred, who was present and involved, why it was a problem, what occurred after, the interventions tried, and the result. Behavior logs provide detailed information on the frequency and severity of a targeted behavior and the context in which that behavior occurs. See Appendix 6.5 for an example of a behavior log.

FLEXIBILITY OF SERVICES AND ENVIRONMENT

Implementation of interventions to manage behavior often requires changing the environment and the method of care provision to meet the needs of the individual. Inflexibility with services and the environment of care are often barriers to continuing the successful behavior plan. For example, one male resident in a specialized assisted living program reacted aggressively to showers and preferred tub baths at night, as was his preference throughout his life. The staff were able to provide this service, and his aggression decreased. However, the facility to which he was discharged could not provide tub baths at night because an extra staff member would have been needed to take the person off the unit to where the tub bath was located. Another example included a male resident who had significant pain secondary to arthritis, which was worse in the morning and triggered aggression during morning care. He was less likely to hit caregivers if he was allowed to get up gradually and out of bed at a later time. However, the dining service in the facility where he was discharged was not able to adjust meal and snack times to allow him to arise later. A third example included a female resident who started calling out and screaming repeatedly in noisy crowded areas, and she decreased this behavior when moved to a quieter area. However, her new residence lacked the option of quiet areas.

We have observed many more examples highlighting how the inability to change the environment and care creates a barrier to implementing EBTs. Thus, it is important to include all services in learning more about the purpose, expectations, and benefits of the EBT being implemented, including food service, housekeeping, and facilities and maintenance. With greater understanding of the process and purpose of EBTs, these service lines can help make adjustments to better support implementation of EBTs. We have found that individuals in these services appreciate the ability to work as part of the team to improve care.

SUSTAINABILITY

We mentioned briefly in the Organizational Support section that with administrative changes, the resources and commitment to providing caregiver training to new staff decreased, interfering with sustainability of the implementation of EBTs for disruptive behaviors. We have found that implementation of EBTs is not a finite goal to be achieved but a journey that will continue to require time, effort, and resources. Many of the EBTs address the importance of sustainability by incorporating follow-up training or booster sessions, ongoing supervision, and peer support. These efforts communicate to caregivers that implementing EBTs is important and creates the expectation that they will use and develop their skills further.

It is evident from the EBT protocols and our clinical experience that ongoing training is critical to sustainability. Caregivers benefit from reviewing training in EBTs after they have implemented it so that their experience can be incorporated into the training. In addition, caregiver training needs to be repeated to ensure that new caregivers possess the required knowledge and skills.

Research has indicated that providing regular supervision for caregivers improves effectiveness (Lichtenberg, 1994). On the basis of our experience, it is important for mental health professionals to remain accessible and involved in working with caregivers as they learn to use and refine their skills in intervening with disruptive behavior. Hands-on modeling and practice helps to solidify training in adult learners and demonstrates the importance of problem solving, flexibility, trial and error, and practice.

We have also seen the benefits of providing peer support. Working with individuals with disruptive behaviors is stressful and associated with a great deal of caregiver burnout. Visser et al. (2008) found that caregivers who received education and peer support reported greater skills and knowledge than those who received education only. When we were able to direct clinical care, we set up a peer-support process group where staff could feel open about sharing their struggles and frustrations, support each other and problem solve together. They were increasingly comfortable with trying new interventions and providing input into the structured behavioral plan. In addition, they learned from each other about different approaches and interventions.

Finally, Kim Curyto has also found that it is important to emphasize that use of EBTs is expected and valued. Performance appraisals for paid caregivers are one way to provide this feedback. However, performance appraisals occur infrequently, which limits their impact on behavior. We have found it extremely helpful to provide immediate, hands-on feedback and training in the moment in which a behavioral intervention is implemented. This type of feedback provides the opportunity to model skills and promotes positive outcomes in the moment.

Research has demonstrated that supervisory support, such as monitoring, individualized feedback, and incentive programs, is helpful in obtaining, supporting, and sustaining high performance levels in training and intervention programs (Allen-Burge, Stevens, & Burgio, 1999; Burgio & Stevens, 1999). Further, Burgio and colleagues have developed a manual that outlines the process of implementing self, peer, and supervisory feedback and incentive systems needed for sustaining the implementation of EBTs (Stevens et al., 1998).

CASE EXAMPLE

The following is a case example that demonstrates implementation of the need-driven model of management of disruptive behaviors in a residential care setting.

Personal History

Geraldine "Geri" Smith was born in Las Vegas. She, her parents, and two sisters moved to Michigan during her elementary school years. Both of her parents were alcoholics. When Geri was in high school, her father began having an affair with another woman and also sexually abused Geri. Geri began abusing alcohol, smoking cigarettes, and running away from home. She was sent out of state to boarding school, and she began working as a nurse's aide. She married three times and had three children with her first husband. Her first and second husbands abused substances and were physically and verbally abusive to her. She continued to abuse alcohol to cope. In her 60s, Geri married a third time, and together, she and her husband began attending church. The congregation became a kind and supportive family to Geri.

Geri began struggling with memory problems and was diagnosed with early-onset Alzheimer's disease in her mid 60s. She initially coped with this troubling diagnosis by returning to drinking. With the support of her church, she sought outpatient treatment for her alcoholism and depression. She had two right-sided strokes and was diagnosed with diabetes, chronic obstructive pulmonary disease, and chronic heart failure. Her cognitive abilities, ability to complete instrumental activities of daily living, and ability to initiate activities of daily living declined. She began wandering during the nighttime. Her husband, worried for her safety, placed her in a nursing home. During her time in the nursing home, she was admitted to an inpatient psychiatric setting twice for treatment of disruptive behavior, including physical aggression, and she was given trials of different psychotropic medications, including antidepressants and antipsychotics. After the second inpatient psychiatric hospitalization, her nursing home refused to take her back. She was accepted for placement at an assisted living program that specialized in care of people with dementia and significant need-driven behaviors.

Initial Assessment

On admission, Geri received a comprehensive assessment of behavior (BEHAVE-AD; CMAI; Disruptive Behavior Scale; Beck et al., 1998), medical conditions, MDS activities of daily living (Morris, Fries, & Morris, 1999), depression (Cornell Scale for Depression in Dementia; Alexopoulos, Abrams, & Young, 1988), anxiety (Rating of Anxiety in Dementia; Shankar, Walker, Frost, & Orrell, 1999), social history, and spirituality. This assessment was completed by different disciplines before and during admission, spanning a 1-week period. Her CMAI score indicated the presence of physically nonaggressive behavior hourly and verbal and physical aggression daily. Behavioral observation and the Rating of Anxiety in Dementia indicated that Geri experienced significant anxiety, but her depression assessment indicated depression was adequately managed at admission.

On cognitive testing, she demonstrated moderate-to-severe cognitive impairment based on an orientation scale and the Test for Severe Impairment (Albert & Cohen, 1992). Her attention was poor, and she had difficulty maintaining focus during conversation due to her significant short-term memory deficits. She had difficulty communicating verbally at times. Psychosocial assessment documented her psychosocial history described above and personal preferences: that religious rituals and music were important to Geri, as well as helping others. This assessment documented that her favorite color was pink and that she loved board games and crafts, such as making jewelry and scrapbooking.

Functional Analysis

Analysis of Geri's behavior focused on antecedents to her disruptive behavior. Over 2 weeks, the team recorded her disruptive behavior, including when and where it occurred, who was present or involved, a detailed description of her behavior, consequences of her behavior, interventions tried, and the observable impact of these interventions along with a subjective rating of the success of each intervention. This documentation revealed three types of disruptive behaviors: verbal and physical aggression, unsafe ambulation, and inappropriate urination.

Verbal and Physical Aggression

Geri's decreased ability to understand verbal commands and process information appeared to trigger disruptive behavior. The staff used this functional analysis to target TREA correlates for aggression (see Figure 6.3), particularly misperception of the situation and invasion of personal space. For example, she was verbally aggressive toward staff and residents when she misunderstood what was expected or when others tried to redirect her. Without adequate prompts and time to process information, she would become physically aggressive. She was verbally and physically aggressive to staff during personal care, for example, during bathing, when she appeared to not understand what was happening. She also demonstrated anxiety when she was around unfamiliar people. This anxiety was likely due to her inability to recall what her relationship was with others and her tendency to mistrust others in light of her history of abuse. She occasionally became angry at staff for "not being who they said they were," which would lead to misperceptions, paranoia, and aggression.

Unsafe Ambulation

About a month into her treatment, staff also became concerned about Geri's rate of ambulation. She often paced so quickly that staff worried about her risk of bumping into people or objects. Their repeated attempts to get her to walk more slowly were ineffective. She got up and down during meals, which bothered other residents. Staff observed that she would sit in the dining room when it was less crowded and busy but that she left during mealtimes, when there were more people present and more noise. She also wandered into other residents' rooms. Following admission, staff assessed and documented the context of these behaviors over 1 to 2 weeks, and their observations indicated that pacing and wandering into other resident rooms occurred more frequently during times of over or understimulation. This was particularly frequent in the evenings between 7 p.m. and 10 p.m., when she was less likely to be engaged in meaningful activity. On the basis of this information, staff chose to target the TREA correlates for physical nonaggressive behavior (see Figure 6.2), including feeling upset, looking for home or a safe place, and looking for something to do.

Inappropriate Urination

Finally, Geri often urinated in inappropriate places when she was unable to find the bathroom due to memory difficulties. She would wander into other residents' rooms and urinate in wastebaskets and dresser drawers.

Treatment Plan

Geri's individualized behavioral plan was based on the functional analysis described above and on the learning behavior and need-driven behavior models. Using the TREA decision trees (see Figures 6.1–6.3), the team identified potential correlates of her behavior and tailored interventions to Geri's personal history. Care plans were developed to address triggers and needs related to her disruptive behavior, taking 3 to 4 weeks to develop and revise the behavior plan to successfully address Geri's behavior symptoms. This occurred in 15- to 30-minute segments of time during the weekly interdisciplinary treatment team meeting.

Verbal and Physical Aggression

One trigger for Geri's disruptive behavior was her anxiety around unfamiliar people. Knowledge that her personal history included interpersonal trauma and subsequent mistrust aided the team in understanding this trigger. Staff looked unfamiliar to her initially, which led her to feel unsafe. After attempting and evaluating a series of interventions, staff identified an effective approach: Namely, when Geri encountered staff, they provided a calm greeting with her nickname and a smile (e.g., "Hi, Geri. It's nice to see you"). She would relax with the personal acknowledgement, smile back, and occasionally was able to engage in short interactions. These types of interactions helped decrease her anxiety and provided a sense of safety and familiarity along with repeated positive experience with staff.

In the past, when she had been upset in her life, Geri had coped by smoking or having a drink. Smoking was not allowed in the facility she was living in prior to her admission. Staff found that chewing gum replaced smoking, and they found ways for her to safely carry gum. When anxious, Geri also benefited from a break in a quiet room, quiet area, or being outside with staff. As her dementia progressed, she also seemed to derive comfort from having her purse with her.

Staff found that a calm greeting and saying her name and their own name also assisted in decreasing misperception during personal care tasks. In addition, staff adjusted care approaches to preserve her personal space and sense of control, the other TREA correlate targeted during the assessment. Staff walked Geri through each step of the care task and allowed her enough time to understand what was expected of her. Knowledge of her personal preferences, such as her preference for showers and her enjoyment of putting on make-up, helped staff to individualize the care approach. Trial and error also occurred, and staff eventually discovered that she preferred washing and dressing in her bedroom rather than the bathroom.

Unsafe Ambulation

The functional analysis indicated that Geri liked to walk with a long stride and a quick pace. As her chronic obstructive pulmonary disease and chronic heart failure progressed, she experienced shortness of breath. When she was short of breath, her pace quickened and she did not respond to verbal cues to stop or slow down. However, staff discovered that if they took Geri's hand and walked very slowly beside her, she would slow down.

Geri's history was helpful in designing effective interventions for her short attention span at meals and her tendency to leave during mealtimes. Staff targeted interventions to make her environment feel more safe and familiar, addressing the potential TREA correlate of looking for home. First, rituals of her faith tradition were important to her. Thus, prayer prior to mealtime helped her settle into eating at a table in the dining room for longer periods of time. Second, Geri was a grazer, with a tendency to choose sweet snacks. If staff sprinkled a little Splenda on her food and talked about "sweetening it up," her intake improved, and she would sit for longer periods of time.

In addition, staff accommodated her preference to eat while walking by having nutritious snacks and finger foods available, so that she could eat throughout the day in addition to her brief times at the dining room table. She was able to serve herself from unlocked cupboards and the fridge. However, staff discovered that if a plate of cookies was left out, Geri had a tendency to eat them all or hide them in her purse for later. If cookies were kept in tins with lids, she was less likely to eat them. Additionally, staff were concerned about her poor hydration. Knowing that Geri's favorite color was pink, the recreation therapist obtained a large plastic pink cup for Geri's use. Together, they painted her name on the cup, and Geri regularly used this cup to enjoy beverages.

Interventions were also designed to address the potential TREA correlate of looking for meaningful activities especially in the evenings when her pacing and wandering increased. Knowing Geri enjoyed singing, staff began singing church hymns and contemporary Christian music with her. Many other enjoyable activities needed to be adjusted to her current cognitive and physical limitations. For example, as Geri loved board games, staff invited her to sit with them and residents to play modified versions of double Solitaire or Scrabble with significant staff assistance. Geri enjoyed scrapbooking and could crop pictures by following a bold outline of the shape desired and applying adhesive with verbal cues. She also enjoyed stringing beads for jewelry, a task that helped further maintain her fine motor skills.

Interventions to avoid pacing and intrusion on other residents were also created for other times during the day. Tasks were modified so that she could assist in the kitchen by helping to set the table. When given step-by-step instructions, Geri began helping out with meal preparation, which she seemed to enjoy. She would also help with laundry, smiling the whole time she was folding towels and clothes.

Inappropriate Urination

To address her inappropriate urination in places such as wastebaskets, the staff clearly marked the bathrooms throughout the home, including the bathroom in her room, with a picture of a toilet and a sign reading, "BATHROOM." This was successful, and subsequently she only urinated in the toilet.

SUMMARY

A number of EBTs for disruptive behaviors in LTC exist. It is often difficult to follow an EBT protocol verbatim, as the level of support, resources, and environment may vary in important ways from the controlled intervention study. The ability to adapt, as well as trial and error using a scientist–practitioner approach, is necessary. Many specific interventions within each EBT can be used as designed. It is also possible to adjust the timing and process of training to match caregiver schedules and available resources, as is illustrated in the case of Geri. Through comprehensive assessment, triggers were identified, and interventions were designed around triggers and based on personal history and current abilities. The assessment was guided by the TREA strategy. Implementation of EBTs for disruptive behaviors will take significant amounts of staff time and resources, particularly during start-up. However, effective management of disruptive behaviors has the potential to improve quality of life; decrease caregiver burden, burnout, and turnover; and decrease the use of restraints, and institutionalization or psychiatric hospitalization. As a result, it would likely decrease cost of care over time.

APPENDIX 6.1: COHEN-MANSFIELD AGITATION INVENTORY
(LONG FORM)

Client name: _____ Date: _____

Informant name: _____

Note: Give to current caregiver or family as indicated.
Instructions: Please read each of the 29 agitated behaviors, and circle
how often (from 1-7) each was manifested by the resident during the last
2 weeks: If filling out with the person say: **"In the last 2 weeks, how often
has the resident demonstrated . . ."**

	Less than once a week	Once or twice a week	Several times a week	Once or twice a day	Several times a day	Several times an hour
Never						
1	2	3	4	5	6	7

*If prevented part of the time, estimate how frequently it would happen if not
prevented.*
Do not include rare behaviors that are clearly explained by situational factors.

___1. **Pacing and aimless wandering** - constantly walking back and forth,
does not indicate normal purposeful walk, include wandering when done in
a wheelchair

___2. **Inappropriate dressing or disrobing** - putting on too many clothes,
putting on clothing in a strange manner (e.g., putting pants on head), taking off clothing in public or when it is inappropriate (if only genitals are
exposed, do not rate; see item # 28.) Do not rate person's ability to dress/
undress as in ADL's.

___3. **Spitting (including while feeding)** - spitting onto floor, other peo-
ple, etc.; do not include salivating of which person has no control, or spitting into tissue, toilet, or onto ground outside.

___4. **Cursing or verbal aggression** - only when using words; swearing,
use of obscenity, profanity, unkind speech or criticism, verbal anger, verbal
combativeness. Nonverbal will be marked under screaming.

From "A Description of Agitation in a Nursing Home," by J. Cohen-Mansfield, M. S. Marx, and A. S.
Rosenthal, 1989, *Journal of Gerontology: Medical Sciences, 44*(3), M77–M84. Copyright 1989 by
Jiska Cohen-Mansfield. Reprinted with permission. Readers should refer to the *Instruction Manual for the
Cohen-Mansfield Agitation Inventory* (Cohen-Mansfield, 1991) for additional information regarding this
inventory.

Never 1	Less than once a week 2	Once or twice a week 3	Several times a week 4	Once or twice a day 5	Several times a day 6	Several times an hour 7

If prevented part of the time, estimate how frequently it would happen if not prevented.

Do not include rare behaviors that are clearly explained by situational factors.

___5. **Constant unwarranted request for attention or help** - verbal or nonverbal unreasonable nagging, pleading, demanding (indicate also for oriented people).

___6. **Repetitive sentences or questions** - repeating the same sentence or question one right after the other (Do not include complaining - see item # 18; even if oriented and even if possibly warranted).

___7. **Hitting (including self)** - physical abuse, striking others, pinching others, banging self/furniture.

___8. **Kicking** - strike forcefully with feet at people or objects.

___9. **Grabbing onto people or things inappropriately** - snatching, seizing roughly, taking firmly, or yanking.

___10. **Pushing** - forcefully thrusting, shoving, moving putting pressure against.

___11. **Throwing things** - hurl, violently tossing up in air, tipping off surfaces, flinging, intentionally spilling food.

___12. **Making strange noises** - including crying, weeping, moaning, weird laughter, grinding teeth.

___13. **Screaming** - loud shrill, shouting, piercing howl.

___14. **Biting** - chomp, gnash, gnaw (people, objects, or self).

___15. **Scratching** - clawing, scraping with fingernails (people, objects, or self).

___16. **Trying to get to a different place** - trying to get out of the building, off the property - sneaking out of room, leaving inappropriately, trying to get into locked areas, trespassing within unit, into offices, other resident's room or closet.

___17. **Intentional falling** - purposefully falling onto floor, include from wheelchair, chair, or bed.

___18. **Complaining** - whining, complaining about self, somatic complaints, personal gripes or complaining about external things or other people.

___19. **Negativism** - bad attitude, doesn't like anything, nothing is right.

___20. **Eating or drinking inappropriate substances** - putting into mouth and trying to swallow items that are inappropriate.

Never 1	Less than once a week 2	Once or twice a week 3	Several times a week 4	Once or twice a day 5	Several times a day 6	Several times an hour 7

If prevented part of the time, estimate how frequently it would happen if not prevented.
Do not include rare behaviors that are clearly explained by situational factors.

___21. **Hurting self or other** - burning self or other, cutting self or other, touching self or other with harmful objects, etc.

___22. **Handling things inappropriately** - picking up things that don't belong to them, rummaging through drawers, moving furniture, playing with food, fecal smearing.

___23. **Hiding things** - putting objects under or behind something.

___24. **Hoarding things** - putting many or inappropriate objects in purse or pockets, keeping too many of an item.

___25. **Tearing things or destroying property** - shredding, ripping, breaking, stomping on something.

___26. **Performing repetitious mannerisms** - stereotypic movement, such as patting, tapping, rocking self, fiddling with something, twiddling with something, rubbing self or object, sucking fingers, taking shoes on and off, picking at self, clothing, or objects, picking imaginary things out of air or off floor, manipulation of nearby objects in a repetitious manner.

___27. **Making verbal sexual advances** - sexual propositions, sexual innuendo, or "dirty" talk.

___28. **Making physical sexual advances or exposing genitals** - touching a person in an inappropriate sexual way, rubbing genital area, inappropriate masturbation, when not alone in own room or bathroom, unwanted fondling or kissing.

___29. **General restlessness** - fidgeting, always moving around in seat, getting up and sitting down inability to sit still.

30. Did agitated behavior occur most often
__In morning
__In afternoon
__In evening
__No time more than others
__Different times for different behaviors

APPENDIX 6.2: COHEN-MANSFIELD AGITATION INVENTORY SCORING SHEET

Client name: _____   Date: _____

	Aggressive Behavior score	Physically Non-Aggressive score	Verbally Agitated score	Other Behavior score
Item	3: _____	1: _____	5: _____	11: _____
	4: _____	2: _____	6: _____	12: _____
	7: _____	16: _____	13: _____	17: _____
	8: _____	21: _____	18: _____	20: _____
	9: _____	26: _____	19: _____	22: _____
	10: _____	29: _____		23: _____
	14: _____			24: _____
	15: _____			27: _____
	25: _____			28: _____

1. Sub-scale Severity Scores (Add above #'s for each column)

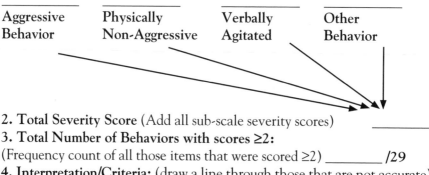

_____ _____ _____ _____
Aggressive   Physically   Verbally   Other
Behavior   Non-Aggressive   Agitated   Behavior

2. Total Severity Score (Add all sub-scale severity scores)   _____

3. Total Number of Behaviors with scores ≥2:
(Frequency count of all those items that were scored ≥2) _____ /29

4. Interpretation/Criteria: (draw a line through those that are not accurate)

Aggressive Behavior occurring at least several times a week
- At least one aggressive behavior scoring 3 or higher
- At least three aggressive behaviors scoring 2

Physically Non-Aggressive Behavior occurring at least once a day
- At least one physically non-aggressive behavior scoring 4 or higher
- At least two physically non-aggressive behaviors scoring 3
- At least four physically non-aggressive behaviors scoring 2

Verbally Agitated Behavior occurring at least once a day
- At least one verbally agitated behavior scoring 4 or higher
- At least two verbally agitated behaviors scoring 3
- At least four verbally agitated behaviors scoring 2

APPENDIX 6.3: REVISED MEMORY AND BEHAVIOR PROBLEM CHECKLIST

BRIEF DESCRIPTIVE INFORMATION

Description and Psychometrics

The Revised Memory and Behavior Problems Checklist (RMBPC; Teri et al., 1992) is a 24-item informant-report measure of observable behavior problems in dementia patients. It is a self-administered caregiver questionnaire, on which the informant rates (a) the frequency of each behavior problem during the past week (1 = not in the past week, to 4 = daily or more often) and (b) their reaction to each behavior (e.g. how bothered or upset the caregiver feels when the behavior occurs with 0 = not at all to 4 = extremely).

The RMBPC provides a method of assessing overall level of behavior problems, as well as specific areas of problems (memory, depression, disruption), and caregiver reactivity associated with these behaviors. It is unique in providing this latter dimension. It is also easy to use and easy to score. Currently, it is being used in a series of longitudinal investigations and treatment outcome studies. It has been translated into French and Mandarin for international use.

RMBPC SCORING

Subscales:

> Memory: 7 items (#1, 2, 3, 4, 5, 6, 7)
> Depression: 9 items (#12, 14, 17, 18, 19, 20, 21, 22, 23)
> Disruption: 8 items (#8, 9, 10, 11, 13, 15, 16, 24)
> Total: 24 items

Frequency Scoring: Sum items with scores of 0 to 4 on subscales and total. If question score is 9, exclude it from the sum and item count.

> Sum items for each subscale as above. Then compute the mean item score for each subscale by dividing by the number of items included in the sum. The range for each subscale is 0 to 4.

> The total frequency score is the sum of all items divided by 24. It also has a range of 0 to 4.

Reaction Scoring: Sum scores on items that had a frequency rating of 1 to 4 on subscales and total. If question score is 0 or 9, exclude it from the sum and item count.

Include only items with **frequency** scores of 1 to 4 in the reaction scoring. Compute the mean reaction score by summing reaction scores of these items and then dividing by the number of items included in the sum. The range for each subscale is 0 to 4.

The total reaction score is computed in the same way, to obtain a possible range of 0 to 4.

Linda Teri, PhD, University of Washington

Resident Name: _____

Interview Date: _____ ____ _____

              Month   Day   Year

Instructions: The following is a list of problems people/patients with a memory loss sometimes have. Please indicate if any of these problems have occurred during the past week. If so, how much has this bothered or upset you when it happened?

Use the following scales for the frequency of the problem and your reaction to it. Please read the description of the ratings carefully.

Frequency Ratings:
    0 = never occurred
    1 = not in the past week
    2 = 1 to 2 times in the past week
    3 = 3 to 6 times in the past week
    4 = daily or more often
    9 = don't know/not applicable

Reaction Ratings:
    0 = not at all
    1 = a little
    2 = moderately
    3 = very much
    4 = extremely
    9 = don't know/not applicable

Please answer all the questions below. Check one box from 0–9 for both **Frequency** and **Reaction**.

Frequency	Reaction	
0 1 2 3 4 9	0 1 2 3 4 9	1. Asking the same question over and over.
0 1 2 3 4 9	0 1 2 3 4 9	2. Trouble remembering recent events (e.g., items in the newspaper or on TV).
0 1 2 3 4 9	0 1 2 3 4 9	3. Trouble remembering significant past events.
0 1 2 3 4 9	0 1 2 3 4 9	4. Losing or misplacing things.
0 1 2 3 4 9	0 1 2 3 4 9	5. Forgetting what day it is.
0 1 2 3 4 9	0 1 2 3 4 9	6. Starting, but not finishing, things.
0 1 2 3 4 9	0 1 2 3 4 9	7. Difficulty concentrating on a task.

Resident Name: _____

Interview Date: _____   ____   _____
                Month   Day   Year

Frequency Ratings:
    0 = never occurred
    1 = not in the past week
    2 = 1 to 2 times in the past week
    3 = 3 to 6 times in the past week
    4 = daily or more often
    9 = don't know/not applicable

Reaction Ratings:
    0 = not at all
    1 = a little
    2 = moderately
    3 = very much
    4 = extremely
    9 = don't know/not applicable

Please answer all the questions below. Check one box from 0–9 for both **Frequency** and **Reaction**.

Frequency	Reaction	
0 1 2 3 4 9	0 1 2 3 4 9	8. Destroying property.
0 1 2 3 4 9	0 1 2 3 4 9	9. Doing things that embarrass you.
0 1 2 3 4 9	0 1 2 3 4 9	10. Waking you or other family members up at night.
0 1 2 3 4 9	0 1 2 3 4 9	11. Talking loudly and rapidly.
0 1 2 3 4 9	0 1 2 3 4 9	12. Appears anxious or worried.
0 1 2 3 4 9	0 1 2 3 4 9	13. Engaging in behavior that is potentially dangerous to self or others.
0 1 2 3 4 9	0 1 2 3 4 9	14. Threats to hurt oneself.
0 1 2 3 4 9	0 1 2 3 4 9	15. Threats to hurt others.
0 1 2 3 4 9	0 1 2 3 4 9	16. Aggressive to others verbally.

Resident Name: _____
Interview Date: _____   ____   _____
　　　　　　　　 Month　　Day　　Year

Frequency Ratings:
　　0 = never occurred
　　1 = not in the past week
　　2 = 1 to 2 times in the past week
　　3 = 3 to 6 times in the past week
　　4 = daily or more often
　　9 = don't know/not applicable

Reaction Ratings:
　　0 = not at all
　　1 = a little
　　2 = moderately
　　3 = very much
　　4 = extremely
　　9 = don't know/not applicable

Please answer all the questions below. Check one box from 0–9 for both
Frequency and **Reaction**.

Frequency	Reaction	
0 1 2 3 4 9	0 1 2 3 4 9	17. Appears sad or depressed.
0 1 2 3 4 9	0 1 2 3 4 9	18. Expressing feelings of hopelessness or sadness about the future (e.g., "Nothing worthwhile ever happens", "I never do anything right").
0 1 2 3 4 9	0 1 2 3 4 9	19. Crying and tearfulness.
0 1 2 3 4 9	0 1 2 3 4 9	20. Commenting about death of self or others (e.g., "Life isn't worth living", "I'd be better off dead").
0 1 2 3 4 9	0 1 2 3 4 9	21. Talking about feeling lonely.
0 1 2 3 4 9	0 1 2 3 4 9	22. Comments about feeling worthless or being a burden to others.
0 1 2 3 4 9	0 1 2 3 4 9	23. Comments about feeling like a failure, or about not having any worthwhile accomplishments in life.
0 1 2 3 4 9	0 1 2 3 4 9	24. Arguing, irritability, and/or complaining.

APPENDIX 6.4: BEHAVIORAL PATHOLOGY IN ALZHEIMER'S DISEASE RATING SCALE

Resident's Name _____

Current Placement _____ Date _____ Sex ☐ M ☐ F

Birthdate _____ Age _____ Evaluator _____

Relationship to Resident: _____

PART 1: Symptomatology: Please check the best response based on the resident's current experience. Specify: _____ weeks.

Part A: Paranoid and delusional

1. "People are stealing things delusion"
   - ☐ (0) Not present
   - ☐ (1) Delusion that people are hiding objects
   - ☐ (2) Delusion that people are coming into the home and hiding objects or stealing objects
   - ☐ (3) Taking and listening to people coming into the home

2. "One's house is not one's home" delusion
   - ☐ (0) Not present
   - ☐ (1) Conviction that the place in which one is living—even temporarily—(e.g. nursing home, hospital) is not where one resides at that moment
   - ☐ (2) Attempt to leave domiciliary to "go home"
   - ☐ (3) Violence in response to attempts to forcibly restrict exit.

3. "Caregiver (or nurse or nursing aide) is an imposter" delusion
   - ☐ (0) Not present
   - ☐ (1) Conviction that caregiver is an imposter (e.g. doesn't work at institution; not responsible for daily care of subject)
   - ☐ (2) Anger towards caregiver for being an imposter
   - ☐ (3) Violence toward caregiver for being an imposter

From "Behavioral Symptoms in Alzheimer's Disease: Phenomenology and Treatment," by B. Reisberg, J. Borenstein, S. P. Salob, & S. H. Ferris, 1987, *Journal of Clinical Psychiatry, 48* (Suppl.), pp. 9–15. Copyright 1986 by Barry Reisberg, MD. Reprinted with permission.

4. Delusion of "abandonment"
   - ☐ (0) Not present
   - ☐ (1) Suspicion that caregiver may abandon the subject (e.g. stop care, desert, forget, leave)
   - ☐ (2) Accusation of a conspiracy to abandon
   - ☐ (3) Accusation of impending or immediate abandonment

5. Delusion of infidelity
   - ☐ (0) Not present
   - ☐ (1) Conviction that caregiver is insincere, disloyal, deceitful, and/or fickle
   - ☐ (2) Anger toward caregiver for being disloyal, insincere, etc.
   - ☐ (3) Violence toward caregiver for being disloyal, insincere, etc.

6. Suspiciousness/paranoia (other than above)
   - ☐ (0) Not present
   - ☐ (1) Suspicious (e.g. hiding objects that he/she may later be unable to locate)
   - ☐ (2) Paranoid (i.e. fixed conviction re suspicions and/or anger as a result of suspicions)
   - ☐ (3) Violence as a result of suspicions
   - ☐ Unspecified? _____

7. Delusions (other than above)
   - ☐ (0) Not present
   - ☐ (1) Vague: not clearly defined
   - ☐ (2) Verbal or emotional manifestations as a result of delusions
   - ☐ (3) Physical actions or violence as a result of delusions
   - ☐ Unspecified? _____

Part B: Hallucinations

8. Visual hallucinations
   - ☐ (0) Not present
   - ☐ (1) Vague: not clearly defined
   - ☐ (2) Clearly defined hallucinations of objects or persons (e.g. sees other people at the table)
   - ☐ (3) Verbal or physical actions or emotional responses to the hallucinations

9. Auditory hallucinations
   - ☐ (0) Not present
   - ☐ (1) Vague: not clearly defined
   - ☐ (2) Clearly defined hallucinations of words or phrases
   - ☐ (3) Verbal or physical actions or emotional responses to the hallucinations

10. Olfactory hallucinations
   - ☐ (0) Not present
   - ☐ (1) Vague: not clearly defined
   - ☐ (2) Clearly defined hallucinations (e.g. smells a fire or "something burning")
   - ☐ (3) Verbal or physical actions or emotional responses to the hallucinations

11. Haptic (sense of touch) hallucinations
   - ☐ (0) Not present
   - ☐ (1) Vague: not clearly defined
   - ☐ (2) Clearly defined hallucinations (e.g. "something is crawling on my body")
   - ☐ (3) Verbal or physical actions or emotional responses to the hallucinations

12. Other hallucinations
   - ☐ (0) Not present
   - ☐ (1) Vague: not clearly defined
   - ☐ (2) Clearly defined hallucinations
   - ☐ (3) Verbal or physical actions or emotional responses to the hallucinations
   - ☐ Unspecified? _____

Part C: Activity Disturbances

13. Wandering away from home or caregiver
   - ☐ (0) Not present
   - ☐ (1) Somewhat, but not sufficient to necessitate restraint
   - ☐ (2) Sufficient to require restraint
   - ☐ (3) Verbal or physical actions or emotional responses to attempts to prevent wandering

14. Purposeless activity (cognitive abulia)
   - ☐ (0) Not present
   - ☐ (1) Repetitive, purposeless activity (e.g. opening and closing pocketbook, packing and unpacking clothing,

repeatedly putting on and removing clothing, opening and closing drawers, insistent repeating of demands or questions)
- □ (2) Pacing or other purposeless activity sufficient to require restraint
- □ (3) Abrasions or physical harm resulting from purposeless activity

15. Inappropriate activity
- □ (0) Not present
- □ (1) Inappropriate activities (e.g. storing and hiding objects in inappropriate places, such as throwing clothing in wastebasket or putting empty plates in the oven; inappropriate sexual behavior, such as inappropriate exposure)
- □ (2) Present and sufficient to require restraint
- □ (3) Present, sufficient to require restraint, and accompanied by anger or violence when restraint is used

Part D: Aggressiveness

16. Verbal outbursts
- □ (0) Not present
- □ (1) Present (including unaccustomed use of foul or abusive language)
- □ (2) Present and accompanied by anger
- □ (3) Present, accompanied by anger, and clearly directed at other persons

17. Physical threats and/or violence
- □ (0) Not present
- □ (1) Threatening behavior
- □ (2) Physical violence
- □ (3) Physical violence accompanied by vehemence

18. Agitation (other than above)
- □ (0) Not present
- □ (1) Present
- □ (2) Present with emotional component
- □ (3) Present with emotional and physical component
- □ Unspecified? _____

Part E: Diurnal Rhythm Disturbances

19. Day/night disturbance
    - ☐ (0) Not present
    - ☐ (1) Repetitive wakenings during the night
    - ☐ (2) 50% to 75% of former sleep cycle at night
    - ☐ (3) Complete disturbance of diurnal rhythm (i.e. less than 50% of former sleep cycle at night)

Part F: Affective Disturbance

20. Tearfulness
    - ☐ (0) Not present
    - ☐ (1) Present
    - ☐ (2) Present and accompanied by clear affective component
    - ☐ (3) Present and accompanied by affective and physical component (e.g. "wrings hands" or other gestures)

21. Depressed mood: other
    - ☐ (0) Not present
    - ☐ (1) Present (e.g. occasional statement "I wish I were dead" without clear affective component)
    - ☐ (2) Present with clear concomitants (e.g. thoughts of death)
    - ☐ (3) Present with emotional and physical concomitants (e.g. suicidal gestures)

Part G: Anxieties and Phobias

22. Anxiety regarding upcoming events (Godot syndrome)
    - ☐ (0) Not present
    - ☐ (1) Present: repeated queries and/or other activities regarding upcoming appointments and/or events
    - ☐ (2) Present and disturbing to caregivers
    - ☐ (3) Present and intolerable to caregivers

23. Other anxieties
    - ☐ (0) Not present
    - ☐ (1) Present
    - ☐ (2) Present and disturbing to caregivers
    - ☐ (3) Present and intolerable to caregivers
    - ☐ Unspecified? _____

24. Fear of being left alone
   □ (0) Not present
   □ (1) Present: vocalized fear of being alone
   □ (2) Vocalized and sufficient to require specific action on part of caregiver
   □ (3) Vocalized and sufficient to require patient to be accompanied at all times

25. Other phobias
   □ (0) Not present
   □ (1) Present
   □ (2) Present and sufficient magnitude to require specific action on part of caregiver
   □ (3) Present and sufficient to prevent patient activities
   □ Unspecified? _____

PART 2: Global Rating

With respect to the above symptoms, they are of sufficient magnitude as to be:
   □ (0) Not at all troubling to the caregiver or dangerous to the patient
   □ (1) Mildly troubling to the caregiver or dangerous to the patient
   □ (2) Moderately troubling to the caregiver or dangerous to the patient
   □ (3) Severely troubling to the caregiver or dangerous to the patient

APPENDIX 6.5: RESIDENT CARE BEHAVIOR LOG

Resident Name: _____

Time & date	Behavior: List and describe	With whom?	Where?	Trigger event(s)	Interventions tried	End result(s)	Effective?	Initials

REFERENCES

Albert, M., & Cohen, C. (1992). The Test for Severe Impairment: An instrument for the assessment of patients with severe cognitive dysfunction. *Journal of the American Geriatrics Society, 40*, 449–453.

Alexopoulos, G. S., Abrams, R. C., Young, R. C., & Shamoian, C. A. (1988). Cornell scale for depression in dementia. *Biological Psychiatry, 23*, 271–284. doi:10.1016/0006-3223(88)90038-8

Algase, D., Beck, C., Kolanowski, A., Whall, A., Berent, S., Richards, K., & Beatty, E. (1996). Need-driven dementia-compromised behavior: An alternative view of disruptive behavior. *American Journal of Alzheimer's Disease and Other Dementias, 11*, 10–19. doi:10.1177/153331759601100603

Allen-Burge, R., Stevens, A. B., & Burgio, L. D. (1999). Effective behavioral interventions for decreasing dementia-related challenging behavior in nursing homes. *International Journal of Geriatric Psychiatry, 14*, 213–228. doi:10.1002/(SICI)1099-1166(199903)14:3<213::AID-GPS974>3.0.CO;2-0

Bartels, S. J., Horn, S. D., Smout, R. J., Dums, A. R., Flaherty, E., Jones, J. K., . . . Voss, A. C. (2003). Agitation and depression in frail nursing home elderly patients with dementia: Treatment characteristics and service. *The American Journal of Geriatric Psychiatry, 11*, 231–238.

Beck, C., Frank, L., Chumbler, N. R., O'Sullivan, P., Vogelpohl, T. S., Rasin, J., . . . Baldwin, B. (1998). Correlates of disruptive behavior in severely cognitively impaired nursing home residents. *The Gerontologist, 38*, 189–198. doi:10.1093/geront/38.2.189

Brotons, M., & Pickett-Cooper, P. (1996). The effects of music therapy intervention on agitation behaviours of Alzheimer's disease patients. *Journal of Music Therapy, 33(1)*, 2–18.

Burgio, L. D., Jones, L. T., Butler, F., & Engler, B. T. (1988). Behavior problems in an urban nursing home. *Journal of Gerontological Nursing, 14*, 31–34.

Burgio, L. D., & Stevens, A. B. (1999). Behavioral interventions and motivational systems in the nursing home. In R. Scultz (Ed.), *Focus on interventions research with older adults* (pp. 284–320). New York, NY: Springer.

Camberg, L., Woods, P., Ooi, W. L., Hurley, A., Volicer, L., Ashley, J., . . . McIntyre, K. (1999). Evaluation of simulated presence: A personalized approach to enhance well-being in persons with Alzheimer's disease. *Journal of the American Geriatrics Society, 47*, 446–452.

Camp, C. J., & Nasser, E. H. (2003). Psychological and nonpharmacological aspects of agitation and behavioral disorders in dementia: Assessment, intervention, and challenges to providing care. In P. Lichtenberg, D. L. Murman, & A. M. Mellow (Eds.), *Handbook of dementia: Psychological, neurological and psychiatric perspectives* (pp. 359–401). Hoboken, NJ: Wiley.

Chan, D. C., Kasper, J. D., Black, B. S., & Rabins, P. V. (2003). Prevalence and correlates of behavioral and psychiatric symptoms in community-dwelling elders with dementia or mild cognitive impairment: The memory and medical care study. *International Journal of Geriatric Psychiatry, 18,* 174–182. doi:10.1002/gps.781

Cohen-Mansfield, J. (1991). *Instruction manual for the Cohen-Mansfield Agitation Inventory.* Rockville, MD: The Research Institute of the Hebrew Home of Greater Washington.

Cohen-Mansfield, J. (2000). Nonpharmacological management of behavioral problems in persons with dementia: the TREA model. *Alzheimer's Care Quarterly, 1,* 22–34.

Cohen-Mansfield, J. (2001). Nonpharmacologic interventions for inappropriate behaviors in dementia. *The American Journal of Geriatric Psychiatry, 9,* 361–381.

Cohen-Mansfield, J., & Deutsch, L. (1996). Agitation: Subtypes and their mechanisms. *Seminars in Clinical Neuropsychiatry, 1,* 325–339.

Cohen-Mansfield, J., Libin, A., & Marx, M.S. (2007). Nonpharmacological treatment of agitation: A controlled trial of systematic individualized intervention. *The Journals of Gerontology. Series A, Biological Sciences and Medical Sciences, 62,* 908–916. doi:10.1093/gerona/62.8.908

Cohen-Mansfield, J., Marx, M.S., & Rosenthal, A.S. (1989). A description of agitation in a nursing home. *The Journals of Gerontology. Series A, Biological Sciences and Medical Sciences, 44,* M77–M84. *doi:10.1093/geronj/44.3.M77*

Cohen-Mansfield, J., & Mintzer, J. (2005). Time for change: The role of nonpharmacological interventions in treating behavior problems in nursing home residents with dementia. *Alzheimer Disease and Associated Disorders, 19,* 37–40. doi:10.1097/01.wad.0000155066.39184.61

Cohen-Mansfield, J., Werner, P., & Marx, M.S. (1989). An observational study of agitation in agitated nursing home residents. *International Psychogeriatrics, 1,* 153–165. doi:10.1017/S1041610289000165

Conely, L.G., & Campbell, L. (1991). The use of restraints in caring for the elderly: Realities, consequences and alternatives. *The Nurse Practitioner, 16,* 48–52. doi:10.1097/00006205-199112000-00012

Cummings, J.L., Mega, M., Gray, K., Rosenberg-Thompson, S., Carusi, D.A., & Gornbein, J. (1994). The neuropsychiatric inventory: Comprehensive assessment of psychopathology in dementia. *Neurology, 44,* 2308–2314.

Curyto, K., Ogland-Hand, S.M., & Vriesman, D.K. (2008). Linking behaviors and interventions: The impact of the dementia living center in its home and community. *Alzheimer's Care Quarterly, 8,* 134–137.

Curyto, K., Van Haitsma, K., & Vriesman, D. (2008). Direct observation of behavior: A review of current methods and measures for use with older adults with dementia. *Journal of Research in Gerontological Nursing, 1,* 1–26.

Daniel, D.G. (2000). Antipsychotic treatment of psychosis and agitation in the elderly. *Journal of Clinical Psychiatry, 61*(Suppl. 14), 49–52.

Davis, L.L., & Burgio, L.D. (1999). Planning cognitive-behavioral management programs for long-term care. *Issues in Mental Health Nursing, 20,* 587–601. doi:10.1080/016128499248385

Davison, T. E., McCabe, M. P., Visser, S., Hudgson, C., Buchanan, G., & George, K. (2007). Controlled trial of dementia training with a peer support group for aged care staff. *International Journal of Geriatric Psychiatry, 22,* 868–873. doi:10.1002/gps.1754

Evans, J. G. (1984). Prevention of age-associated loss of autonomy: Epidemiological approaches. *Journal of Chronic Diseases, 17,* 357–363.

Garland, K., Beer, E., Eppingstall, B., & O'Connor, D. W. (2007). A comparison of two treatments of agitated behavior in nursing home residents with dementia: Simulated family presence and preferred music. *The American Journal of Geriatric Psychiatry, 15,* 514–521. doi:10.1097/01.JGP.0000249388.37080.b4

Gerdner, L. A., Buckwalter, K. C., & Reed, D. (2002). Impact of a psychoeducational intervention on caregiver response to behavioral problems. *Nursing Research, 51,* 363–374. doi:10.1097/00006199-200211000-00004

Gitlin, L. N., Winter, L., Burke, J., Chernett, N., Dennis, M. P., & Hauck, W. W. (2008). Tailored activities to manage neuropsychiatric behaviors in persons with dementia and reduce caregiver burden: A randomized pilot study. *The American Journal of Geriatric Psychiatry, 16,* 229–239.

Hamilton, M. (1960). A rating scale for depression. *Journal of Neurology, Neuro-surgery, and Psychiatry, 23,* 56–62. doi:10.1136/jnnp.23.1.56

Hamilton, M. (1967). Development of a rating scale for primary depressive illness. *The British Journal of Social and Clinical Psychology, 6,* 278–296. doi:10.1111/j.2044-8260.1967.tb00530.x

Hebert, L. E., Scherr, P. A., Bienias, J. L., Bennett, D. A., & Evans, D. A. (2003). Alzheimer disease in the US population: Prevalence estimates using the 2000 census. *Archives of Neurology, 60,* 1119–1122. doi:10.1001/archneur.60.8.1119

Helmes, E., Csapo, K. G., & Short, J. A. (1987). Standardization and validation of the multidimensional observation scale for elderly subjects (MOSES). *Journal of Gerontology, 42,* 395–405.

Huang, H. L., Shyu, Y. L., Chen, M., Chen, S., & Lin, L. (2003). A pilot study on a home-based caregiver training program for improving caregiver self-efficacy and decreasing the behavioral problems of elders with dementia in Taiwan. *International Journal of Geriatric Psychiatry, 18,* 337–345. doi:10.1002/gps.835

Kolanowski, A. M., Richards, K. C., & Sullivan, S. C. (2002). Derivation of an intervention for need-driven behavior: Activity preferences of persons with dementia. *Journal of Gerontological Nursing, 28,* 12–15.

Lawton, M. P., & Nahemow, L. (1973). Ecology and the aging process. In L. Eisdorfer & M. P. Lawton (Eds.), *The psychology of adult development and aging* (pp. 619–674). Washington, DC: American Psychological Association. doi:10.1037/10044-020

Lawton, M. P., Van Haitsma, K., & Klapper, J. (1996). Observed affect in nursing home residents with Alzheimer's disease. *Journal of Gerontology, 51,* 3–14.

Lawton, M.P., Van Haitsma, K., Klapper, J., Kleban, M.H., Katz, I.R., & Corn, J.A. (1998). A stimulation-retreat special care unit for elders with dementing illness. *International Psychogeriatrics, 10,* 379–395. doi:10.1017/S104161029800547X

Levkoff, S., Chen, H., Fisher, J., & McIntyre, J. (2006). *Evidence-based behavioral health practices for older adults: A guide to implementation.* New York, NY: Springer.

Lichtenberg, P.A. (1994). *A guide to psychological practice in geriatric long term care.* Binghamton, NY: Haworth Press.

Lichtenberg, P.A., Kemp-Havican, J., MacNeill, S.E., & Schafer Johnson, A. (2005). Pilot study of behavioral treatment in dementia care units. *The Gerontologist, 45,* 406–410. doi:10.1093/geront/45.3.406

Logsdon, R.G., McCurry, S.M., & Teri, L. (2007). Evidence-based psychological treatments for disruptive behaviors in individuals with dementia. *Psychology and Aging, 22,* 28–36. doi:10.1037/0882-7974.22.1.28

Logsdon, R.G., Teri, L., Weiner, M.F., Gibbons, L.E., Raskind, M., Peskind, E.,...Thal, L.J. (1999). Assessment of agitation in Alzheimer's disease: The Agitated Behavior in Dementia scale. Alzheimer's disease cooperative study. *Journal of the American Geriatrics Society, 47,* 1354–1358.

McCabe, M.P., Davison, T.E., & George, K. (2007). Effectiveness of staff training for behavioral problems among older people with dementia. *Aging & Mental Health, 11,* 505–519. doi:10.1080/13607860601086405

Morris, J.N., Fries, B.E., & Morris, S.A. (1999). Scaling ADLs within the MDS. *The Journals of Gerontology. Series A, Biological Sciences and Medical Sciences, 54,* M546–M553.

Morris, J.N., Hawes, C., Fries, B., Phillips, C., Mor, V., Katz, S.,...Friedlob, A.S. (1990). Designing the national resident assessment instrument for nursing homes. *The Gerontologist, 30,* 293–307. doi:10.1093/geront/30.3.293

Mungas, D., Weiler, M., Franzi, C., & Henry, R. (1989). Assessment of disruptive behavior associated with dementia: The disruptive behavior rating scales. *Journal of Geriatric Psychiatry and Neurology, 2,* 196–202. doi:10.1177/089198878900200405

Ogland-Hand, S.M., & Zeiss, A.M. (2000). Interprofessional health care teams in long-term care. In V. Molinari (Ed.), *Professional psychology in long term care* (pp. 257–277). New York, NY: Hatherleigh Press.

Opie, J., Doyle, C., & O'Connor, D.W. (2002). Challenging behaviours in nursing home residents with dementia: A randomized controlled trial of multidisciplinary interventions. *International Journal of Geriatric Psychiatry, 17,* 6–13. doi:10.1002/gps.493

Opie, J., Rosewarne, R., & O'Connor, D.W. (1999). The efficacy of psychosocial approaches to behavior disorders in dementia: A systematic literature review. *Australian & New Zealand Journal of Psychiatry, 33,* 789–799. doi:10.1046/j.1440-1614.1999.00652.x

Proctor, R., Burns, A., Powell, H.S., Tarrier, N., Faragher, B., Richardson, G.,... South, B. (1999). Behavioural management in nursing and residential homes:

A randomized controlled trial. *The Lancet*, *354*, 26–29. doi:10.1016/S0140-6736(98)08237-3

Prodger, N., Hurley, J., Clarke, C., & Bauer, D. (1992). Queen Elizabeth behavioural assessment graphical system. *The Australian Journal of Advanced Nursing*, *9*, 4–11.

Putman, L., & Wang, J. T. (2007). The closing group: Therapeutic recreation for nursing home residents with dementia and accompanying agitation and/or anxiety. *American Journal of Alzheimer's Disease & Other Dementias*, *22*, 167–175. doi:10.1177/1533317507300514

Reisberg, B., Borenstein, M. D., Salob, S. P., Ferris, S. H., Franssen, E., & Georgotas, A. (1987). Behavioral symptoms in Alzheimer's disease: Phenomenology and treatment. *Journal of Clinical Psychiatry*, *48*(suppl.), 9–15.

Rewilak, D. (2007). Behavior management strategies. In D. K. Conn et al. (Eds.), *Practical psychiatry in the long-term care home* (3rd ed., pp. 217–237). Ashland, OH: Hogrefe & Huber.

Rovner, B. W., Steele, C. D., Shmuely, Y., & Folstein, M. (1996). A randomized trial of dementia care in nursing homes. *Journal of the American Geriatrics Society*, *44*, 7–13.

Shankar, K. K., Walker, M., Frost, D., & Orrell, M. W. (1999). The development of a valid and reliable scale for rating anxiety in dementia (RAID). *Aging & Mental Health*, *3*, 39–49. doi:10.1080/13607869956424

Sixsmith, A., Stilwell, J., & Copeland, J., (2004). Rementia: Challenging the limits of dementia care. *International Journal of Geriatric Psychology*. *8*, 993–1000.

Stevens, A. B., Burgio, L. D., Bailey, E., Burgio, K. L., Paul, P., Capilouto, E., . . . Hale, G. (1998). Teaching and maintaining behavior management skills with nursing assistants in a nursing home. *The Gerontologist*, *38*, 379–384. doi:10.1093/geront/38.3.379

Streim, J. (2004, May). *New evidence regarding the safety of pharmacologic interventions for management of the behavioral aspects of dementia*. Presented at the Annual Meeting of the American Geriatrics Society, Las Vegas, NV.

Teri, L., Gibbons, L. E., McCurry, S. M., Logsdon, R. G., Buchner, D. M., Barlow, W. E., . . . Larson, E. B. (2003). Exercise plus behavioral management in patients with Alzheimer disease: A randomized controlled trial. *JAMA*, *290*, 2015–2022. doi:10.1001/jama.290.15.2015

Teri, L., Huda, P., Gibbons, L., Young, H., & van Leynseele, J. (2005). STAR: A dementia-specific training program for staff in assisted living residences. *The Gerontologist*, *45*, 686–693. doi:10.1093/geront/45.5.686

Teri, L., Logsdon, R. G., Uomoto, J., & McCurry, S. (1997). Behavioral treatment of depression in dementia patients: A controlled clinical trial. *Journals of Gerontology. Series B, Psychological Sciences*, *52*, P159–P166. doi:10.1093/geronb/52B.4.P159

Teri, L., McCurry, S. M., Logsdon, R. G., & Gibbons, L. E. (2005). Training community consultants to help family members improve dementia care: A randomized controlled trial. *The Gerontologist*, *45*, 802–811. doi:10.1093/geront/45.6.802

Teri, L., Truax, P., Logsdon, R., Uomoto, J., Zarit, S., & Vitaliano, P. P. (1992). Assessment of behavioral problems in dementia: The Revised Memory and Behavior Problem-Checklist (RMBPC). *Psychology and Aging, 7,* 622–631. doi:10.1037/0882-7974.7.4.622

Visser, S. M., McCabe, M. P., Hudgson, C., Buchanan, G., Davison, T. E., & George, K. (2008). Managing behavioural symptoms of dementia: Effectiveness of staff education and peer support. *Aging & Mental Health, 12,* 47–55. doi:10.1080/13607860701366012

Volicer, L., Simard, J., Pupa, J., Medrek, R., & Riordan, M. (2006). Effects of continuous activity programming on behavioral symptoms of dementia. *Journal of the American Medical Directors Association, 7,* 426–431. doi:10.1016/j.jamda.2006.02.003

Woods, P., & Ashley, J. (1995). Simulated presence therapy: Using selected memories to manage problem behaviors in Alzheimer's disease patients. *Geriatric Nursing, 16,* 9–14. doi:10.1016/S0197-4572(05)80072-2

Zarit, S., Todd, P. A., & Zarit, J. M. (1986). Subjective burden of husbands and wives as caregivers: A longitudinal study. *The Gerontologist, 26,* 260–266. doi:10.1093/geront/26.3.260

Zeiss, A. M., & Steffen, A. M. (1996). Interdisciplinary health care team: The basic unit of geriatric care. In L. L. Cartensen, B. A. Eldstein, & L. Dornbrand (Eds.), *The practical handbook of clinical gerontology* (pp. 424–450). Thousand Oaks, CA: Sage.

7

EVIDENCE-BASED PSYCHOLOGICAL TREATMENTS FOR DISTRESS IN FAMILY CAREGIVERS OF OLDER ADULTS

DAVID W. COON, MAUREEN KEAVENY, IRENE RIVERA VALVERDE, SHUKOFEH DADVAR, AND DOLORES GALLAGHER-THOMPSON

Over 45 million Americans provide on average about 21 hours per week of unpaid care to aging adults debilitated by physical and mental health ailments in the United States (National Alliance for Caregiving & AARP, 2009). Family caregiving is clearly the backbone of long-term care, providing the most important source of assistance for people with chronic conditions that require consistent care. When the economic value of informal (unpaid) family care is defined as the costs of replacing this care with formal (paid) care at a cost of $10 per hour, the estimated value of family care in 2007 was $375 billion. This amount is more than total Medicaid spending ($311 billion), including both federal and state contributions for medical and long-term care, and it approached the total amount of Medicare program expenditures ($432 billion; Houser & Gibson, 2008). In addition to the monetary cost associated with caregiving, the price to family caregivers often includes negative physical, emotional, and social outcomes, such as depressive symptoms, anxiety, anger, poorer health, social isolation, and heightened rates of mortality (Bakas, Pressler, Johnson, Nauser, & Shaneyfelt, 2006; Coon et al., 2004; Gallagher, Rose, Rivera, Lovett, & Thompson, 1989; Gallagher, Wrabetz, Lovett, Del-Maestro, & Rose, 1989; Gaugler, 2010; Haley et al., 2004; Schulz & Beach, 1999; Vitaliano, Zhang, & Scanlan, 2003).

The debilitating consequences of caregiver distress and their reluctance to seek assistance result in circumstances in which family caregivers become society's hidden patients. The distress of providing care for a family member is often cumulative, arising from multiple factors: the increasing toll of stress and strain due to the care recipient's disease progression (Bainbridge, Krueger, Lohfeld, & Brazil, 2009; Riedijk et al., 2006); the loss of a sense of control due to the unpredictable course of illnesses such as Alzheimer's disease (Bakas et al., 2006) and the unexpected behavioral challenges exhibited by the care recipient (Lu & Wykle, 2007; Quinn, Clare, & Woods, 2009); the absence of social support that provides relief from caregiving tasks or the opportunity to safely express caregiving frustrations and concerns (Roth, Mittelman, Clay, Madan, & Haley, 2005; Wight, Aneshensel, & LeBlanc, 2003); the tug-of-war experienced by many family caregivers who are struggling to juggle multiple roles and responsibilities (National Alliance for Caregiving, 2010); and the feelings of helplessness associated with a lack of preparedness in terms of the energy and skills necessary to meet caregiving demands (Mausbach et al., 2007; Son et al., 2007). The rise in the proportion of older adults in U.S. society and the increasing diversity of that segment of the population have not only led to a growing demand for informal caregivers (Administration on Aging, 2009a; Centers for Disease Control and Prevention, & Merck Company, 2007; Spillman & Black, 2005) but has also spawned a variety of interventions to address the needs of caregivers who are assisting loved ones in divergent sociocultural contexts (Coon, Ory, & Schulz, 2003).

With the growing number of interventions available for family caregivers, the purpose of this chapter is first to identify evidence-based psychological interventions designed to reduce caregiver distress. Moreover, two authors share their approach in implementing one of evidenced-based caregiver interventions, thus exemplifying the translation of research into evidence-based practice. Finally, this chapter includes resources designed to assist interested readers in translating evidence-based caregiver interventions into everyday practice.

EVIDENCE-BASED INTERVENTIONS
FOR FAMILY CAREGIVERS OF OLDER ADULTS

This section provides an overview of evidence-based psychological interventions designed to reduce distress in family caregivers of impaired older adults and extends previous work (Coon & Evans, 2009; Gallagher-Thompson & Coon, 2007) in this arena by reviewing caregiver interventions studies through 2008. In contrast to other chapters in this book, participants in the studies reviewed here may or may not have been older adults themselves but rather were family members who provided assistance to cognitively or physically impaired older adults. Moreover, the multidisciplinary gerontological literature on family caregiving has spawned a variety of intervention approaches (e.g., psychoeducational–skill building, psychotherapy, case management, support groups, respite) to alleviate family caregiver distress; however, in keeping with other reviews in this book, we narrowed our final evidence-based treatment (EBT) coding and analysis to studies of interventions that target caregiver distress that were grounded in psychological theories or models of behavior change.

In brief, this chapter mirrors our earlier work (please see Gallagher-Thompson & Coon, 2007, review for details) by (a) emphasizing treatments that use psychological theories or frameworks of behavior change; (b) using a more rather than less inclusive definition of caregiver distress by encompassing both negative outcomes (e.g., depression, caregiver burden, anger, stress) and positive outcomes (e.g., coping skills, self-efficacy, quality of life, support seeking, and social support satisfaction) related to family caregiving for impaired older adults; (c) classifying caregiver interventions into three overarching categories (psychoeducational–skill building, psychotherapy–counseling, and multicomponent) that are consistent with the established caregiving intervention literature (e.g., Bourgeois et al., 1996; Coon, Ory, & Schulz, 2003; Gatz et al., 1998; Schulz, Martire, & Klinger, 2005; Sörensen, Pinquart, & Duberstein, 2002); and (d) considering the interventions within these overarching categories to be consistent enough in their approaches to be grouped and evaluated together as an EBT for family caregivers of impaired older adults. These categories and related exemplars are described in the remainder of this section.

Tables 7.1, 7.2, and 7.3 provide summaries of the EBT findings for caregiver distress. Each table corresponds to one of the three overarching classifications of caregiver interventions. Table 7.1 delineates five subcategories that emerged within the overarching classification of psychoeducational–skill-building studies. Note that some studies in this table appear more than once because they tested multiple interventions in their clinical trials. Table 7.2 describes the psychotherapeutic–counseling studies, and Table 7.3 highlights the multicomponent studies. Updated and adapted from our previous reviews (Coon & Evans, 2009; Gallagher-Thompson & Coon, 2007), these tables describe the interventions and denote reductions, improvements, or both, in the specified outcomes that were identified at one or more of the postintervention assessment points. Each table also provides notations in regard to studies with samples from countries other than the United States as well as studies that report findings on culturally or ethnically diverse samples within this country. Moreover, all outcomes listed are for the family caregivers themselves unless otherwise specified. Finally, these tables present an

TABLE 7.1

Psychoeducational Skill-Building Caregiver (CG) Intervention Studies

Authors	Sample	Conditions	Manual protocol	Length of treatment	Outcome measure	Finding
Behavioral management skill training						
Beauchamp et al., 2005	N = 307 (299 completed) CG; M age = 46.9; female = 73%; child = 67%; Caucasian = 80%, African American = 4%, Hispanic = 8%	Condition 1: CG's friend: dealing with dementia (CFDwD; n = 150); web-based multimedia intervention providing text and videos modeling positive caregiving strategies; individualized tailoring through questionnaires Condition 2: wait-list control (WLC; n = 149)	Condition 1: full description of intervention in Beauchamp et al. (2005); grounded in stress appraisal and coping theory	30 days; 3 online modules available to be viewed multiple times within the time frame	CG stress appraisal; CG self-efficacy; Revised Ways of Coping checklist (measures on problem-focused strategies and social support); Caregiver Strain Instrument (Bass et al., 1998); Positive Aspects of Caregiving (Tarlow et al., 2004); Center for Epidemiologic Studies Depression Scale (CES-D); Suicidal ideation (Lewinsohn et al., 1996); State–Trait Anxiety Inventory (STAI)	CFDwD > WLC for CG self-efficacy, intention to get support, and CG gain at post

| Bourgeois et al., 2002 | N = 93 (63 completed); dementia CGs, majority spouse; M age = 73 years | All CGs had one 3-hr workshop; Condition 1: patient change (PC), taught behavior management skills Condition 2: self-change (SC), taught increasing pleasant events, problem solving, and relaxation Condition 3: control—workshop only | Lewinsohn et al. (1986); D'Zurilla (1986) | 12 weeks; Weeks 3–12: 1-hr home visit with CG in all 3 conditions | Direct measure of effect: CG mood rating (adapted from Lewinsohn et al., 1986); indirect measure included STA Expression Inventory (STAXI); STAI; Perceived Stress Scale; CES-D; CG Self-Efficacy Assessment; CG Health Index | PC > control for CG positive mood at post and 6-month follow-up; SC > control for mood at post-, 3-month, and 6-month follow-up; in terms of indirect measures, positive effects for PC and SC on depression (posttest), CG strain (3 months); PC > control on self-efficacy for patient management (3 and 6 months) and perceived stress (posttest); SC > control on strain at 6 months |

(continues)

TABLE 7.1
Psychoeducational Skill-Building Caregiver (CG) Intervention Studies *(Continued)*

Authors	Sample	Conditions	Manual protocol	Length of treatment	Outcome measure	Finding
Davis et al., 2004	N = 71 > 50, dementia CGs; care recipient (CR) Mini-Mental State Examination (MMSE) ≤ 24, 4 or more behavioral problems; CGs lived with CR	Condition 1: In-home training (IHT) Condition 2: Telephone training (TT) Condition 3: Social support calls: control condition "friendly calls"	Full description of intervention in Davis et al. (2004); grounded in stress appraisal and coping theory	12 weeks; IHT: training in problem solving, behavior and anger management, and relaxation skills; TT: same content but by phone	Screen for CG burden (burden and distress), Geriatric Depression Scale (GDS), Caregiver Life Satisfaction	At post and 3 months; IHT > TT > control on burden and distress
Gonyea et al., 2006	N = 91 (80 completed); dementia CGs 4 hr per week of direct care to CR with dementia, MMSE ≥ 10, 1 neuropsychiatric symptom; CG *M* age = 64.4; mostly women (67%); spouse (59%), adult children (32%)	Condition 1: behavioral intervention group (BI; n = 40) Condition 2: psychoeducational group, general information on aging and Alzheimer's (control; n = 40); trial targeted CR neuropsychiatric symptoms and CG distress; only CG outcomes are reported here	Condition 1: full description of intervention in Gonyea et al. (2006); based on Coping with Caregiving (Gallagher-Thompson et al., 2003)	Condition 1 (BI): 5 small group sessions, 90 min each session Condition 2 (control): 5 small group sessions, 90 min each session	Neuropsychiatric Inventory (Cummings et al., 1994) severity and distress; Zarit Burden Interview (ZBI; O'Rourke & Tuokko, 2003)	BI > control on CG distress

Study	Sample	Conditions	Intervention details	Outcome measures	Results
Graff et al., 2006	N = 135 (114 completed) CG/CR dyads; CR ≥ 65, dementia diagnosis, mild (9–24) and moderate (25–40) scores on Brief Cognitive Rating Scale (BCRS), GDS ≤ 12; CG M age = 63.7; mostly female (70%); partners (59%), daughters (32%)	Condition 1: Graff et al. (2006)	Condition 1: occupational therapy (OT; n = 68); therapy included OT for the CR and psychoeducational skill building (problem solving, coping strategies) for the CG Condition 2: WLC (n = 67)	Condition 1: ten 1-hr sessions over 5 weeks; Sessions 1–4 focus on goals and selection of meaningful activities; Session 5–10 learn compensatory and environmental strategies to reach goals	CG competence (Vernooij-Dassen et al., 1996); CES-D	OT > WLC on CG feelings of competence at 6 weeks and 12 weeks after start of program
Perren et al., 2006	N = 128, CR–CG dyads; CR with mild-to-moderate dementia, lives together or within walking distance; CG M age = 68.4; CR M age = 74.7; 63% of CG and 44% of CR were women; 90% of CG were spouses	Condition 1: Perren et al. (2006) Condition 2: Wettstein et al. (2005)	Condition 1: caregiver education session (CES; n = 65; disease education, support-seeking skills, relationship skills) Condition 2: memory training booklet (control; n = 63)	Condition 1: eight 2-hr weekly group sessions Condition 2: dyad mailed booklet and asked to practice weekly for 8 weeks; materials are delivered in German	Positive and negative affect from the Swiss health survey (Weiss et al., 1990); Schedule for the Evaluation of Individualized Quality of Life (Meier et al., 1999); scales combined for an overall CG well-being measure	CES > control for overall CG well-being

(continues)

TABLE 7.1
Psychoeducational Skill-Building Caregiver (CG) Intervention Studies *(Continued)*

Authors	Sample	Conditions	Manual protocol	Length of treatment	Outcome measure	Finding
Teri et al., 1997	$N = 88$, CG–CR pairs; CRs met criteria for probable Alzheimer's disease and major or minor depression; $N = 72$ pairs completed; CG M age = 67, CR M age = 76; 31% of CGs were men; 69% were women	Condition 1: Behavior Therapy/Problem Solving (BTPS) Condition 2: Behavior Therapy/Pleasant Events (BTPE Condition 3: usual care (UC) Condition 4: waiting list (WL); this randomized clinical trial targeted patient outcomes but had a significant effect on depression for CGs; only CG outcome is reported here	Manual for BTPE; focus of finding and experiencing shared pleasant events for CG–CR pair; BTPS, less structured CGs use problem solving to alleviate depression in CR	60-min weekly sessions for 9 weeks for Conditions 1 and 2	Hamilton Depression Rating Scale (Hamilton, 1960)	CGs greater improvement in depression in BTPS and BTPE; BTPS = BTPE

	Depression management skill training				
Coon, Thompson, et al., 2003	N = 169, all women, all dementia CGs; M age = 64 years; 60% wives, 40% daughters	Condition 1: anger management class (AMC; n = 41); cognitive and behavioral techniques to recognize and manage frustration; cognitive reappraisal and relations. Condition 2: depression management class (DMC (n = 45); cognitive and behavioral techniques to manage depression; increase pleasant events and problem solving. Condition 3: WLC (n = 44)	Condition 1 (AMC): Anger Management cognitive behavioral therapy (CBT; Novaco, 1975; Feindler & Ecton, 1986). Condition 2 (DMC): Behavior Therapy (Beck et al., 1979; Lewinsohn, 1974; specific manuals for these interventions available from the authors. Condition 1 (AMC): ten 2-hr sessions. Condition 2 (DMC): ten 2-hr sessions; both AMC and DMC are small-group interventions. Condition 3: wait-list	STAXI, Multiple Affect Adjective checklist (Hostility and Depression subscales), Revised Ways of Coping Checklist (measure of adaptive-positive and negative coping), Self-Efficacy for caregiving	At posttest, both AMC and DMC > WLC: less depression and higher self-efficacy; AMC > DMC and WLC for increase in positive coping strategies over time; anger expression style and level of depression moderated the relative effects of both interventions on mood and coping

(continues)

TABLE 7.1
Psychoeducational Skill-Building Caregiver (CG) Intervention Studies *(Continued)*

Authors	Sample	Conditions	Manual protocol	Length of treatment	Outcome measure	Finding
Gallagher-Thompson et al., 2003	*N* = 213, female dementia CGs (91 Hispanic Latino, 122 Caucasian Anglo); *M* age = 57 years; for Anglos, majority were spouses; for Latinos, majority were daughters or daughters-in-law; majority of Latinos identified as Mexican American, and additional analysis was conducted comparing this group with Anglos	Condition 1: Coping with Caregiving class (CWC; *n* = 105); combined features of AMC and DMC (Coon et al., 2003) focused on cognitive restructuring, behavior, and mood management skills Condition 2: enhanced support group (ESG; *n* = 108); patterned after typical community-led groups but had professional facilitator and met weekly, not monthly	Condition 1 (CWC): CBT (Beck et al., 1979; Lewinsohn, 1974) Condition 2 (ESG): CG support groups (Alzheimer's Association); manuals for both conditions are available from the authors in English and Spanish	Condition 1 (CWC): ten 2-hr group sessions Condition 2 (ESG): ten 2-hr group sessions; both CWC and ESG are small-group interventions and were delivered in English and Spanish as needed	CES-D; Revised Memory and Behavior Problem Checklist (RMBPC-CB; Teri et al., 1992); Bother scale, Revised Ways of Coping Checklist (measure of adaptive– positive and negative coping), social support satisfaction and negative interaction	Overall CWC > ESG for reducing depressive symptoms, increasing adaptive coping, and reducing negative coping; no differences by ethnicity and no effect of ESG > CWC; for analysis with Anglo and Mexican American participants only, CWC > ESG in reducing depressive symptoms, increasing positive coping, and reducing negative interactions and problem behavior bother

Study	Sample	Intervention	Measures	Outcomes
Gallagher-Thompson et al., 2008	N = 184 (156 completed); female dementia CGs (89 Hispanic Latinas, 95 non-Hispanic White); M age = 58; for Hispanic Latina CGs, 22.4% were spouses; for non-Hispanic White CGs; 52.6% were spouses	Condition 1: Updated CWC (n = 97) Condition 2: telephone support condition (TSC; n = 87); Empathic support delivered via telephone with CGs	Condition 1: Gallagher-Thompson et al. (2000, 2001, 2003, 2008); Gallagher-Thompson et al. (2001); all materials were available in English and Spanish	Condition 1 (CWC): thirteen 2-hr group sessions Condition 2 (TSC): seven 15–20 min telephone calls every 2 weeks; CGs also were mailed educational materials	CES-D; Perceived Stress Scale; RMBPC-CB subscale; Skill Utilization Questionnaire (SUQ)	CWC > TSC in reducing CG depression, perceived stress, and bother
Gallagher-Thompson et al., 2007	N = 55 (45 completed); all Chinese female CGs who provided 8 hr/week of care for at least 6 months; CR MMSE ≤ 23 and unable to perform one or more activities of daily living (ADLs) or two or more instrumental ADLs (IADLs), or dementia diagnosis; CG provide care	Condition 1: in-home behavioral management program (IHBMP; n = 22) focused on skills to help CG cope with stress Condition 2: telephone-based comparison treatment (TSC; n = 23)	Condition 1: Gallagher-Thompson et al. (2007); Gallagher-Thompson et al. (2001); Gallagher-Thompson et al. (2003); specific manuals for these interventions are available from the first author	Condition 1 (IHBMP): 3–4 months, including seven 90-min sessions covering 6 modules Condition 2 (TSC): 12 weeks, including initial and 6 phone calls every 2 weeks	CES-D; Perceived Stress Scale; Conditional Bother Subscale (CBS); CG self-efficacy	IHBMP > TSC in reduction of CG bother

(continues)

Authors	Sample	Conditions	Manual protocol	Length of treatment	Outcome measure	Finding
	for 8 hr/week for 6 months; CGs completing program; mean age = 59; 31.1% were spouses					
Gallagher-Thompson et al., 2000	N = 161, physically and/or cognitively impaired CGs (134 women, 27 men); about half were spouses, and half were adult children; M age = 60 years	Condition 1: Increasing Life Satisfaction group (LS; n = 56): focus on increasing pleasant events, identifying and resolving obstacles Condition 2: problem-solving skills group (PS; n = 59); taught six-step model (e.g., define problem, brainstorm solutions, evaluate, and modify) Condition 3: WLC (n = 46): no contact	Condition 1 (LS): behavior therapy (Lewinsohn, 1974) Condition 2 (PS): problem solving (D'Zurilla, 1986)	Condition 1 (LS): 10 sessions, 2 hr each Condition 2 (PS): 10 sessions, 2 hr each	Schedule for Affective Disorders and Schizophrenia (SADS; interview for depression diagnosis; Endicott & Spitzer, 1978), Perceived Stress Scale (Cohen et al., 1983), burden from the Caregiver Task Checklist (Poulshock & Deimling, 1984), coping scales from Health and Daily Living Questionnaire (Moos et al., 1984)	LS > PS and WLC on improvement in depression diagnoses (SADS); LS > WLC on increasing behavioral coping and reducing burden; PS > WLC on increasing cognitive and behavioral coping

Study	Sample	Conditions	Intervention basis	Intervention format	Measures	Results
Márquez-González et al., 2007	N = 74 (39 completed) Spanish dementia CGs; 3 hr of care for at least 8 months; CG; M age = 56.5, mostly female (79.5%), spouses = 47.8%, sons = 46.5%	Condition 1: modification of dysfunctional thoughts about caregiving intervention (MDTC; n = 34); modules focused on managing dysfunctional thoughts and improving CG coping skills Condition 2: WLC (n = 40)	Condition 1: manual, in part, derived from Gallagher-Thompson et al. (2003); Losada (2005); Dick & Gallagher-Thompson (1995); Kaplan & Gallagher-Thompson (1995)	Condition 1: eight 2-hr group sessions	CES-D; Memory and Behavior Problems Checklist (MBPC; Zarit & Zarit, 1982); Dysfunctional Thoughts about Caregiving Questionnaire (DTCQ; Losada et al., 2006)	MDTC > WLC reduction in CG dysfunctional thoughts of caregiving and negative appraisal of behavioral problems
Progressively lowered stress threshold model						
Buckwalter et al., 1999	N = 245, dementia family caregivers; M age = 64 years, >4 hr care–week, global deterioration score < 3	Condition 1: progressively lowered stress threshold (PLST; n = 132); individualized needs assessment tool to guide teaching, demonstration of skills related to individualized care plan Condition 2: routine care condition (RC; n = 108);	Condition 1: manual based on PLST model (Hall & Buckwalter, 1987)	Condition 1 (PLST): 3–4 hr of in-home intervention focused on developing low stimulus care plan; biweekly phone calls for 6 months Condition 2 (RC): in-home visits receiving general information and same telephone follow-up	POMS Depression subscale (McNair et al., 1971); GDS; Yesavage et al., 1983)	At 6 months, PLST > RC on POMS depression; at 6 and 12 months, PLST > RC on GDS

(continues)

TABLE 7.1

Psychoeducational Skill-Building Caregiver (CG) Intervention Studies *(Continued)*

Authors	Sample	Conditions	Manual protocol	Length of treatment	Outcome measure	Finding
		information community services and referrals for case management and support groups				
Huang et al., 2003	*N* = 48, dementia CGs from Northern Taiwan	Condition 1: In-home PLST (IH; *n* = 24); clinician identified targeted behavioral problems and plan to address Condition 2: control condition (control; *n* = 24); social contact phone calls every 2 weeks and written material	Manual based on PLST model (Hall & Buckwalter, 1987)	Condition 1 (IH): 2-session in-home training separated by 1 week lasting 2–3 hr Condition 2 (control): written educational materials; both received biweekly telephone calls	Chinese version of Cohen-Mansfield Agitation Inventory (CMAI); Agitation Management Self-Efficacy Scale, developed by the authors for each behavioral problem identified on CMAI, CG asked how confident to handle problems	CG self-efficacy for management of behavioral problems increased in PLST > control; at posttest and 3 months, PLST > control for reducing physically nonaggressive behavior, verbally aggressive and nonaggressive behavioral, and overall CMAI

Anger management skill training

Study	Sample	Conditions		Intervention	Measures	Outcomes
Coon, Thompson, et al., 2003	See entry above in depression management skills section	See entry above in depression management skills section	See entry above in depression management skills section	See entry above in depression management skills section	See entry above in depression management skills section	At posttest, both AMC and DMC >WLC: less anger and hostility, and higher self-efficacy; AMC >DMC and WLC for increase in positive coping strategies over time; anger expression style and level of depression moderated the relative effects of both interventions on mood and coping
Steffen, 2000	$N = 33$, 40–82 years old; 5 hr per week of direct care to CR with dementia	Condition 1: home-based anger management (HM; $n = 12$) Condition 2: Class-based anger management (CL; $n = 9$)	Conditions: Anger Management CBT (Novaco; 1975, 1977, 1985; Ecton & Feindler, 1990)	Condition 1 (HM): 8 videotapes, 30 min each + 20 min phone call by therapist to reinforce learning and respond to questions	Caregiver Anger Interview, Beck Depression Inventory (BDI); and self-efficacy for responding to disruptive patient behaviors	HM and CL > WL on reducing levels of anger and increasing CG self-efficacy for managing CR disruptive behaviors. HM > WL on depression

(continues)

Authors	Sample	Conditions	Manual protocol	Length of treatment	Outcome measure	Finding
		In both Conditions 1 and 2, CGs watched videos teaching anger management skills; in HM, this was done at home; in CL condition, it was done in a small group Condition 3: waitlist condition (WL; *n* = 12)		Condition 2 (CL): 8 sessions, 90 min each to watch videos and discuss. Videos taught cognitive and behavioral skills to manage anger and frustration		
			Mixed			
Fung & Chien, 2002	*N* = 60 enrolled; 52 male and female dementia CGs (19 men and 33 women) completed; all were Chinese from Hong Kong	Condition 1: mutual support (MS; *n* = 30); psychological support, education, sharing and discussion, and problem solving	Based on Almberg et al. (1997); Hinrichsen & Niederehe (1994); and Toseland et al. (1989)	Condition 1 (MS): 12 weeks, 1 hr each, in small groups Condition 2 (control): received usual care	Neuropsychiatric Inventory– Caregiver Distress Scale (NPI-D) in Chinese and WHO Quality of Life scale (WHOQOL) in Chinese	MS > control on NPI-D (CG distress) and WHOQOL; CGs in MS had significant reduction in distress levels for managing delusions,

hallucinations, agitation, and overexcitement as well as increases in psychological and social quality of life

DCMP > SC reducing CG burden and improving CG quality of life

Chinese versions of the following: Family Caregiver Burden Inventory (Chou et al., 2002); WHOQOL; Social Support Questionnaire (Sarason et al., 1987)

Condition 1 (DCMP): in addition to standard care (pharmacotherapy, social and recreation activities for CR, and written educational material for CG), DCMP group received twelve 2-hr biweekly sessions based on CG–CR dyad needs (e.g., problem solving, stress management); additional biweekly home visits by case managers and

Condition 1 (DCMP) based on Belle et al. (2006) and Fung & Chien (2002) intervention

Condition 2: control (n = 30); treatment as usual, including social work, nursing, and social services

Condition 1: dementia care management program (DCMP; n = 44) Condition 2: standard care (SC; n = 44)

N = 88, Chinese dementia CGs; M age = 43.6; 64% were female; spouses = 32% and children = 36%

Chien & Lee, 2008

(continues)

TABLE 7.1
Psychoeducational Skill-Building Caregiver (CG) Intervention Studies *(Continued)*

Authors	Sample	Conditions	Manual protocol	Length of treatment	Outcome measure	Finding
				monthly health assessments were provided Condition 2 (SC): standard care and 6 monthly education sessions on dementia care		
Ostwald et al., 1999	*N* = 117; CR has mild–severe dementia, CG average age was 65; *n* = 94 families completed the program	Condition 1: Minnesota Family Workshop (MFW; *n* = 72); education, family support, and skills training for CGs and their families; included information about dementia; practical skill development to handling caregiving; workshops involved interdisciplinary faculty and	Condition 1 (MFW): Stress mediation model (Aneshensel, Pearlin, Mullan, Zarit, & Whitlatch, 1995; Folkman, Lazarus, Gruen, & DeLongis, 1986)	Condition 1 (MFW): 7 sessions, 2 hr each, delivered in a workshop format by using written curriculum, videos, exercises, and homework	Revised Caregiver Burden Scale; CESD; RMBPC reaction-response	At follow-up, MFW > WLC on burden and CG response to disruptive behaviors

Study	Sample	Conditions		Measures	Results
Hepburn et al. (2001)	See Ostwald et al. (1999)	See Ostwald et al. (1999)	focused on family involvement by using group-process techniques to involve all family participants as active learners and resources for primary CGs Condition 2: wait-list control (WLC; n = 45)	See Ostwald et al. (1999)	See Ostwald et al. (1999)	See Ostwald et al. (1999); in addition, Beliefs about Caregiving Scale subscales nurturing and monitoring	In addition to results in Ostwald et al. (1999), MFW > WL on depression and nurturing at 5-month follow-up
Toseland et al., 1989	N = 56; CGs randomly assigned to 1 of 3 groups, with 52 CGs who completed treatment; CGs were all adult daughters and daughters-in-law of a parent	Condition 1: groups led by professionals (n = 18) Condition 2: groups led by peers. (n = 18) Condition 3: respite only (n = 20)	Conditions 1 and 2 relied heavily on supportive interventions, such as ventilation of stressful experiences, validation of experiences,	All groups met for 8 weekly 2-hr sessions	Zarit Burden Interview (ZBI; Bedard et al., 2001; Problems with Caregiving) Bradburn Affect Balance, Brief Symptom Inventory, Pressing	No difference on perceived burden; peer and professional groups > respite only on affect balance, global severity, and positive symptom

(continues)

TABLE 7.1
Psychoeducational Skill-Building Caregiver (CG) Intervention Studies *(Continued)*

Authors	Sample	Conditions	Manual protocol	Length of treatment	Outcome measure	Finding
	with a chronic disability who resided in the community; *M* age = 51.3		praise, and support Condition 1 had additional education and problem solving using 6-step model Condition 2 peer group was less structured		Problem Change Index, and other personal change variables	index of Brief Symptom Inventory and personal change variables
Smith & Toseland, 2006	*N* = 97 (89 completed) CG; Caregiver Strain Index ≥ 7 and CR have 2 or more ADL–IADL impairments; *M* age of spouse CG = 66.2; *M* age of adult child CG = 54.9; mostly female (88.4%); 63% adult children and 37% spouses	Condition 1: telephone support group (TSG; multicomponent intervention, includes education, coping strategies, problem solving, and support Condition 2: wait-list control (WLC; *n* = 44)	Condition 1 (TSG): Smith and Toseland (2006); modified from Toseland et al. (1992); manuals available from authors	Condition 1 (TSG): 12 weekly 90-min telephone group sessions; group leader manuals and participant workbooks used during the telephone session Condition 2 (WLC): usual services by senior services center	Medical Outcomes Study Social Support Survey; ZBI; CES-D; STAI; Pressing Problems Index (Toseland et al., 2001, 2004)	TSG > WLC in reducing CG burden and strain, as well as in reducing CG depression; additionally, TSG > WLC in improving positive social interactions for CGs

TABLE 7.2

Psychotherapy–Counseling Caregiver (CG) Intervention Studies:
Cognitive Behavioral Therapy (CBT) Methods

Authors	Sample	Conditions	Manual protocol	Length of treatment	Outcome measure	Finding
Akkerman & Ostwald, 2004	$N = 38$ dementia CGs (35 completed); CG mean age = 58.1 years; 33 women, 5 men; African American = $n = 7$, Asian $n = 1$, Caucasian $n = 25$, Hispanic $n = 5$	Condition 1: 9-week group CBT intervention Condition 2: wait-list control (WLC)	Condition 1 (CBT): intervention addressed physical, cognitive, and behavioral components associated with CG anxiety; each component was reviewed with CGs over a 3-week period; CG practiced skills appropriate for each of the three components Condition 2 (WLC): received treatment after follow-up	Condition 1 (CBT): 9 weekly 2-hr sessions focusing on behavioral, physical, and cognitive components associated with CG anxiety— sessions focused on each component over a 3-week period; CGs practiced skills to reduce anxiety applicable to each of the 3 components	The Beck Anxiety Inventory and Hamilton Anxiety Scale were administered at baseline, Week 10 postintervention, Week 16 follow-up	CBT > WLC for improvement on Beck Anxiety Inventory and Hamilton Anxiety Scale

(continues)

TABLE 7.2
Psychotherapy–Counseling Caregiver (CG) Intervention Studies:
Cognitive Behavioral Therapy (CBT) Methods   *(Continued)*

Authors	Sample	Conditions	Manual protocol	Length of treatment	Outcome measure	Finding
Gallagher-Thompson & Steffen, 1994	$N = 66$; family CGs with diagnosed clinical depression according to current psychiatric categories; M age = 62 years; 90% were women; care recipient (CR) were either physically or cognitively disabled	Condition 1: CBT ($n = 36$) Condition 2: brief psychodynamic therapy (BPT; $n = 30$)	Manuals available from the authors	16–20 sessions of individual therapy, twice per week for the first 4 weeks, then once per week for the duration of treatment (4 months)	Schedule for Affective Disorders Schizophrenia (SADS)—SADS change interview, Hamilton Rating Scale for Depression (HRSD), Beck Depression Inventory (BDI), Geriatric Depression Scale	For CG > 44 months, CBT > BPT on BDI, HRSD, and GDS; for CGs < 44 months, BPT > CBT on same symptom measures; CGs in both improved in depression diagnoses (SADS)—at post, 71% no longer depressed

| López & Crespo, 2008 | N = 86; Spanish CGs; CGs scores on BI > 9 or Hospital Anxiety and Depression Scale–Anxiety Subscale (HAD-A) > 7; noninstitutionalized CR over 60 years and at least 1 or more ADL impairment; CG M age = 53.3; mostly female (89.5%) and children (62.85%) CGs | Condition 1: traditional weekly sessions (TWS; $n = 42$): one-to-one CBT aimed to improve CG's relaxation skills, pleasant activities, cognitive appraisals of caregiving situations, social support, communication, and coping strategies. Condition 2: minimal therapist contact (MTC; $n = 44$): similar material to TWS provided to CGs with minimal therapist contact | Condition 1 (TWS): treatment handbooks used in sessions with therapist. Condition 2 (MTC): materials provided to CGs during minimal contact session; López & Crespo (2008) | Condition 1 (TWC): eight 60-min weekly face-to-face psychotherapy sessions. Condition 2 (MTC): three 90-min face-to-face session every 4 weeks; three telephone contacts lasting 10 min in between sessions | Anxiety subscale of HAD-A; BDI; Zarit Burden Interview; Brief COPE (Carver, 1997); Support questionnaire, Short Form-Revised (SSQSR; Saranson et al., 1987); Rosenberg Self-Esteem Scale (RSE; Rosenberg, 1965) | TWS > MTC in reducing CG anxiety at post, as well as at 3 months and 12 months follow-up; additionally, TWS > MTC in reducing CG depression at post and at 1 month follow-up |

(continues)

TABLE 7.2

Psychotherapy–Counseling Caregiver (CG) Intervention Studies:
Cognitive Behavioral Therapy (CBT) Methods   *(Continued)*

Authors	Sample	Conditions	Manual protocol	Length of treatment	Outcome measure	Finding
Marriott et al., 2000	$N = 41$; CGs caring for patients with Alzheimer's disease, selected for presence of psychological morbidity; M age = 56.5 years, over 80% female; all were from the United Kingdom	Condition 1: CBT-based intervention (CBTIG) built on stress vulnerability–family coping skills model with CG-care recipient (CR) dyads ($n = 13$) Condition 2: in-depth semi-structured interview control (INT; $n = 14$) Condition 3: no interview control (CTL; $n = 14$)	Protocol derived from CBT family intervention for schizophrenia (Tarrier et al., 1986); included teaching CGs stress management techniques, self-monitoring, and relaxation training; coping skills to help respond to CR behaviors; and exercises to help cope with loss and changes in their own quality of life	Condition 1 (CBTIG): consisted of 14 sessions (1 every 2 weeks) Condition 2 (INT): used one interview to explore family dynamics Condition 3 (CTL): nothing provided	General Health Questionnaire (GHQ); BDI	At posttest and follow-up, CBTIB > INT and CTL on GHQ and BDI (less distress and depression)

TABLE 7.3
Multicomponent Caregiver (CG) Intervention Studies

Authors	Sample	Conditions	Manual protocol	Length of treatment	Outcome measure	Finding
Belle et al., 2006	N = 642, dementia CGs; 518 CGs had completed all 5 outcomes needed to calculated CG's overall quality of life; Resources for Enhancing Alzheimer's Caregivers Health (REACH) criteria; Latino–Hispanic n = 212; 168 completed), non-Hispanic White–Caucasian (n = 219; 182 completed), and African American–Black (n = 211; 168 completed) were included in the sample	Condition 1: REACH Phase 2 interventions (REACH II; n = 323), including providing information, didactic instruction, role playing, problem solving, skills training, stress management techniques, and telephone support groups Condition 2: wait-list control (WLC; n = 319). Both conditions available in English or Spanish	Yes; Belle et al. (2006)	Condition 1 (REACH II): over 6 months CGs received 12 total sessions with 9 in-home 90-min sessions, 3 30-minute telephone sessions, as well as 5 structured telephone support group sessions Condition 2 (WLC): CGs provided packets of educational material and 2 brief (< 15 min) telephone "check-in" calls at 3 months and 5 months after randomization	Primary outcome: Overall CG quality of life (CGQOL) based on 10-item Center for Epidemiological Studies Depression Scale (CES-D); brief Zarit Burden Index; self-care items; social support items on received support, satisfaction, and negative interactions; 3 questions to assess primary domains of Revised Memory and Behavior Problem Checklist (i.e., memory, depression, and disruption) Secondary outcomes: CES-D (CG clinical depression); institutional placement of CR at 6-month follow-up	REACH II > WLC in improvement of CGQOL for Latino–Hispanic and non-Hispanic White–Caucasian CG; for African American–Black spousal CGs, REACH II > WLC in improvement on CGQOL; WLC > REACH II on prevalence of CG clinical depression at follow-up

(continues)

TABLE 7.3
Multicomponent Caregiver (CG) Intervention Studies (Continued)

Authors	Sample	Conditions	Manual protocol	Length of treatment	Outcome measure	Finding
Eisdorfer et al., 2003	N = 225, dementia CGs; REACH criteria; only Cuban American (n = 114) and Caucasian (n = 111) sample	Condition 1: Minimal telephone support (MTS) Condition 2: structural ecosystems family therapy (SET) designed to identify and restructure specific familial interactions and interactions with other systems that may be linked with CG burden; identify specific CG problems experienced, usable resources available and formal supports, and CG and family capacity to collaborate in the caregiving effort	Manuals are available from the authors	Condition 1 (MTS): Biweekly supportive telephone calls Condition 2 (SET): 13 contacts for an average total of 14 hr; they met weekly for 4 months, biweekly for 2 months, and monthly for 6 months Condition 3 (SET + CTIS): Includes treatment from Condition 2 and CTIS use across all features for 56 contacts averaging 19 total hr	CES-D	At 6 months, SET + CTIS > MTS and SET on CES-D; for White daughters at 6 months, SET > MTS on CES-D; for Cuban daughters, Cuban husbands, White wives, and White daughters at 6 months, SET + CTIS > MTS on CES-D; for Cubans at 18 months, SET + CTIS > MTS on CES-D

| Mittelman et al., 2004 | $N = 406$, spousal CGs of Alzheimer's patients; 380 included 1-year follow-up, 328 at 3-year and 223 at 5-year follow-up; continuation of previous study (Mittelman et al., 1995) with 206 CGs; $N = 200$ additional CGs included in this study; new analysis strategy using growth curves | Condition 1: treatment (Rx; $n = 203$) enhanced counseling and support
Condition 2: usual care—support (UC; $n = 203$)
Condition 3: SET combined with computer telephone integrated systems (CTIS; SET + CTIS) | Condition 1 (Rx): both individual and family counseling plus support group; additional help, advice, or counseling provided as needed and initiated by CG or family member (ad hoc counseling); education and conflict resolution major components; role-play to teach how to deal with problem behaviors
Condition 2 (UC): routine support and information; no formal counseling but could choose to participate in support groups and ad hoc counseling | No predefined end to treatment; 2 scheduled individual sessions with CG: 1 after intake and 1 at 4 months; 4 scheduled family sessions within the first 4 months and tailored to problems revealed at intake; other contacts as requested; CGs followed over 5 years, with assessments occurring every 4 months in the first year and every 6 months thereafter until 2 years after death of patient or they refused or were unable to participate | Study focused on depression on measured by Geriatric Depression Scale (GDS; Yesavage et al., 1983) | At 1 year, enhanced counseling and support (Rx) is better than UC on GDS (less depression); effects sustained for 3.1 years |

abridged outline with an overview of EBT interventions for family caregivers by focusing on the key components of studies within each of the overarching intervention categories.

Psychoeducational–Skill Building

These interventions focus on increasing caregivers' knowledge of a specific disease or disorder (e.g., Alzheimer's disease, prostate cancer, stroke) and teaching caregivers key coping skills for managing the common emotional, behavioral, or both types of problems associated with caring for people with that disease or disorder. Psychoeducational–skill-building interventions teach behavior or mood management skills, problem-solving skills, and/or skills for environmental modification. Many times, skill building is combined with emotional support as well as basic information about caregiving, the disease or disorder impacting their care recipients, and relevant community resources. However, all the studies in this overarching category emphasize skill building as one of their core components.

The psychoeducational–skill-building intervention category contained the largest number of studies that meet EBT criteria, and it grew the most since the 2007 review, adding nine studies to this overarching category. Studies in this category often derived from cognitive and behavioral theories and practices, emphasize education and skill training of the caregiver, and frequently focus on improving adaptive coping skills and reducing the use of avoidant coping strategies. As depicted in Table 7.1, these studies can be grouped further into five subcategories because at least two studies met EBT criteria within each of the following subcategories: behavior management skill training, depression management (increasing life satisfaction) skill training, progressively lowered stress threshold (PLST) studies, anger management skill training, and mixed studies. Behavior management interventions emphasized teaching behavior management skills to address care recipient behavior problems (e.g., how to change antecedents of care recipient problem behaviors or caregiver responses to these behaviors), and/or caregiving challenges (e.g., problem-solving skills, pleasant event scheduling). Depression management interventions stressed the development of caregiver mood-management skills to alleviate depression, including cognitive reappraisal, increasing pleasant events, relaxation training, and problem solving. Anger management interventions focused on the recognition of sources of frustration and the use of a variety of cognitive and behavioral skills to reduce anger and hostility, such as challenging unhelpful thinking, engaging in more positive self teaching, and communicating assertively. PLST interventions implemented a model that centers on modifying environmental demands to help ameliorate the stress experienced by dementia patients. The final category, *mixed,* was defined as such because they placed a greater emphasis on education and support in comparison to the skill-building components of their interventions. These subcategories were formed by carefully considering the study's theoretical framework, outcomes targeted, and the relative mix of skill-building components, and they can be useful to clinicians, researchers, and students who are learning more about the range of effective programs that fall under the overarching psychoeducational–skill-building category.

Unfortunately, published reports provide inconsistent information about the interventionists who are delivering caregiver-intervention protocols. The experience level of interventionists in the psychoeducational–skill-building category varied widely, ranging from trained peer counselors (e.g., Toseland, Rossiter, & Labrecque, 1989), research associates (e.g., Buckwalter et al., 1999), and trained staff (e.g., Bourgeois, Schulz, Burgio, & Beach, 2002; Davis, Burgio, Buckwalter, & Weaver, 2004), to experienced nurses (e.g., Fung & Chien, 2002; Huang, Shyu, Chen, Chen, & Lin, 2003), interdisciplinary professional faculty (e.g., Ostwald, Hepburn, Caron, Burns & Mantell, 1999), doctoral level psychologists, master's level clinicians, or supervised clinical interns or graduate level trainees (Coon, Thompson, Steffen, Sorocco, & Gallagher-Thompson, 2003; Gallagher-Thompson et al., 2003; Steffen, 2000), and experienced geriatricians (e.g., Teri, Logsdon, Uomoto, & McCurry, 1997).

As one EBT example from the psychoeducational–skill-building category, Table 7.4 outlines the basic components of Coping With Caregiving (CWC), a 10-week, group-psychoeducational intervention for family caregivers of persons with dementia that meets 2 hours each week and is grounded in cognitive and behavioral theories (Gallagher-Thompson et al., 2003). CWC integrated the core components of two other EBTs for family caregivers of persons with dementia: a depression management intervention and an anger management intervention (Coon, Thompson, Steffen, Sorocco, & Gallagher-Thompson, 2003). CWC and the anger management intervention are the interventions implemented in the cases described later in this chapter.

In brief, CWC taught caregivers several cognitive behavioral mood management skills through emphasizing the following two approaches: (a) reducing negative affect by learning how to relax in stress situations, appraise the care recipient's behavior more realistically, and use assertive communication skills; and (b) increasing positive mood through learning the contingency between mood and activities, developing ways to do more small pleasant activities daily, and learning to set self-change goals and reward oneself for accomplishments along the way. Caregivers were encouraged to practice these skills and apply them to their daily caregiving experiences. The CWC was compared with an enhanced support group that was patterned after Alzheimer's Association community-based support groups for family caregivers of dementia patients. It was enhanced by meeting weekly rather than monthly and asking participants

TABLE 7.4
Coping With Caregiving: Intervention Phases, Class Goals,
and Home Practice

Intervention phases	Goals of the class–group meeting	Home practice
Introduction and thinking tools		
Class 1	Overview of dementia, discuss sources of frustration and anger, and practice relaxation	Daily relaxation log
Classes 2–4	Learn to identify unhelpful thoughts about caregiving, change unhelpful thoughts into more helpful or adaptive ways of thinking, and see the links between thinking and caregiver and care recipient behavior	Relaxation log, daily thought record
Doing tools: Communication		
Classes 5–6	Understand types of communication (passive, assertive, and aggressive) and role play how to be more assertive in caregiving situations and with others	Assertive communication
Doing tools: Pleasant events		
Classes 6–9	Learn the relationship between pleasant events and mood, identify pleasant events and activities, and understand and overcome personal barriers to increasing or infusing pleasant events in one's life	Daily mood rating, pleasant events tracking form
Class 10	Review skills covered across the classes	Relaxation log, daily thought record, pleasant events tracking, and assertive communication
Reinforcement and maintenance		
8 boosters	Maintain and continue to fine tune skills and transfer these skills to daily caregiving situations	Transfer and practice skills in everyday life

to attend all 10 sessions. Both the CWC and the enhanced support group were conducted separately in either English or Spanish for self-identified Latinas–Hispanic women and non-Hispanic White women. In comparison with support group participants, CWC caregivers reported a reduction in depressive symptoms and an increased use of positive coping strategies. Although not a focus of the outcome study, CWC did provide booster sessions on a monthly basis for 8 months following the 10 weekly sessions to help maintain, fine tune, and apply skills to everyday caregiving situations.

Psychotherapy Counseling

The caregiver intervention studies in the psychotherapy–counseling category implemented specific types of individual or group therapy or counseling. All but one intervention that met EBT criteria in the psychotherapy–counseling category used cognitive behavioral therapy (CBT) or were strongly CBT based, and all measured caregiver depression or anxiety symptoms as outcomes. In contrast to the studies in the psychoeducational–skill-building category that were derived from CBT theories, the behavior therapy, cognitive therapy and CBT studies in the psychotherapy-counseling category placed more emphasis on the development and use of the therapeutic relationship in the treatment process. One additional study conducted with family caregivers of older dependent adults in Spain was added to this category since the 2007 review (López & Crespo, 2008). The CBT-based caregiver interventions in this category use many of the strategies, techniques, and tools that are found in other chapters in this book, such as those that address depression and anxiety. However, all of the interventions reviewed here are implemented within the framework of family caregiving for older adults. The one brief psychodynamic therapy study (Gallagher-Thompson & Steffen, 1994) in this category suggests the need for additional replication of this approach that could warrant future subcategorization of this EBT category into CBT and brief psychodynamic treatments. On average, the interventionists in studies that meet EBT criteria within the psychotherapy–counseling category appeared to be more highly trained than those in the two other categories and included doctoral-level psychologists, master's-level clinicians, or supervised clinical interns or graduate-level trainees.

As an example, the one group-therapy intervention in this category that met EBT criteria is Akkerman and Ostwald's (2004) brief CBT intervention designed to reduce anxiety in community-dwelling family caregivers of patients with Alzheimer's disease. This 2-hour, 9-week intervention was delivered in small groups of four to eight caregivers and used a multidimensional model to address the physical, cognitive, and behavioral components of caregiver anxiety. The weekly groups included didactic presentations related to the model's three components, with each component being reviewed over a 3-week period. Participants were provided printed material and asked to practice anxiety reduction skills that were tied to each of the model's components. At postintervention assessment (Week 10), caregivers in the CBT group therapy reported lower levels of anxiety on both self-report and clinician-administered assessments in comparison with caregivers in a wait-list control condition.

Multicomponent

Multicomponent caregiver interventions incorporate two or more conceptually different approaches that are combined into one intervention package. For example, an intervention that brings together skill building with respite, family counseling, and support group attendance would be included in this category. Previous reviews of the caregiving intervention literature (e.g., Acton & Kang, 2001; Bourgeois, Schulz, & Burgio, 1996; Schulz, 2000; Sörensen et al., 2002) support the use of a multicomponent category. As in the psychotherapy-counseling category, interventionists on studies in the multicomponent category tended to be more experienced than those in the psychoeducational–skill-building category for at least two of the three studies (Eisdorfer et al., 2003; Mittelman, Roth, Coon, & Haley, 2004), relying primarily on doctoral level psychologists, master's level clinicians, or supervised clinical interns or graduate level trainees. Given the small number in this category, the development of well-integrated multicomponent approaches and the replication of the three EBT-identified multicomponent treatments warrant additional investigation.

In the 2007 review, two studies were determined to have met EBT criteria; and, a third study published in late 2007 is added here. Each of these interventions drew from at least two distinct perspectives to develop the overall package. For example, the enhanced counseling and support treatment by Mittelman et al. (2004) consisted of three key components. The first component was composed of two individual and four family counseling sessions that included relatives identified by the family caregiver; however, the older adult with dementia did not attend these sessions. These sessions were tailored to meet the caregiver's needs, such as learning ways to manage patient problem behaviors or promoting family communication. In addition, counselors provided caregivers and family members with information and education regarding Alzheimer's disease and community resources at these sessions. The second intervention component was a weekly support group to help provide ongoing emotional support and education. The third component was the provision of ongoing ad hoc counseling for caregivers and their families to help them manage crises and the various changes in the symptoms of their family members with dementia. At the end of a year, participants in the enhanced counseling and support treatment condition reported fewer depressive symptoms than participants in a usual care condition; follow-up analyses indicated that these effects were sustained for 3.1 years (Mittelman et al., 2004).

A second example in this category, the REACH II (Resources for Enhancing Alzheimer's Caregiver Health) intervention (Belle et al., 2006) funded by the National Institute on Aging and the National Institute of Nursing Research, was also published since the 2007 review. The REACH

II intervention grew out of the original REACH study, in which several different intervention approaches were tested at six different sites to help identify the most promising ones for decreasing caregiver depression and burden. Findings from these studies, published as a set in *The Gerontologist* in 2003 (see Schulz et al., 2003, for an overview), guided the REACH II multicomponent intervention. This intervention was designed to impact one primary outcome: a multicomponent quality-of-life indicator incorporating separate measures of caregiver depression, burden, self-care, and social support and care-recipient problem behaviors. Secondary outcomes included caregiver clinical depression, as measured by scores on the Center for Epidemiological Studies Depression Scale (CES-D) that are judged to be at a level that requires clinical intervention (Andresen, Malmgren, Carter, & Patrick, 1994; Irwin, Artin, & Oxman, 1999) and frequency of institutional placement of the care recipient at 6 months.

Over 600 family caregivers participated with the sample composed of at least 200 caregivers from each of the following racial or ethnic backgrounds: Latino–Hispanic, Black–African American, or non-Hispanic White–Caucasian. This study is one of the largest to date to be completed with a multiethnic, multiracial sample of family members caring for loved ones with dementia. The intervention program was offered in English or Spanish and consisted of 12 individual sessions–meetings with the primary caregiver (nine in home at 1.5 hours each; three telephone sessions at a half hour each) as well as five structured telephone support group sessions. It included a variety of strategies, such as basic education about dementia and safety in the home setting, skill training to learn how to manage care-recipient troublesome behaviors (e.g., developing alternative, more adaptive responses to the care recipient's wandering or repetitive questioning), cognitive strategies to learn how to reframe unhelpful thinking patterns (e.g., challenging thoughts like, "It's hopeless and there's nothing I can do to improve things"), strategies for managing stress (e.g., relaxation skills), and strategies for increasing needed social support (e.g., how to ask for help more effectively from family members). Which strategies to use and in which order were decided collaboratively between the caregiver and interventionist after review of available information.

Evaluation of the REACH II intervention is more complicated than other studies given that an overall quality-of-life indicator (and not distinct measures of specific constructs) was used as the primary outcome (Belle et al., 2006). Findings indicate that both Latino–Hispanic and non-Hispanic White–Caucasian caregivers in the intervention condition had significantly greater improvement in quality of life than those in the project's control condition ($p < .001$, $p = .037$, respectively). This was not the case among African American–Black caregivers overall, where only spousal caregivers improved significantly more than did their control counterparts ($p = .003$). Why other relatives did not show significant improvement needs additional study. With regard to effect size, the quality-of-life indicator improved 0.3 standard deviation more in Latino–Hispanic participants and 0.20 more in non-Hispanic White–Caucasian caregivers who were in the intervention condition compared with those in the control condition. In terms of secondary outcomes, the overall prevalence of clinical depression at follow-up was significantly greater among control group participants than those in the intervention (22.7% vs. 12.6%, p = .001). No clear effects were found for delay of institutional placement, most likely because follow-up was brief (only 6 months). However, it is reasonable to expect that longer term follow-up would be necessary to demonstrate this effect.

EBT REVIEW: CONCLUDING THOUGHTS AND RELEVANT RESOURCES

In sum, there are a growing number of caregiving-EBT approaches available for psychologists and their colleagues interested in translating empirically based treatments into their organizations or private practices. As in our previous review and similar to other published reviews and meta-analyses (e.g., Schulz, Martire, & Klinger, 2005; Sörensen, Pinquart, & Duberstein, 2002), the three categories of psychoeducational–skill building, psychotherapy–counseling, and multicomponent interventions demonstrated the most benefit in terms of effectively impacting caregiver distress. This review also provides additional evidence for the integration of skill-building strategies (e.g., care-recipient behavior management, caregiver mood-management strategies) into family caregiver interventions. Skill building appeared in a variety of interventions across all three EBT categories.

In the course of this and our 2007 review and related commentary (Coon & Evans, 2009; Gallagher-Thompson & Coon, 2007), we uncovered a number of key issues and next steps for caregiver interventions that are relevant to clinicians, clinical researchers, and policymakers. For example, the most frequently implemented caregiver interventions in today's society (respite, support groups, and case management), although not a focus of either the 2007 or this review, were examined for professional presentation purposes. This examination found that they do not currently meet EBT status; however, specific studies on how to best integrate these services into multicomponent intervention approaches are warranted. In addition, while the number of theory-based caregiving interventions continues to grow, most of the current caregiver research remains grounded in stress and coping or stress-process models. Ongoing research continues to uncover the multidimensional nature of caregiving, suggesting the need to modify extant theories and to develop new theoretical models to better capture relationships between intervention strategies and outcomes—particularly at different points across the caregiving trajectory. New or adapted models may lead us to a better understanding of the psychiatric and the physical morbidities associated with family care, as well as the dynamic interplay between the two (Coon & Evans, 2009; Coon, Ory, & Schulz, 2003). This need is underscored in research with culturally diverse caregivers, for whom current models may not be adequate since they often do not include constructs such as acculturation and health literacy as possible moderators of response. Recent articles such as those by Hilgeman et al. (2009) and Montoro-Rodriguez and Gallagher-Thompson (2009) raise a variety of issues related to these concerns while attempting more in-depth evaluations of popular stress and coping models within the context of caregiving.

Most intervention research with family caregivers of impaired older adults focuses on caregivers for persons with dementia. Empirical research on interventions to address the concerns of caregivers of other types of older patients, including those with psychiatric problems and other kinds of chronic illness, is sorely lacking. Likewise, the vast majority of identified EBTs were conducted with non-Hispanic White samples. There is an ongoing need for research–practice partnerships to help design new EBTs (or tailor existing ones) to address the needs of other cultural groups. Few treatment studies have involved other cultural groups residing in the United States or included large samples of multiple groups in the same trial. Notably, there is a paucity of research on Native American and Asian American caregivers; in addition, given the great heterogeneity of these groups (e.g., those of Chinese, Japanese, Vietnamese, Hmong, Asian Indian, and other ancestry within Asian Americans), this lack of information about their needs as caregivers and what interventions might be most applicable to meet those needs cannot continue. Yet, a limited amount of work is emerging with these groups, such as that of Gallagher-Thompson and colleagues (Gallagher-Thompson et al., 2007, 2010) with Chinese American caregivers. In two separate randomized trials (one that focused on adapting the CWC for in-home use and the other that adapted the CWC for use through a DVD, illustrating the same skills used in the CWC but again "tailored" for the Chinese family), they found that caregivers generally responded in a very positive manner. In the home-based study, there was significant reduction in depressive symptoms from pre- to postintervention (Gallagher-Thompson et al., 2007). In the DVD study, there was significant reduction in perceived stress due to caregiving from pre to post (Gallagher-Thompson et al., 2010). Although both studies used relatively small sample sizes, results are promising and clearly warrant replication with larger samples. Even less empirical research has been conducted with the other Asian groups mentioned—partly due to language and cultural barriers specific to each group. Yet, in the decades ahead, older Asian Americans will increase substantially in numbers, and with that increase will come an increase in those family members providing care. It is clear that this work, as well as work with Native American caregivers, needs priority in the near future.

In addition, very little is known about the longer term impact of the vast majority of the EBTs identified here, providing little insight about how to best sustain caregivers' positive physical and mental health outcomes across the course of caregiving. Moreover, even less is known about interventions that target key caregiver transitions, including initiation of the caregiving role, care recipient placement, or caregiver bereavement. Nevertheless, efforts to sustain caregivers' behavior change or maintenance of intervention gains undoubtedly will require multiple intervention strategies and multiple disciplines (e.g., psychology, social work, nursing, medicine) working in partnership. In everyday practice, maintenance of gains often requires follow-up contacts or "booster sessions" to address the changing circumstances of the caregiving dyad.

The social significance of family caregiver EBTs, including their impact on nursing home placement and their cost-effectiveness, needs further investigation across EBT categories to help ensure their sustainability and dissemination. Mittelman and her colleagues, by using the multicomponent intervention described earlier (Mittelman et al., 2004), evaluated and found positive intervention effects for the delay of nursing home placement (Mittelman, Ferris, Shulman, Steinberg, & Levin, 1996; Mittelman, Haley, Clay, & Roth, 2006). Also, a recent analysis of the REACH II intervention that used an incremental cost-effectiveness ratio demonstrated that at a cost of $4.96 per day per caregiver, caregivers in the intervention received an additional hour of noncaregiving time per day. Clearly, these findings are important to all caregivers, but they are particularly relevant to working caregivers and those struggling with their own physical and mental health concerns (Nichols et al., 2008).

Finally, effective, sustainable translation of EBTs into community settings requires strategic partnerships among practitioners, clinical researchers, and policymakers. These partnerships help to ensure solid communication between evidence-based practice and practice-based evidence, where practitioners' insights are also valued in the identification of intervention approaches and related outcomes (Coon & Evans, 2009). Related to such partnerships are the recent efforts of the U.S. Administration on Aging (AoA; 2009b), which has developed funding mechanisms through its Alzheimer's Disease Supportive Services Program (ADSSP) for Evidence-Based Projects to help examine the translation of several caregiver EBTs identified in this review into the community (e.g., Belle et al., 2006; Gallagher-Thompson et al., 2003; Mittelman et al., 2004). For example, one of our EBTs described earlier, the CWC program (renamed CarePRO: Care Partners Reaching Out), is being translated into the community through partnership with the local Alzheimer's Association chapters and the state units on aging in both Arizona and Nevada as well as the local area agencies on aging in Arizona. This effort is primarily designed to embed CarePRO into chapter and area agency program activities across both states through appropriate training and supervision across 3 years of service to approximately 600 family caregivers. A key component of the ADSSP is the evaluation of the translation of evidence-based models such as CarePRO as they are embedded into service networks. The ADSSP encourages the use of the RE-AIM framework (Glasgow et al., 2006; Glasgow, Vogt, & Boles, 1999; Klesges, Estabrooks, Glasgow, & Dzewaltowski, 2005), suggesting that the evaluation of the translatability and public health impact of its initiatives is best examined by considering the following dimensions: Reach (representativeness of the target population enrolled), Efficacy/Effectiveness (effectiveness of the intervention on caregiver outcomes), Adoption (of the intervention by target settings, institutions, and staff), Implementation (in terms of the consistency and cost of delivery of the intervention), and Maintenance (of intervention effects in individuals and settings over time). The steps taken by the AoA's ADSSP may ultimately be tied to policy-level programs like the National Family Caregiver Support Program, which allocates money to states to work in partnership with area agencies on aging and local community-service providers to provide services to family caregivers and could also provide partnerships with mental health professionals to deliver interventions and help sustain the positive effects of caregiver interventions.

In conclusion, this review can help guide psychologists and other professionals locate specific interventions that are more likely to reduce family caregiver distress and enhance well-being. It also can help health care and social service organizations, as well as private practice groups, identify appropriate staff to hire to support family caregiving intervention activities, and guide relevant staff training and supervision activities. Ongoing dialogues among practitioners, clinical researchers, and policymakers can also foster the identification of practical interventions for diverse settings as well as the relevant and realistic outcome measures for translation of empirically based caregiver interventions into everyday practice (Coon & Evans, 2009).

The next section of this chapter provides case examples of the translation of two EBTs with two different cultural groups and is followed by examples of tools used in these and related psychoeducational–skill-building interventions (Appendices 7.1–7.4). Tools found in other chapters, particularly those tools that are CBT based (e.g., those in Chapter 4 on depression), are also often introduced as part of CBT-based caregiver interventions. Besides contacting the authors listed in the previously referenced articles grouped by EBT category, providers interested in implementing any of the caregiver intervention EBTs are referred to the following two websites: Rosalynn Carter Institute for Caregiving, Caregiver Intervention Database (http://www.rosalynncarter. org/caregiver_intervention_database/) and the Substance Abuse and Mental Health Services Administration's (SAMHSA) National Registry of Evidence-based Programs and Practices (http://www.nrepp.samhsa.gov/).

Developers of interventions are frequently adding empirical support for their work and refining interventions to facilitate translation into a variety of situations and settings, as well as tailoring interventions to meet the needs of our increasingly diverse population of family caregivers. These websites are useful repositories of caregiver interventions; however, neither website uses the EBT criteria implemented in this chapter, and they do not house exactly the same list of EBTs presented here.

Finally, the American Psychological Association has developed the Family Caregiver Briefcase for Psychologists as an online resource for psychologists who provide services to family caregivers. The "briefcase" covers a variety of useful material and references, including information relevant to not only family caregivers of older adults but also to those family caregivers who are assisting children and young and middle-aged adults (http://www. apa.org/pi/about/publications/caregivers/index.aspx).

ADAPTING EBT FOR PRACTICE: TWO CASE PRESENTATIONS

Case Example 1: Maria

Maria is a very frustrated 70-year-old monolingual Spanish-speaking caregiver. She is caring for her older sister Rose, who has "significant memory loss" likely to be due to Alzheimer's disease. Maria was educated in Mexico, where she completed the fourth grade, but she has lived in the United States for about 50 years and is now a U.S. citizen. She completed her GED at age 65, in Northern California, where she and her family had been migrant workers for many years. Maria's husband had passed on about 5 years before she sought help for caregiving, even though he had severe diabetes, and she provided considerable care to him before he died. Maria contacted Irene Valverde, a bilingual, bicultural outreach worker for the Coping With Frustration project being conducted in an agricultural region in Northern California after she noticed it written up in the church bulletin. She was relieved that she was able to connect with someone who spoke Spanish and that there was a program that might help her learn how to better manage her stress and related distress (particularly her frustration and anger) as her sister's condition worsened over time.

At the first group meeting of the Coping With Frustration class (which was a forerunner to the CWC program described earlier, which focused on teaching skills for managing frustrations related to caregiving), Maria stated that she had never been in a group where people discuss their problems freely, and although she was hesitant at first, she soon participated, especially after she realized "their problems are the same as mine." She told the group that "Rosa is just impossible! She forgets things and refused to accept reason." Maria said she was constantly on the verge of losing her temper, felt trapped by the situation, and was not getting much help from other family members. She cried a lot at the first meeting, and she seemed very relieved to be heard and understood by others with similar issues.

Besides building in time for caregivers to share their experience (called *platicar* in Spanish), other cultural adaptations of the intervention program included (a) significant time spent on discussing what is dementia and what to expect (because lack of accurate information clearly contributes to negative evaluation of the situation), (b) use of Spanish-language materials in the workbook given to the caregivers, and (c) use of bilingual–bicultural leaders for the intervention program. Following training in this model by Gallagher-Thompson, Valverde became one of the first in that region to implement the program. As the program changed and other versions became available, she continued to remain involved and take advantage of opportunities to learn more about how she could assist Latino caregivers. In fact, she has remained involved in several follow-up research-demonstration projects with Latino caregivers, and she has made significant contributions to the process of culturally tailoring these programs for their intended audience. She is currently employed as a coordinator for a new project that involves Latino caregivers in Northern California and continues to use skills she learned in these programs in her work.

The major skills taught in the Coping With Frustration program included anger management (e.g., recognizing feelings of frustration and developing adaptive ways to cope with them) and learning to communicate more effectively with other family members (e.g., to get needed help). It was important for Maria to learn that she could modulate her anger: It did not have to get as strong as it was getting. The group was taught how to recognize "danger signs" and what to do (e.g., deep breathing, counting to 10, distracting themselves) so that the danger signs did not escalate. They were then taught that it's okay not to answer all the questions the demented person has, and it is most important to realize that the demented person often does not make sense. Once Maria and other group members really understood that a great deal of the rambling, or challenging, or repeated questioning they were experiencing with their loved one was due to the disease and was not personal and they used the course skills, they were able to turn their anger into compassion for the other individual.

The skill of learning to communicate more effectively was also key to this program's success. Most Latina women are accustomed to being in a "service" role, and they do not generally ask for help, which they believe would be a sign that they are not adequate to do the job, or that they are complaining, or some other culturally taboo interpretation (Hilgeman et al., 2009; Montoro-Rodriguez & Gallagher-Thompson, 2009). Coping With Frustration, like many psychoeducational–skill-building programs, makes extensive use of role playing to make learning interactive and more realistic for each individual. Virtually every member of Maria's group wanted to work on how to ask for help from family members. This extended into how to seek respite, which was available in the region because of a special small grant–demonstration project. Practicing how to be assertive (rather than passive or aggressive) was a very important part of this learning experience—although the term *assertiveness training* was not culturally acceptable, so it was modified into how to communicate more effectively—a goal that resonated with each of the caregivers.

At the conclusion of the class series, participants reported significant changes in caregiver distress, including reductions in anger–frustration and depressive symptoms. In addition, six of the 10 caregivers, including Maria, were well on their way to obtaining in-home support services from the county to help with daily care of their loved one. Several commented that it was a "blessing from God" that they had encountered this program and these particular facilitators. To mark their satisfactory completion of the 10-class series, each caregiver was given a "diploma" or certificate of completion. Maria said this was very meaningful to her and showed her that she could "do it"—that is, learn to take better care of herself while at the same time doing a better job of caring for her sister.

Although we did not conduct any formal long-term follow-up with these caregivers, we know from periodic communication with Valverde and other class leaders (who still live in that community and continue to work with Latino caregivers) that services for Latino caregivers are "going strong" in the region and are expected to expand as the Latino population in California continues to grow.

Case Example 2: Sima

Sima is a 56-year-old Iranian woman who immigrated to the United States after the Islamic Revolution began about 30 years ago. She was educated in Iran and worked as a social worker there, but despite being bilingual (English and Farsi) she was not able to continue her profession when she came to the United States. She has three grown children and was the primary caregiver for her 80-year-old father, who suffered with dementia. He had been an educator in Iran, and the loss of his cognitive abilities was particularly difficult for his family and him. Sima's mother had multiple medical problems and was physically unable to provide ongoing care to her husband;

however, she was cognitively intact and wanted to be part of the decision making. Sima responded to a flyer posted at a community center that serves the local Persian–Iranian population advertising an educational program for family members who care for older adults with significant memory problems. Sima and two of her close women friends said they did not know much about memory problems in later life, except to think of them as "normal aging." Still, all three women said they would like to talk about their experiences in a small group. From this initial show of interest, and with strong support from the community center's staff, the program developed.

The program was patterned after the CWC psychoeducational EBT, but with several significant modifications to make content and method of delivery more culturally appropriate for this particular group of dementia family caregivers—a group about which virtually nothing is written. In Iranian families, for example, caregiving is culturally normative and flows from the sense of duty and responsibility one has to family members. Bringing in an outsider to assist with personal care is strongly frowned on, so there is little use of these and other services that exist to ease caregivers' burdens. In the initial group in which Sima participated (see Azar & Dadvar, 2008, for more details) emphasis was placed on maintaining the essence of the CWC program but presenting the information in ways that it was more likely to be heard and accepted by members of this community.

Fourteen Iranian caregivers participated in the first small-group series, which was conducted in English (by Gallagher-Thompson), with simultaneous translation by Dadvar. This proved to be an inefficient way to transmit information; therefore, in the second small group of 12, the entire class was conducted in Farsi, their native language. In the interim, all written materials were translated and back-translated as well, with significant modifications in terminology. For instance, taking care of oneself is not highly valued in Persian culture, which emphasizes the collective needs of the family above those of the individual. Therefore, conceptually, emphasis had to be placed on the value to the family of the caregiver by learning new skills and being able to manage his or her stress more effectively.

In both groups, participants reported that it was the first time they were able to speak openly about their caregiving stress. Both men and women caregivers attended the classes. At first it was feared that the men would dominate the discussion, as is culturally normative. However, because of the caregivers' great need to talk about common situations they all shared, the leaders were able to set up a rule of equal time for all and go around the group at each meeting so that even the more reticent caregivers were given a chance to share their experiences. Sima was one of the participants who helped lead the way due at least in part to her bilingual abilities and level of education in comparison with many of the other participants. She was also very articulate, and as a result, helped leaders to develop an atmosphere of trust within the group. Moreover, Sima was able to take some of the vignettes (that had worked so well in English) and modify the way the story was told so that the rest of the group could understand better. She frequently went back and forth between the two languages and often commented on the difficulties of doing an adequate job with maintaining original meanings while at the same time modifying wording where appropriate.

On a more personal note, Sima gained a great deal from learning the skill of cognitive restructuring, which was featured prominently in both groups. A particularly intriguing concept for many of the participants was the notion that thoughts influenced feelings and behaviors, so that by examining and when necessary modifying one's thoughts, one could change one's feelings and subsequent actions. The ideas are complex to teach in any language, but in Farsi the challenge was increased. One challenge was how to best use the thought diary that is typically used for this part of the class, because their handwriting goes from right to left (not left to right, as in English). This meant that the thought diary, which runs sequentially from left to right in terms of antecedents/beliefs/consequences, had to be redesigned to accommodate the way Persian is written. Relatively speaking, more time was needed to teach the concepts and to practice them than in groups conducted with non-Persian caregivers, leading to a situation in which some of the other content was emphasized less, to give ample time for this skill to be learned and practiced in the group.

A final challenge was the need to find a way to integrate some discussion of spirituality into the CWC program. It became clear from the first group that Islamic beliefs about morality, spirituality, and the role of God in one's everyday life are important for many and are part of the strength of this culture, which has survived for thousands of years. Yet, most Western-oriented mental health professionals are not trained to work with spiritual constructs and to integrate them into clinical practice. Many discussions occurred about how best to do this. Again, Sima both contributed to the conceptual process and gained from doing some of this integration on a personal level, herself. The eventual decision was that written materials would not be changed to add this content, but it would be allowed (even encouraged) in the small-group discussions, since it was an integral part of the coping system used by most of the caregivers in the groups.

By the conclusion of the two initial groups, Sima was volunteering some of her personal time at the community center to continue the program and was instrumental in arranging for additional training to be conducted with the bilingual–bicultural social workers on staff there. Continued contact with this community center reveals that the program is offered periodically, with Sima serving as a bridge between caregivers in that community who might be fearful of seeking services and the staff at the center who can help them once they come forward.

CHALLENGES IN THE APPLICATION OF MANUALIZED INTERVENTION PROGRAMS TO THE "REAL WORLD" OF CLINICAL PRACTICE

There are several issues that warrant discussion here to help clinicians use the information presented in this chapter more effectively in their clinical work. First is the issue of how to get adequate training in the EBT in question. Irene Valverde was trained in social work and case management and had prior experience working with patients with dementia and their families, but she needed training and supervised experience in how to work in a behavior change model. Dadvar was trained as a psychologist and therefore was familiar with behavior change models, but she had virtually no experience working with dementia family caregivers. So, to prepare for CWC project implementation, additional training was needed in the specific areas noted above. This was provided by Gallagher-Thompson as part of the preparatory phase of program implementation. For example, Valverde was first a participant observer in a Coping With Frustration class series (held in English) and then coleader with an experienced leader in a second class series, conducted in Spanish. She was given relevant materials to read and, thus, she conducted her own self-study during this time. On the basis of her self-report and others' observations, it was concluded that she was ready to be an independent leader after completing the second class series. This process took about 6 months.

In contrast, Dadvar's preparation involved obtaining more background information about dementia and caregiving stress. Under Gallagher-Thompson's direction, she embarked on a comprehensive self-study program in which she was provided with informational materials about these topics to read and videos and DVDs to review. She also attended several support group meetings offered by the local Alzheimer's Association chapter and met with Gallagher-Thompson on a regular basis to discuss what she was learning and how it could be adapted for Persian culture. This program took about 3 months to complete.

At this point it should be noted that training in both instances was not a one-way process but a two-way street. Gallagher-Thompson learned a great deal as well during these time periods about cultural issues that are key to implementing psychoeducational programs effectively with caregivers from these different cultural backgrounds.

In real-world clinical practice, it is not easy to retool and learn a new set of skills. It may be difficult to take time (and to pay for) needed guidance from a competent consultant, and/or attend workshops and other training opportunities available for learning the new skill set. Learning to do a manualized treatment requires a commitment of both time and resources. If there is support for this from the clinician's employer, then it seems to be more feasible, in contrast to a clinician in solo private practice. For example, the Veterans

Affairs (VA) National Healthcare System initiated a comprehensive training program in cognitive behavioral therapy for depression about 3 years ago that requires attendance at a 3-day workshop plus commitment to about 4 months of 90-minute weekly conference calls at which time consultation is provided to a group of four clinicians who have provided audiotapes of their patient sessions. Tapes are rated by expert clinician consultants who provide detailed feedback about the therapist's competence in CBT, with the goal of attaining a nationally recognized standard of basic competence in this model of psychotherapy. Clearly, this is a time- and resource-intensive program; it was adopted by the VA (after consideration of other training models) because empirical data indicate that this type of training (didactic followed by experiential over a period of time) is most effective for teaching clinicians what they need to know in order to implement the model effectively.

Similar programs and opportunities exist for those primarily in private practice. As noted earlier in this chapter, there are two national websites to consult for more specific information: SAMHSA (for information on a host of evidence-based mental health training programs) and the Rosalynn Carter Institute (for information on evidence-based programs focused on interventions for family caregivers). Although these programs require a commitment of time and money, they are, at present, the best way for clinicians who are not in research settings to begin to retool and gain the skills they need to be able to implement the EBT effectively in their work.

A second issue is how to best use existing manuals that are available to clinicians and that describe in detail what to do for each EBT. Are they used all of the time (by trained clinicians)? Most of the time? What is realistic in the real world of clinical practice?

It is well-known that in research projects and clinical trials, written protocols exist for the interventionists to follow. Fidelity checks are built in to assess how well the protocol is being followed, and regular (often mandatory) supervision or consultation meetings or phone calls are also built in to the study, so that interventionists have a designated time for problem solving and a safe place to bring up challenges with protocol implementation. Building in these safeguards usually results in sufficient protocol adherence so that the internal validity of the study is not compromised.

In contrast, in routine clinical practice, there are no regular fidelity checks to evaluate protocol adherence, and generally there are no routine supervision or consultation procedures with EBT experts. This is particularly true for licensed professionals who shoulder clinical responsibility for their clients' mental health. So the question remains: In nonresearch settings, to what extent are existing CWC manuals actually being followed? Both of the interventionists in this chapter are no longer working on the specific projects described earlier: Valverde is currently a coordinator for a very different project with Latino–Hispanic caregivers, and Dadvar works as a psychologist both in an acute psychiatric hospital and in private practice. However, both have worked with Gallagher-Thompson to train staff in other social service agencies, which provides us the opportunity to comment on this issue. The answer is complex and depends on the circumstances.

We offer the following observations related to the use of EBT protocols and their manuals. First, training in EBT protocols is the cornerstone of success in the real world of clinical practice, just as it is in research projects. The agency/employer/individual clinician must recognize this and be willing to commit the time and resources necessary to complete appropriate training programs successfully.

Second, following that, we note that most clinicians make a sincere good-faith effort to follow the protocol they have been provided. However, clinical situations occur that may require at least temporary deviations from the protocol. For example, in CWC classes, we have had caregivers come into a scheduled class in crisis—current or potential elder abuse, or an intensifying depression, being good cases in point. Does the CWC leader simply ignore this content and continue to follow the manual as it's written? Clearly, this would not be in the caregiver's best interests. So what is the clinician to do?

In the CWC model, there are typically two coleaders: One can work privately and individually with the caregiver in crisis, whereas the second continues with the class structure. When there is only one leader, that person has a commitment both to the individual caregiver in crisis and to the rest of the group; thus, one effective way to handle this is to do the following: (a) conduct a brief relaxation exercise for the whole group at the beginning of the class; (b) follow the protocol for the first half of the meeting; and (c) meet individually with the distressed caregiver at the break, to further assess the situation—while explaining to the group that this is the plan. If the crisis truly requires immediate attention, the leader must decide what to do with the second half of the class time. Generally, the solo clinician in this situation will end the class then and work individually with the distressed caregiver, asking other caregivers for their understanding and patience. The leader can explain that participants will not miss any content and indicate that the time allocation for content discussion in subsequent class meetings will be adjusted to allow for this.

This approach sends a message to others in the CWC that when there is a real crisis, help will be provided. On the other hand, if assessment indicates that it's less of an emergency than was first thought, the leader is encouraged to continue with the class protocol as planned and also have an individual follow-up meeting or telephone call with the distressed caregiver to do problem solving and to make referrals that may be needed to assist the person further. In all such cases, clinical judgment is needed to determine the best course of action at that time.

In short, clinicians are advised to not just dump the protocol and focus the entire CWC time on the distressed caregiver—except in rare instances where there is an imminent danger to self or others. Options such as those discussed above (and others not mentioned but perhaps in common practice in the setting in which the clinician works) should be considered and implemented as appropriate. A final recommendation on this issue is that clinicians work with training consultants to develop specific guidelines in advance for handling various crisis scenarios when implementing groups; clearly, these guidelines will need to be tailored appropriately to meet their particular clinical practice situations. Having such a game plan reduces stress and assists the clinician with decision making. Although not all possible crises can be anticipated, the most common ones can (e.g., increase in depressive symptoms, potential elder abuse, possible suicidal ideation or an actual suicide plan), and by having guidelines in mind, they can be handled in ways that are effective for both the very stressed caregiver and the CWC group as a whole.

The third issue for clinicians in the real world to consider is this: What if the manualized intervention program is not enough to meet caregivers' service needs? This may well be true, and acknowledging this recognizes a limitation of most EBTs that has been raised for some time. EBTs for family caregiver distress were typically developed to focus on a specific problem or issue (e.g., reducing caregiver burden, stress, or depression)—not the entire range of problems that caregivers face today. For example, CWC (and its variations) was developed to teach adaptive cognitive and behavioral coping skills to distressed dementia family caregivers. It was not designed as a treatment for clinical levels of depression (although reduction in symptoms has been reported in most published studies), nor was it intended to be a kind of support group such as those sponsored by the Alzheimer's Association. It does not provide extensive referrals for other services, such as respite or day care, and it was not designed to help caregivers of persons with other chronic illnesses (although it is entirely possible that some of the skills taught can transfer to these other situations). Therefore, CWC may need to be supplemented with other services that are needed by individual caregivers. In most research studies, such referrals are typically given at the conclusion of the project—not while the caregiver is in active intervention—so that intervention effects can be more clearly ascertained. However, for most clinicians who are practicing in nonacademic settings, the following question may arise: When is the best time to do these referrals?

There are pros and cons to doing referrals for concurrent services while the caregiver is in a CWC class. We recommend that the clinician carefully weigh these issues before making a decision. In our opinion, participating in the CWC program is an intensive new kind of learning experience for most caregivers, requiring their time and commitment both to attend the weekly meeting and practice the coping skills outside of the group meetings. To simultaneously be trying to effect a referral to a day care or respite program also takes time and energy. It may not be wise to attempt to do both at the same time because either or both may suffer from the caregiver's divided attention and the demands on her time that both require. Therefore, it may be best that any nonurgent referrals be postponed until the CWC is completed, especially if cost is a concern. On the other hand, it may help adherence to the CWC program if the caregiver has additional support while in the program. For example, if the caregiver has difficulty getting to the group meetings because she has no respite care or in-home support services, it may help her attendance to have the in-home support services begin while she is in the CWC—so that she can participate more fully in the CWC program. Similarly, we know of situations where CWC has been offered at day care program sites effectively coordinating both CWC and respite for caregivers. Of course, caregivers may continue to use these respite services after the CWC series ends, thereby further enhancing CWC participants' well-being.

A second consideration regarding concurrent versus postponed referrals is the question of priorities: If the clinician is offering the CWC program to a given caregiver, there must be a reason why that intervention was selected at that time. Most likely, it was the clinician's judgment that this is the program most likely to benefit the caregiver. If the clinician thought the caregiver would benefit from other programs, it is reasonable to assume that those would be prioritized over involvement in CWC. This is a matter of clinical judgment in that caregivers may benefit from a variety of programs, but the question of when each should be introduced, how many to participate in at any one time, and when to end one and begin another is not yet well understood. For example, additional research is needed to better understand the use of caregiver programs in (a) planned succession (e.g., an intervention designed for couples facing early stage dementia follow by CWC for the caregiver as the disease progresses); or (b) a stepped care model, whereby the clinician determines whether a participant needs additional assistance in tandem with or in lieu of CWC at this time (e.g., respite care to afford caregiver participation in CWCs exercises to build everyday pleasant events or individual CBT for the treatment of severe, recalcitrant clinical depression).

In sum, it is our opinion that once the CWC has been selected as the intervention of choice, it is best for the caregiver to be encouraged to participate fully in that program. As CWC is ending, appropriate referrals can then be discussed, with the recognition that caregiving is a long-term process, and therefore, over the course of time, additional services may well be both necessary and appropriate. In fact, we find that through CWC, family caregivers often develop the skills that help them identify, seek out, and obtain the additional informal and formal support they need to help them in their caregiving role.

APPENDIX 7.1: FIVE-COLUMN THOUGHT RECORD

Situation	Feelings	Current thoughts	Challenge & replace with more helpful thoughts	New feelings
Describe the events that led to your unpleasant feelings.	What are you feeling (frustrated, angry, anxious, etc.)?	Identify your thoughts in the situation.	What is a more helpful way of thinking about the situation?	What are you feeling now (frustrated, angry, anxious, etc.)?

APPENDIX 7.2: TRACKING PLEASANT ACTIVITIES AND MONITORING YOUR MOOD

Using the nine-point scale, please rate your mood for each day. If you felt good, put a high number on the chart below. If you felt "so-so," mark a 5. And if you felt low or depressed, mark a lower number.

Name: _____

Pleasant Activities or Events	Days						
	1	2	3	4	5	6	7
1.							
2.							
3.							
4.							
5.							
6.							
7.							
8.							
9.							
10.							
Total # Pleasant Activities Each Day							
* Mood Score							

☹ 1   2   3   4   5   6   7   8   9 ☺

very sad   "so-so"   very happy

APPENDIX 7.3: BEHAVIOR DIARY

Date/Day of week	Time	Person Present	What happened before the behavior? Trigger ⟶	What was the behavior? Behavior ⟶	How did you and your care recipient respond? Response	What was the strategy you used to manage the behavior?
						What happened when you used the strategy? (What was the outcome?)

APPENDIX 7.4: IDEAL COMMUNICATION–ASSERTIVENESS PRACTICE SHEET

Identify	Describe	Express	Assert	Listen
Identify a particular situation. Identify with whom and when you want to be assertive.	Describe below what you think and feel about the situation.	Express what you would like the listener to do for you. If you can offer something in return, express that.	Assert why you need what you are asking and how it can be of help.	Listen carefully to the response. If they can fulfill the request, THANK THEM; and state how/when you will do what you offered to them. If the listener is unresponsive or cannot fulfill the request, then negotiate. What is possible and when? What will work?

REFERENCES

Acton, G.J., & Kang, J. (2001). Interventions to reduce the burden of caregiving for an adult with dementia: A meta-analysis. *Research in Nursing & Health, 24,* 349–360. doi:10.1002/nur.1036

Administration on Aging. (2009a). *Alzheimer's Disease Supportive Services Program: Evidence-based cooperative agreements to better serve people with Alzheimer's disease and related disorders.* Washington, DC: Department of Health and Human Services.

Administration on Aging. (2009b). *A profile of older Americans: 2009.* Washington, DC: Department of Health and Human Services.

Akkerman, R.L., & Ostwald, S.K. (2004). Reducing anxiety in Alzheimer's disease family caregivers: The effectiveness of a nine-week cognitive-behavioral intervention. *American Journal of Alzheimer's Disease & Other Dementias, 19,* 117–123. doi:10.1177/153331750401900202

Almberg, B., Grafstrom, M., & Winbald, B. (1997). Major strain and coping strategies as reported by family members who care for aged demented relatives. *Journal of Advanced Nursing, 26,* 394–411.

Andresen, E.M., Malmgren, J.A., Carter, W.B., & Patrick, D.L. (1994). Screening for depression in well older adults: Evaluation of a short form of the CES-D (Center for Epidemiologic Studies Depression Scale). *American Journal of Preventive Medicine, 10,* 77–84.

Aneshensel, C.S., Pearlin, L.I., Mullan, J.T.; Zarit, S.H., & Whitlatch, C.J. (1995) *Profiles in caregiving: The unexpected career.* San Diego, CA: Academic Press.

Azar, A., & Dadvar, S. (2007). A psychoeducational program for Iranian family caregivers living in northern California. *Clinical Gerontologist, 31,* 95–100. doi:10.1080/07317110802072249

Bainbridge, D., Krueger, P., Lohfeld, L., & Brazil, K. (2009). Stress process in caring for an end-of-life family member: Application of a theoretical model. *Aging & Mental Health, 13,* 537–545. doi:10.1080/13607860802607322

Bakas, T., Pressler, S.J., Johnson, E.A., Nauser, J.A., & Shaneyfelt, T. (2006). Family caregiving in heart failure. *Nursing Research, 55,* 180–188. doi:10.1097/00006199-200605000-00004

Bass, D.M., McClendon, M.J., Flatley-Brennan, P., & McCarthy, C. (1998). The buffering effect of a computer support network on caregiver strain. *Journal of Aging and Health, 10,* 20–43.

Beauchamp, N., Irvine, A.B., Seeley, J., & Johnson, B. (2005). Worksite-based internet multimedia program for family caregivers of persons with dementia. *The Gerontologist, 45,* 793–801. doi:10.1093/geront/45.6.793

Beck, A.T., Rush, A.J., Shaw, B., & Emery, G. (1979). *Cognitive therapy for depression.* New York, NY: Guilford Press.

Bédard, M., Molloy, D.W., Squire, L., Dubois, S., Lever, J.A., & O'Donnell, M. (2001). The Zarit Burden Interview: A new short version and screening version. *The Gerontologist, 41,* 652–657.

Belle, S. H., Burgio, L., Burns, R., Coon, D., Czaja, S. J., Gallagher-Thompson, D., . . . Zhang, S. (2006). Enhancing the quality of life of dementia caregivers from different ethnic or racial groups. *Annals of Internal Medicine, 145,* 727–738.

Bourgeois, M. S., Schulz, R., & Burgio, L. (1996). Interventions for caregivers of patients with Alzheimer's disease: A review and analysis of content, process, and outcomes. *The International Journal of Aging and Human Development, 43,* 35–92. doi:10.2190/AN6L-6QBQ-76G0-0N9A

Bourgeois, M. S., Schulz, R., Burgio, L., & Beach, S. (2002). Skills training for spouses of patients with Alzheimer's disease: Outcomes of an intervention study. *Journal of Clinical Geropsychology, 8,* 53–73. doi:10.1023/A:1013098124765

Buckwalter, K. C., Gerdner, L., Kohout, F., Richards Hall, G., Kelly, A., Richards, B., & Sime, M. (1999). A nursing intervention to decrease depression in family caregivers of persons with dementia. *Archives of Psychiatric Nursing, 13,* 80–88. doi:10.1016/S0883-9417(99)80024-7

Carver, C. S. (1997). You want to measure coping but your protocol's too long: Consider the Brief Cope. *International Journal of Behavioral Medicine, 4,* 92–100.

Centers for Disease Control and Prevention, & the Merck Company. (2007). *The state of aging and health in America 2007.* Whitehouse Station, NJ: Merck Company Foundation.

Chien, W. T., & Lee, Y. M. (2008). A disease management program for families of person in Hong Kong with dementia. *Psychiatric Services, 59,* 433–436. doi:10.1176/appi.ps.59.4.433

Chou, K. R., Jiann-Chyun, L., & Chu, H. (2002). The reliability and validity of the Chinese version of the Caregiver Burden Inventory, *Nursing Research, 51,* 324–331.

Coon, D. W., & Evans, B. (2009). Empirically based treatments for family caregiver distress: What works and where do we go from here? *Geriatric Nursing, 30,* 426–436. doi:10.1016/j.gerinurse.2009.09.010

Coon, D. W., Ory, M., & Schulz, R. (2003). Family caregivers: Enduring and emergent themes. In D. W. Coon, D. Gallagher-Thompson, & L. Thompson (Eds.), *Innovative interventions to reduce dementia caregiver distress: A clinical guide* (pp. 3–27). New York, NY: Springer.

Coon, D. W., Rubert, M., Solano, N., Mausbach, B., Kraemer, H., Arguëlles, T., . . . Gallagher-Thompson, D. (2004). Well-being, appraisal, and coping in Latina and Caucasian female dementia caregivers: Findings from the REACH study. *Aging & Mental Health, 8,* 330–345. doi:10.1080/13607860410001709683

Coon, D., Thompson, L. W., Steffen, S., Sorocco, K., & Gallagher-Thompson, D. (2003). Anger and depression management: Psychoeducational skill training interventions for women caregivers of a relative with dementia. *The Gerontologist, 43,* 678–689. doi:10.1093/geront/43.5.678

Cummings, J., Mega, M., Gray, K., Rosenberg-Thomson, S., Carusi, D., & Gornbein, J. (1994). The Neuropsychiatric Inventory: Comprehensive assessment of psychopathology in dementia. *Neurology, 44,* 2308–2314.

Davis, L. L., Burgio, L. D., Buckwalter, K. C., & Weaver, M. A. (2004). A comparison of in-home and telephone-based skill training interventions with caregivers of persons with dementia. *Journal of Mental Health and Aging, 10*, 31–44.

Dick, L. P., & Gallagher-Thompson, D. (1995). Cognitive therapy with the core beliefs of a distressed, lonely caregiver. *Journal of Cognitive Psychotherapy: An International Quarterly, 9*, 215–227.

D'Zurilla, T. (1986). *Problem solving therapy: A social competence approach to clinical intervention*. New York, NY: Springer.

Ecton, R. B., & Feindler, E. L. (1990). Anger control training for temper control disorders. In E. L. Feindler & G. R. Kalfus (Eds.), *Adolescent behavior therapy handbook* (pp. 351–371). New York, NY: Springer.

Eisdorfer, C., Czaja, S. J., Loewenstein, D. A., Rubert, M. P., Arguelles, S., Mitrani, V. B., & Szapocznik, J. (2003). The effect of a family therapy and technology-based intervention on caregiver depression. *The Gerontologist, 43*, 521–531. doi:10.1093/geront/43.4.521

Endicott, J., & Spitzer, R. (1978). A diagnostic interview: The Schedule for Affective Disorders and Schizophrenia. *Archives of General Psychiatry, 35*, 837–844.

Feindler, E. L., & Ecton, R. B. (1986). *Adolescent anger control: Cognitive behavioral techniques*. New York, NY: Pergamon Press.

Folkman, S., Lazarus, R. S., Gruen, R. J., & DeLongis, A. (1986). Appraisal, coping, health status, and psychological symptoms. *Journal of Personality and Social Psychology, 50*, 571–579.

Fung, W., & Chien, W. (2002). The effectiveness of a mutual support group for family caregivers of a relative with dementia. *Archives of Psychiatric Nursing, 26*, 134–144. doi:10.1053/apnu.2002.32951

Gallagher, D., Rose, J., Rivera, P., Lovett, S., & Thompson, L. W. (1989). Prevalence of depression in family caregivers. *The Gerontologist, 29*, 449–456. doi:10.1093/geront/29.4.449

Gallagher, D., Wrabetz, A., Lovett, S., Del Maestro, S., & Rose, J. (1989). Depression and other negative affects in family caregivers. In E. Light & B. D. Lebowitz (Eds.), *Alzheimer's disease treatment and family stress: Directions for research* (pp. 218–244). Rockville, MD: U.S. Department of Health & Human Services.

Gallagher-Thompson, D., Arean, P., Rivera, P., & Thompson, L. W. (2001). A psychoeducational intervention to reduce distress in Hispanic family caregivers: Results of a pilot study. *Clinical Gerontologist, 23*, 17–32.

Gallagher-Thompson, D., & Coon, D. W. (2007). Evidence-based treatments to reduce psychological distress in family caregivers of older adults. *Psychology and Aging, 22*, 37–51. doi:10.1037/0882-7974.22.1.37

Gallagher-Thompson, D., Coon, D. W., Solano, N., Ambler, C., Rabinowitz, Y., & Thompson, L. W. (2003). Change in indices of distress among Latino and Anglo female caregivers of elderly relatives with dementia: Site-specific results from the REACH national collaborative study. *The Gerontologist, 43*, 580–591. doi:10.1093/geront/43.4.580

Gallagher-Thompson, D., Gray, H. L., Dupart, T., Jimenez, D., & Thompson, L. W. (2008). Effectiveness of cognitive/behavioral small group intervention for reduction in non-Hispanic White and Hispanic/Latino women dementia family caregivers: Outcomes and mediators of change. *Journal of Rational-Emotive & Cognitive-Behavior Therapy, 26*, 286–303. doi:10.1007/s10942-008-0087-4

Gallagher-Thompson, D., Gray, H. L., Tang, P. C. Y., Pu, C. Y., Leung, L. Y. L., Wang, P. C., . . . Thompson, L. W. (2007). Impact of in-home behavioral management versus telephone support to reduce depressive symptoms and perceived stress in Chinese caregivers: Results of a pilot study. *The American Journal of Geriatric Psychiatry, 15*, 425–434. doi:10.1097/JGP.0b013e3180312028

Gallagher-Thompson, D., Lovett, S., Rose, J., McKibbon, C., Coon, D., Futterman, A., & Thompson, L. W. (2000). Impact of psychoeducational interventions on distressed family caregivers. *Journal of Clinical Geropsychology, 6*, 91–110. doi:10.1023/A:1009584427018

Gallagher-Thompson, D., & Steffen, A. M. (1994). Comparative effects of cognitive-behavioral and brief psychodynamic psychotherapies for depressed family caregivers. *Journal of Consulting and Clinical Psychology, 62*, 543–549. doi:10.1037/0022-006X.62.3.543

Gallagher-Thompson, D., Wang, P.-C., Liu, W., Cheung, V., Peng, R., China, D., & Thompson, L. W. (2010). Effectiveness of a psychoeducational skill training DVD program to reduce stress in Chinese American dementia caregivers. *Aging & Mental Health, 14*, 263–273. doi:10.1080/13607860903420989

Gatz, M., Fiske, A., Fox, L., Kaskie, B., Kasl-Godley, J., McCallum, T., & Wetherell, J. L. (1998). Empirically validated psychological treatments for older adults. *Journal of Mental Health and Aging, 4*, 9–46.

Gaugler, J. E. (2010). The longitudinal ramification of stroke caregiving: A systematic review. *Rehabilitation Psychology, 55*, 108–125. doi:10.1037/a0019023

Glasgow, R. E., Green, L. W., Klesges, L. M., Abrams, D. B., Fisher, E. B., Goldstein, M. G., . . . Orleans, C. T. (2006). External validity: We need to do more. *Annals of Behavioral Medicine, 31*, 105–108. doi:10.1207/s15324796abm3102_1

Glasgow, R. E., Vogt, T. M., & Boles, S. M. (1999). Evaluating the public health impact of health promotion interventions: The RE-AIM Framework. *American Journal of Public Health, 89*, 1322–1327. doi:10.2105/AJPH.89.9.1322

Gonyea, J. G., O'Connor, M. K., & Boyle, P. A. (2006). Project CARE: A randomized controlled trial of a behavioral intervention group for Alzheimer's disease caregivers. *The Gerontologist, 46*, 827–832. doi:10.1093/geront/46.6.827

Graff, M. J. L., Vernooij-Dassen, M. J. M., Thijssen, M., Dekker, J., Hoefnagels, W. H. L., & Olde Rikkert, M. G. M. (2006). Community based occupational therapy for patients with dementia and their care givers: Randomized controlled trial. *BMJ, 333*, 1196–1201. doi:10.1136/bmj.39001.688843.BE

Haley, W. E., Gitlin, L. N., Wisniewski, S. R., Feeney Mahoney, D., Coon, D. W., . . . Ory, M. (2004). Well-being, appraisal, and coping in African-American and

Caucasian dementia caregivers: Findings from the REACH study. *Aging & Mental Health, 8*, 316–329. doi:10.1080/13607860410001728998

Hall, G.R., & Buckwalter, K.C. (1987). Progressively lowered stress threshold: A conceptual model for care of adults with Alzheimer's disease. *Archives of Psychiatric Nursing, 1*, 399–406.

Hamilton, M. (1960). A rating scale for depression. *Journal of Neurology, Neurosurgery and Psychiatry, 23*, 56–62.

Hepburn, K.W., Tornatore, J., Center, B., & Ostwald, S.W. (2001). Dementia family caregiver training: Affecting beliefs about caregiving and caregiver outcomes. *Journal of the American Geriatrics Society, 49*, 450–457. doi:10.1046/j.1532-5415.2001.49090.x

Hilgeman, M.M., Durkin, D., Sun, F., DeCoster, J., Allen, R.S., Gallagher-Thompson, D., & Burgio, L. (2009). Testing a theoretical model of the stress process in Alzheimer's caregivers with race as a moderator. *The Gerontologist, 49*, 248–261. doi:10.1093/geront/gnp015

Hinrichsen, G.A., & Niederehe, G. (1994). Dementia management strategies and adjustment of family members of older patients. *Gerontologist, 34*, 95–102.

Houser, A., & Gibson, M.J. (2008). *Valuing the invaluable: The economic value of family caregiving, 2008* update. AARP Public Policy Institute. Retrieved from http://assets.aarp.org/rgcenter/il/i13_caregiving.pdf

Huang, H.L., Shyu, Y.I., Chen, M.C., Chen, S.T., & Lin, L.C. (2003). A pilot study on a home-based caregiver training program for improving caregiver self-efficacy and decreasing the behavioral problems of elders with dementia in Taiwan. *International Journal of Geriatric Psychiatry, 18*, 337–345. doi:10.1002/gps.835

Irwin, M., Artin, K.H., & Oxman, M.N. (1999). Screening for depression in the older adult: Criterion validity for the 10-item Center for Epidemiological Studies Depression Scale (CES-D). *Archives of Internal Medicine, 159*, 1701–1704.

Kaplan, C.P., & Gallagher-Thompson, D. (1995). Treatment of clinical depression in caregivers of spouses with dementia. *Journal of Cognitive Psychotherapy, 9*, 35–44.

Klesges, L.M., Estabrooks, P.A., Glasgow, R.E., & Dzewaltowski, D. (2005). Beginning with the application in mind: Designing and planning health behavior change interventions to enhance dissemination. *Annals of Behavioral Medicine, 29*, 66–75. doi:10.1207/s15324796abm2902s_10

Lewinsohn, P.M. (1974). A behavioral approach to depression. In R.J. Friedman & M.M. Katz (Eds.), *The psychology of depression: Contemporary theory and research* (pp. 157–178). New York, NY: Wiley.

Lewinsohn, P.M., Muñoz, R.F., Youngren, M.A., & Zeiss, A. (1986). *Control your depression*. New York, NY: Prentice-Hall.

Lewinsohn, P.M., Rohde, P., & Seeley, J.R. (1996). Adolescent suicidal ideation and attempts: Prevalence, risk factors and clinical implications. *Clinical Psychology: Science and Practice, 3*, 25–46.

López, J., & Crespo, M. (2008). Analysis of the efficacy of a psychotherapeutic program to improve the emotional status of caregivers of elderly dependent relatives. *Aging & Mental Health, 12*, 451–461. doi:10.1080/13607860802224292

Losada, A. (2005). *Influencia de los pensamientos disfuncionales sobre el cuidado en el malestar psicológico de cuidadores de personas mayores con demencia. Resultados de un studio transversal y de intervención* [Influence of dysfunctional thoughts about caregiving on dementia caregivers' psychology distress. Results of a correlational and an intervention study]. Unpublished doctoral dissertation, Universidad Autónoma de Madrid, Spain.

Losada, A., Montorio, I., Knight, B.G., Márquez, M., & Izal, M. (2006). Explanation of caregivers' distress from the cognitive model: The role of dysfunctional thoughts. *Psicologia Conductual, 14*, 115–128.

Lu, Y.F.Y., & Wykle, M. (2007). Relationship between caregiver stress and self-care behaviors in response to symptoms. *Clinical Nursing Research, 16*, 29–43. doi:10.1177/1054773806295238

Márquez-González, M., Losada, A., Izal, M., Pérez-Rojo, G., & Montorio, I. (2007). Modification of dysfunctional thoughts about caregiving in dementia family caregivers: Description and outcomes of an intervention programme. *Aging & Mental Health, 11*, 616–625. doi:10.1080/13607860701368455

Marriott, A., Donaldson, C., Tarrier, N., & Burns, A. (2000). Effectiveness of cognitive-behavioural intervention in reducing the burden of carers of patients with Alzheimer's disease. *The British Journal of Psychiatry, 176*, 557–562. doi:10.1192/bjp.176.6.557

Mausbach, B.T., Patterson, T.L., Von Kanel, R., Mills, P.J., Dimsdale, J.E., Ancoli-Israel, S., & Grant, I. (2007). The attenuating effect of personal mastery on the relations between stress and Alzheimer's caregiver health: A five-year longitudinal analysis. *Aging & Mental Health, 11*, 637–644. doi:10.1080/13607860701787043

McNair, D.M., Lorr, M., & Droppleman, L.F. (1971). *The Profile of Moods States manual*. San Diego, CA: Educational and Industrial Testing Service.

Meier, D., Vodoz, V., & Spiegel, R. (1999). Development of a Short Measurement of Individual Quality of Life (SEIQoL Short Form). In K. Iqbal, D.F. Swabb, B. Winblad & H.M. Wisniewski (Eds.), *Alzheimer's disease and related disorders* (pp. 817–821). London, England: Wiley.

Mittelman, M.S., Ferris, S.H., Shulman, E., Steinberg, G., & Levin, B. (1996). A family intervention to delay nursing home placement of patients with Alzheimer disease: A randomized controlled trial. *JAMA, 276*, 1725–1731. doi:10.1001/jama.1996.03540210033030

Mittelman, M.S., Haley, W.E., Clay, O.J., & Roth, D.L. (2006). Improving caregiver well-being delays nursing home placement of patients with Alzheimer disease. *Neurology, 67*, 1592–1599. doi:10.1212/01.wnl.0000242727.81172.91

Mittelman, M.S., Roth, D.L., Coon, D.W., & Haley, W.E. (2004). Sustained benefit of supportive intervention for depressive symptoms in caregivers of patients with Alzheimer's disease. *The American Journal of Psychiatry, 161,* 850–856. doi:10.1176/appi.ajp.161.5.850

Montoro-Rodriguez, J., & Gallagher-Thompson, D. (2009). The role of resources and appraisals in predicting burden among Latina and non-Hispanic white female caregivers: A test of an expanded socio-cultural model of stress and coping. *Aging & Mental Health, 13,* 648–658. doi:10.1080/13607860802534658

National Alliance for Caregiving. (2010). *The MetLife study of working caregivers and employer health care costs: new insights and innovations for reducing health care costs for employers.* Retrieved from http://caregiving.org/pubs/data.htm

National Alliance for Caregiving & AARP. (2009). *Executive summary: Caregiving in the U.S.* Retrieved from http://caregiving.org/pubs/data.htm

Nichols, L.O., Chang, C., Lummus, A., Burns, R., Martindale-Adams, J., Graney, M.J., . . . Czaja, S. (2008). The cost effectiveness of a behavior intervention with caregivers of Alzheimer's patients. *Journal of the American Geriatrics Society, 56,* 413–420. doi:10.1111/j.1532-5415.2007.01569.x

Novaco, R. (1975). *Anger-control: The development and evaluation of an experimental treatment.* Lexington, MA: Lexington Books.

O'Rourke, N., & Tuokko, H. (2003). Psychometric properties of an abridged version of the Zarit Burden Interview within a representative Canadian caregiver sample. *The Gerontologist, 43,* 121–127. doi:10.1093/geront/43.1.121

Ostwald, S.K., Hepburn, K.W., Caron, W., Burns, T., & Mantell, R. (1999). Reducing caregiver burden: A randomized psychoeducational intervention for caregivers of persons with dementia. *The Gerontologist, 39,* 299–309. doi:10.1093/geront/39.3.299

Perren, S., Schmid, R., & Wettstein, A. (2006). Caregivers' adaptation to change: The impact of increasing impairment of persons suffering from dementia on their caregivers' subjective well-being. *Aging & Mental Health, 10,* 539–548. doi:10.1080/13607860600637844

Quinn, C., Clare, L., & Woods, B. (2009). The impact of the quality of relationship on experiences and wellbeing of caregivers of people with dementia: A systematic review. *Aging & Mental Health, 13,* 143–154. doi:10.1080/13607860802459799

Riedijk, S.R., De Vugt, M.E., Duivenvoorden, H.J., Niermeijer, M.F., Van Swieten, J.C., Verhey, F.R.J., & Tibben, A. (2006). Caregiver burden, health-related quality of life and coping in dementia caregivers: A comparison of frontotemporal dementia and Alzheimer's disease. *Dementia and Geriatric Cognitive Disorders, 22,* 405–412. doi:10.1159/000095750

Roth, D.L., Mittelman, M.S., Clay, O.J., Madan, A., & Haley, W.E. (2005). Changes in social support as mediators of the impact of a psychosocial intervention for spouse caregivers of person with Alzheimer's disease. *Psychology and Aging, 20,* 634–644. doi:10.1037/0882-7974.20.4.634

Sarason, I.G., Sarason, B.R., Shearin, E.N., & Pierce, G.R. (1987). A brief measure of social support: Practical and theoretical implications. *Journal of Social and Personal Relationships, 4,* 497–510. doi:10.1177/0265407587044007

Schulz, R. (Ed.). (2000). *Handbook on dementia caregiving: Evidence-based interventions for family caregivers.* New York, NY: Springer.

Schulz, R., & Beach, S. R. (1999). Caregiving as a risk factor for mortality: the caregiver health effects study. *JAMA, 282,* 2215–2219. doi:10.1001/jama.282.23.2215

Schulz, R., Burgio, L., Burns, R., Eisdorfer, C., Gallagher-Thompson, D., Gitlin, L. N., & Mahoney, D. F. (2003). Resources for Enhancing Alzheimer's Caregiver Health (REACH): Overview, site-specific outcomes, and future directions. *The Gerontologist, 43,* 514–520. doi:10.1093/geront/43.4.514

Schulz, R., Martire, L., & Klinger, J. (2005). Evidence-based caregiver interventions in geriatric psychiatry. *Psychiatric Clinics of North America, 28,* 1007–1038. doi:10.1016/j.psc.2005.09.003

Smith, T. L., & Toseland, R. W. (2006). The effectiveness of a telephone support program for caregivers of frail older adults. *The Gerontologist, 46,* 620–629. doi:10.1093/geront/46.5.620

Son, J., Erno, A., Shea, D. G., Femia, E. E., Zarit, S. H., & Stephens, M. A. P. (2007). The caregiver stress process and health outcomes. *Journal of Aging and Health, 19,* 871–887. doi:10.1177/0898264307308568

Sörensen, S., Pinquart, M., & Duberstein, P. (2002). How effective are interventions with caregivers? An updated meta-analysis. *The Gerontologist, 42,* 356–372. doi:10.1093/geront/42.3.356

Spillman, B. C., & Black, K. G. (2005). *Staying the course: Trends in family caregiving* (#2005-17). Washington, DC: AARP.

Steffen, A. M. (2000). Anger management for dementia caregivers: A preliminary study using video and telephone interviews. *Behavior Therapy, 31,* 281–299. doi:10.1016/S0005-7894(00)80016-7

Tarlow, B. J., Wisniewski, S. R., Belle, S. H., Rubert, M., Ory, M. G., & Gallagher-Thompson, D. (2004). Positive aspects of caregiving: Contributions of the REACH Project in the development of new measures of Alzheimer's caregiving. *Research on Aging, 26,* 429–453. doi:10.1177/0164027504264493

Tarrier, N., & Barrowclough, C. (1986). Providing information to relatives about schizophrenia: Some comments. *British Journal of Psychiatry, 149,* 458–463. doi:10.1192/bjp.149.4.458

Teri, L., Logsdon, R. G., Uomoto, J., & McCurry, S. M. (1997). Behavioral treatment of depression in dementia patients: A controlled clinical trial. *Journal of Gerontology, 52,* 159–166.

Teri, L., Traux, P., Logsdon, R., Uomoto, J., Zarit, S., & Vitaliano, P. P. (1992). Assessment of behavioral problems in dementia: The Revised Memory and Behavior Problems Checklist. *Psychology and Aging, 7,* 622–631.

Toseland, R., Labrecque, M., Goebel, S., & Whitney, M. (1992). An evaluation of a group program for spouses of frail elderly veterans. *The Gerontologist, 32,* 382–390.

Toseland, R., McCallion, P., Smith, T., & Banks, S. (2004). Supporting caregivers of frail older adults in an HMO setting. *American Journal of Orthopsychiatry, 74,* 349–364.

Toseland, R., McCallion, P., Smith, T., Huck, S., Bourgeois, P., & Garstka, T. (2001). Health education group for caregivers in an HMO. *Journal of Clinical Psychology, 57,* 551–570.

Toseland, R. W., Rossiter, C. M., & Labrecque, M. S. (1989). The effectiveness of peer-led and professionally led groups to support family caregivers. *The Gerontologist, 29,* 465–471. doi:10.1093/geront/29.4.465

Vernooij-Dassen, M. J. M., Persoon, J. M., & Felling, A. J. (1996) Predictors of sense of competence in caregivers of demented individuals. *Social Science Medicine, 43,* 41–49.

Vitaliano, P. P., Zhang, J., & Scanlan, J. M. (2003). Is caregiving hazardous to one's physical health? A meta-analysis. *Psychological Bulletin, 129,* 946–972. doi:10.1037/0033-2909.129.6.946

Weiss, W., Spuhler, T., Gruet, F., Guidani, D., & Noack, H. (1990). *Enquête auprès de la population 'La santé et la promotion de la santé'. Etude intercantonale sur les indicateurs de santé (IGIP-PROMES)* [Population survey on health and health promotion. Swiss study on health indicators]. *Rapport final.* Lausanne, Switzerland: Institut Suisse de la Santé Publique et des Hôpitaux ISH/SKI.

Wettstein, A., Konig, M., Schmid, R., & Perren, S. (2005). *Belastung und Wohlbenfinden bei Angehörigen von Menschen mit Demenz. Eine Interventionsstudie* [Burden and Well-being in Caregivers of Persons With Dementia: An Intervention Study]. Zurich, Switzerland: Ruegger.

Wight, R. G., Aneshensel, C. S., & LeBlanc, A. J. (2003). Stress buffering effects of family support in AIDS caregiving. *AIDS Care, 15,* 595–613. doi:10.1080/09540120310001595096

Yesavage, J. A., Brink, R. A., Rose, T. L., Lum, O., Huang, V., Adey, M., & Leirer, V. (1983). Development and validation of a geriatric depression screening scale: A preliminary report. *Journal of Psychiatric Research, 17,* 37–49.

Zarit, S. H., & Zarit, J. M. (1982). Families under stress: Interventions for caregivers of senile dementia patients. *Psychotherapy: Theory, Research and Practice, 19,* 461–471. doi:10.1037/h008459.

INDEX

Supportive therapy, 16, 18
Sustainability, 193–194, 260–261

Talerico, K., 104
Teamwork, 189–190
Teri, L., 48, 52, 91, 92, 169–172, 232
Thompson, L. W., 90–95, 99, 104,
    120–125, 233, 239
Thorp, S. R., 16
Thought record worksheet, 272
TIB (time in bed), 49–50
Tierney, L., 98
Time (spent in training), 25, 146
Time in bed (TIB), 49–50
Time management, 29
Tomhave, J. A., 92, 95
Toseland, R. W., 243–244
Total sleep time (TST), 49–50
Tracking pleasant activities
    worksheet, 273
Training. See also Relaxation training
    in anger management, 252
    in anxiety disorder EBT
        implementation, 23
    for behavioral disturbances,
        188–189
    in behavior therapy, 178–179
    for family caregiver interventions,
        267–268
    for memory function, 133, 137–141,
        145–147
    for neural plasticity, 132
    resistance to, 142–143
    setting for, 143
    in sustainability of implementation,
        193–194
TREA (treatment routes for explora-
    tion of agitation intervention),
    183–185
Treatment
    in insomnia case study, 67–72
    noncompliance with, 60–61
    poor outcomes of, 147
    rationale of, 104–105
    resistance to, 60–61, 104–105,
        142–143
    setting for, 54–55
    teamwork in, 189–190

Treatment plan
    in disruptive behaviors case example,
        197–198
    in insomnia case study, 65–66
Treatment routes for exploration of
    agitation intervention (TREA),
    183–185
Trevino, K., 186
TST (total sleep time), 49–50

Unhelpful thoughts worksheet, 117
Unsafe ambulation, 196–199
Uomoto, J., 92
Urination, inappropriate, 199

VA (Veterans Affairs), 22, 267–268
Valverde, Irene, 263, 267
Vangel, S. J., 91
Van Schaik, 104
Van't Veer-Tazelaar, P. J., 18, 20
Verbal aggression, 168, 196
Verbal agitation, 167, 183
Veterans Affairs (VA), 22, 267–268
Viney, L. L., 104
Visser, S. M., 171, 194
Visual imagery, 137
Vitiello, M. V., 48, 52
Volicer, L., 175

Walton, E., 52
Wang, J. J., 103
Watt, L. M., 103
Webster, J. D., 100
West, R., 139
Westerhof, G. J., 100
Wetherell, J. L., 14
Wilson, N. M., 52
Woods, P., 173
Working memory. See also Memory
    function
    with cognitive behavioral therapy,
        90, 93
    with reminiscence therapy, 100
Worksheets
    for behavioral disturbances, 201–217
    for family caregivers, 272–275
    for geriatric depression, 117–125
    for problem solving, 39–40
    for sleep disturbances, 73–77
Worry, 27. See also Anxiety disorders

ABOUT THE EDITORS

Forrest Scogin, PhD, is a professor of psychology and coordinator of the Clinical Geropsychology Concentration at the University of Alabama. His research has been primarily in the areas of psychotherapy, depression, and mental health and aging. He has received funding to support his activities from the National Institutes of Health, the Bureau of Health Professions, and the Retirement Research Foundation. He is a fellow of American Psychological Association (APA) Divisions 12 (Society of Clinical Psychology) and 20 (Adult Development and Aging) and the Gerontological Society of America. He has served as the chair of APA's Committee on Aging and as president of the Society of Clinical Geropsychology.

Avani Shah, PhD, is an assistant professor of social work at the University of Alabama. Her research focuses on increasing the number of clinical psychologists and social workers available to meet the health care needs of older adults and to improve access to specialized behavioral health services for medically underserved older adult populations. She is also interested in improving mental health treatment access through clinical interventions for depression, memory, and independent living for aging populations in the context of health (cardiovascular disease, stroke, hypertension, diabetes, and smoking).